VETERINARY CLINICAL DIAGNOSTIC TECHNOLOGY

VETERINARY CLINICAL DIAGNOSTIC TECHNOLOGY

Dr. B. Prasad
B.V.Sc. & A.H., M.V.Sc., Ph.D. (Medicine)
Professor & Head
Department of Medicine
College of Veterinary & Agriculture Science, (COVAS)
H.P.K.V., Palampur-176062.

CBS

CBS Publishers & Distributors Pvt. Ltd.
New Delhi • Bengaluru • Chennai • Kochi • Kolkata • Mumbai
Hyderabad • Nagpur • Patna • Pune • Vijayawada

ISBN: 81-239-1371-0

First Edition: 1992
Reprint: 1996, 2006, 2007, 2016

Published by:
Satish Kumar Jain for CBS Publishers & Distributors Pvt. Ltd.,
4819/XI Prahlad Street, 24 Ansari Road, Daryaganj, New Delhi - 110002
delhi@cbspd.com, cbspubs@airtelmail.in • www.cbspd.com
Ph.: 23289259, 23266861, 23266867 • Fax: 011-23243014

Corporate Office: 204 FIE, Industrial Area, Patparganj, Delhi - 110 092
Ph: 49344934 • Fax: 011-49344935
E-mail: publishing@cbspd.com • publicity@cbspd.com

Branches:

- ***Bengaluru:*** 2975, 17th Cross, K.R. Road, Bansankari 2nd Stage, Bengaluru - 70 • Ph: +91-80-26771678/79 • Fax: +91-80-26771680 E-mail: cbsbng@gmail.com, bangalore@cbspd.com
- ***Chennai:*** No. 7, Subbaraya Street, Shenoy Nagar, Chennai - 600030 Ph: +91-44-26681266, 26680620 • Fax: +91-44-42032115 E-mail: chennai@cbspd.com
- ***Kochi:*** Ashana House, 39/1904, A.M. Thomas Road, Valanjambalam, Ernakulum, Kochi • Ph: +91-484-4059061-65 Fax: +91-484-4059065 • E-mail: cochin@cbspd.com
- ***Kolkata:*** 6-B, Ground Floor, Rameshwar Shaw Road, Kolkata - 700014 Ph: +91-33-22891126/7/8 • E-mail: kolkata@cbspd.com
- ***Mumbai:*** 83-C, Dr. E. Moses Road, Worli, Mumbai - 400018 Ph: +91-9833017933, 022-24902340/41 • E-mail: mumbai@cbspd.com

Representatives:

- Hyderabad: 0-9885175004
- Nagpur: 0-9021734563
- Patna: 0-9334159340
- Pune: 0-9623451994
- Vijayawada: 0-9000660880

Printed at:
Neekunj Print Process, Delhi

To My Mother

Whenever I see past, I see,
A barefoot run for kilometres,
From village to a railway station,
And parallel to slow moving train,
Not to board into, but;
To handover her son's hostel-key.

CONTENTS

1

INTRODUCTION

The application of appropriate clinical tools and established techniques in systematic way enables clinicians to recognise the diseased organs distinctly from that of healthy one. Basically, a clear concept of anatomy, physiology and the normal behaviour of the animal is essential. Both quantitative and qualitative changes occur during disease conditions, which are appreciated in terms of signs/symptoms, help determining the disease condition. The determination of the nature of ailment is technically called, **"a diagnosis."**

In order to formulate and adopt rational treatment, it is essential for the clinician to undertake careful and complete examination of the patient to acertain the disease. The veterinarian, especially, faces difficulties in handling the various species of animals, viz. domestic, zoo and wild animals. However, during clinical investigation, some general principles are being applied. Before going for the examination of the patient, the past, immediate and environmental circumstances must be kept in consideration. These, in most instances help significantly in making a diagnosis.

Attempts should be made for exact diagnosis, that is to acertain not only the site of disease but also to establish its causative agent(s). In the absence of determination of causative agent(s), the treatment of the disease will only be empirical. The diagnosis are of following types:

Confirmatory: When the disease is diagnosed with certainty.

Presumptive: The diagnosis is based on physiological status of animals and response to treatment e.g. Milk fever in cows and buffaloes. They respond to calcium therapy promptly.

Tentative: If the disease is not diagnosed with certainty. It may change.

Symptomatic: The confirmation of disease is based on prominent symptoms present but the basic reason and location are not known, e.g. pale conjunctival mucous membrane is indicative of anaemia, which may be due to suppressed blood-production, haemorrhage,haemolysis or blood protozoan diseases etc.

Most often the owners are interested in knowing the outcome of the disease. Whether the disease is curable, how long treatment is required, the expenditure involved and so on. Forecasting the probable duration and outcome of a disease is called **prognosis**. And for making accurate **prognosis** it is imperative for the veterinarians to make sure diagnosis, which will guide them for suitable therapeutic and prophylactic measures.

Clinically, there are certain classical symptoms which directly help in making diagnosis. Such symptom is generally known as **pathognomonic** symptom e.g. protrusion of third eyelid of horse in tetanus.

It is obvious that diagnosis requires practical experience, fundamental knowledge of subject and application of technical know-how intelligently. The students, therefore, are advised to make theirselves familiar with the normal behaviour of different species of animals which will be helpful in the determination and tackling of disease conditions.

2

TECHNIQUES OF RESTRAINT

Clinical examination of animals is rather impossible without proper control. The different species of animals resist differently during the clinical examination procedure. A clinician is judged by way of his approach to the animals. The examiner must approach the animal with confidence, offering some feed (cattle and buffalo), expressing melody words or patting gently, particularly to dogs. Use of harsh sound, kicking or beating has no place during the examination procedure. When the above methods are helpless and when there is risk of accidental injury, appropriate methods of restraint must be used. However, it must be borne in mind that one method of restraint for one species of animal is not applicable to other species of animals.

Mechanical Restraint

Improper use of mechanical instruments and techniques may cause injury to the animals. Therefore, a veterinarian must know how to use particular means of restraint in order to ensure suitable condition for examining the animal. The owner first be asked about vices, if any, of the animal like kicking, sideways pressing, butting, biting etc. The veterinarian must be sure that he, his helpers and the animals are out of risk of injury.

Catching Individual Animal

Exotic cattle and their crosses can be caught without much problem by grasping the head or the nose. However, this method is practically impossible for Haryana breed and hilly cattle and furious buffaloes. Animals which are not in close human contact pose much difficulty. They can be controlled at feeding or milking time. By offering some palatable feed or driving into shed, catching is facilitated. Helpers may use noose around the horns or the halters can be used. If these fails, the animal may be driven to a metallic crush, fixed or mobile (Fig 2.1). For zoo animals, either cage (monkey) or squeeze cage (tiger/lion) is required. Wild animals may need medicated bait or use of stunning guns.

In Group

In order to conduct routine examination or for conducting mass vaccination, it is necessary to restrain all animals individually one after the other. This can be achieved by forcing the animals to pass through a crush made of iron pipe, ending in a closed pen. It may be either fixed or portable. The height and breadth of the crush are such that jumping or back movement is not possible. There is provision of space at the end of the pen from where a veterinarian can conduct examination or inoculations.

Ways of Approach

Cattle and buffalo: A well restrained cow or buffalo must be approached from the right side (milking side).

Fig. 2.1 Iron crush for cattle

One should not approach from the left side without patting at the back. A nervous or furious cow/buffalo usually puts side kicks or even short back-kicks. Furious bull may butt with head or horns and press against a wall or the floor.

Individual Restraint Techniques

Head grip: Head grip or nose grip or neck rope is necessary for examination of cattle and buffalo. If available, the nose holder is to be used. The head must be drawn forward and upward as the cattle has more strength when its neck is at low level. In furious cattle a permanent nose-ring with or without a pole, is being fitted with the help of nose ring plier Plate-I.

In the horse, a twitch is applied on to the ear or on to the lower or upper lip. A loop of soft rope, about three feet long, is attached to a wooden handle or rod. It is applied on the appropriate point and twisted so as to cause sufficient pain to divert the animal's attention from the part of the animal body, which is to be examined. In order to protect against kicks from the hind feet, both in horse and ox, the forefoot is held up on the side on which, the clinician is willing to examine.

The pig is restrained by means of rope twitch or a pair of pincer applied to the upper jaw or the snout.

Dog is being controlled with tape muzzle (Fig. 2.2) or leather muzzle. Furious dog, which does not allow muzzling, can be controlled with floor-ring for medication. Small animals can be placed on table dorso-ventrally or laterally for examination.

The birds like parrot, fowls and others are examined using leather gloves.

Limbs

Whenever the limb is to be raised, the floor must not be slippery. The leg is raised either manually or with the help of simple rope. The hind limbs can be restrained with the application of simple twitch (Fig. 2.3) or with flank-fold clamp, which prevents kicking, while examining the udder or teats.

Raising of hind limb can be made with a wooden pole, either as such or tied with a rope.

Tail: During examination of hind limbs, uro-genital tract, rectal palpation and udder, tail poses difficulty. It not only soils the clinician but also hinders mechanically. It can be controlled by an assistant or can be tied with hock using suitable rope. Use of V clamp at the base of the tail, solves the problem.

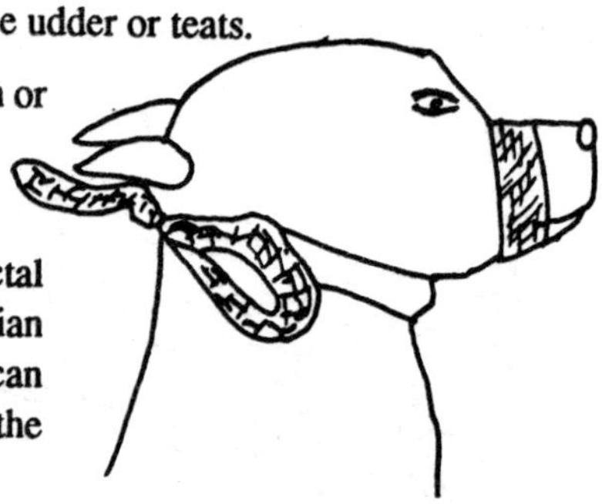

Fig. 2.2 Tape muzzle for dog.

Leading of Animals

Cattle and buffalo should be led by means of halter of rope, chain or leather. The size of the halter should be appropriate and the nose-brim loop should not be too tight. The leading rope is attached on the left side and the man should walk on its left side. The furious bulls, bullocks should be led by an active and strong attendant. The eyes must be covered with leather/canvass eye-cups. The lead is to be attached with nose-ring. An assistant should be there to meet emergency need. The horse can be lead with the reign and the dog with a leather lead.

Fig. 2.3 Leg twitch.

Casting

Wherever certain examination viz. shoeing, nail clipping, management of dystocia or prolapse is not teasible in standing position, the casting of animal is imperative. There are number of methods of casting for different species of animals. The ground must be even and well bedded with soft paddy straw or thick rubber mat to avoid injury. The cattle and buffalo should be casted slowly unlike the horse to escape fracture of horns, ribs, pelvic bones and injury to the diaphragm and gravid uterus.

Cattle/Buffalo

The adults, youngs and heifers are casted on the right side while for the pregnant and recently calved animal, left side casting is preferred. For adult cattle and buffalo, 3-4 persons are required for casting, depending on the method used.

Herting method: A nylon or jute rope will serve the purpose. The noose of one end is placed around the horns. The other end moves behind making three rings, one just before, the other just behind the shoulder and the third around the last lumber vertebra. This end is pulled slowly by an assistant. The hitch knots should be about 6" - 8" away from the median line, on the side choosen up. The head should be turned to the up side.

Madsen Method: This can be applied when hobbles are available for the fetlocks. The fore legs are tied with rope making twist-wind. Two nylon ropes of 3-4 m long, tied to the hind fetlock hobbles and passed underneath and around the rope locking forelegs. The other ends of the rope are drawn backward by two assistants. The head is turned opposite to the side being downward. This allows the animal a sudden fall.

Buffalo: Generally buffalo does not allow gentle handling. Thus the method, used for casting, forces a sudden fall. For this, two ropes of 24"-30" long, one for both forelegs and the other for both hind legs are applied by twist. A long rope is tied with the rope between forelegs and rolled twice crossing the rope twisted between hind legs. The other end of the rope is being pulled caudally with one or two persons and the animal is forced to move. In this way, all the legs assemble and the animal falls suddenly. Adequate bedding must be provided so as to avoid injury to the animal.

Operation Table

For small animals, portable hydraulic table is available. The table is attached with warming arrangement for winter. The table is available from equipments manufacturers.

Most of the teaching colleges of the country have installed fixed operation table. The table is equipped with hydraulic system for lowering, raising or tilting in one or two planes. It can move horizontally also. Rings and ropes are attached at suitable places to restrain whole body of the animal. The floor is properly bedded and has a capacity to bear the weight upto 800-1000kg.

Instruments Helping the Animal Stand

Manual lift or change of side is possible only in small animals and calves. The adult cattle, buffalo and horses need mechanical help for the purpose.

The casted or paretic cow can be dragged from one to the other place by putting on a strong guny-bag mat. A strong rope is attached around the periphery of mat for easy grip. With the help of assistants, the place can be changed.

Often the animal needs persuation for standing. This can be done manually by slapping at the neck or the chest and shouting and closing the nostrils. If these fail, electric goads can be applied on the ventral abdomen skin. If this also fails, a strong rope is tied tightly around the body of the animal and 4-6 persons may lift the animal. However, the number of persons required, depends on the weight of the animal. But the method is of not much help in heavy buffaloes.

The animals showing downer syndrome can raise their fore parts of the body but unable to do so with the hind limbs. Such animals may be put on their hind legs for required time using Bagshawe's hip clamp or chainpulley and rope. This clamp and chainpulley are commercially available.

References

Kelly, W.R. (1984) *Veterinary Clinical Diagnosis. 3rd ed.* Bailliere, Tindall, London.

Rosenberger, G. (1979). *Clinical Examination of Cattle.* Verlag Paul Parey, Berlin and Hamberg.

3

CLINICAL ANAESTHESIA

In veterinary clinical practice, sedation, immobilization, surface, local and general anaesthesia are required. For immobilization, both instruments and drugs are used, while for various types of anaesthesia, the chemicals are used.

Sedation: The following drugs can be used for sedation of animals. The selection of drugs is based on species of animals. Either intramuscular or intravenous route is preferred. The action sets within 5-10 minutes of intravenous administration while intramuscular injection takes 15-45 minutes lasting for 2-6 hours.

Common Drugs used as Sedative

Group	Brand name	Dose	Route
Chlorpromazine	Largactil (M&B)	0.5-2 mg/kg	i/m or i/v
Triflupromazine	Siquil (Sarabhai)	0.1-0.5 mg/kg	i/m or i/v
Trimeprazine	Vallergan (M&B)	1-2 mg/kg	i/m or i/v
Diazepam	Campose	0.5-1 mg/kg	i/m or i/v

Local Anaesthesia

For painless and better operative procedures, e.g. docking, amputation of leg, rumenotomy and dehorning, local anaesthetics are used. Local anaesthesia may be categorised into surface, infiltration, nerve block and extra epidural anaesthesia.

Common Local Anaesthetics used in Animals

Compound	Brand name	% concentration in type of anaesthesia			
		Surface	Infiltration	Nerve Block	Extradural
Procaine HCI	Novocaine (Hoechst)	-	1-2	3-6	2-4
Lignocaine HCI		5	2	-	-
Tetracaine	Pantocain	0.5-2	-	-	-
	Neocain	2-5	1	2-5	2
Butamine	Tutocain (Bayer)	5	1-2	1-5	1-3
Carticaine	Ultracain (Hoechst)	-	2-4	2-4	2-4
Ethylchloride		Spray as such			

Surface Anaesthesia

Instillation of surface anaesthetic into the conjunctival sac or nasal mucosa facilitate examination of eye and the nasal cavity. Swabing of prepucial mucous membrane with anaesthetics and ethylchloride spray on the skin can be used for minor operations.

Infiltration Anaesthesia

The area of operation is infiltered either sub-cutaneously or intramuscularly. Massaging promotes the onset of anaesthesia. For operation on the extremities, the anaesthetics can be used intravenously after applying a tourniquet (Fig. 3.1) above the site of operation. This enhances the onset of anaesthesia.

Fig. 3.1 Tourniquet

Nerve Block

The conduction of nerve impulse between the site of operation and brain/spinal cord is blocked. About 5-20 ml of anaesthetic is placed along the course of nerve e.g. cornual (Fig. 3.2) block for dehorning in cattle, digital nerve block for claw amputation.

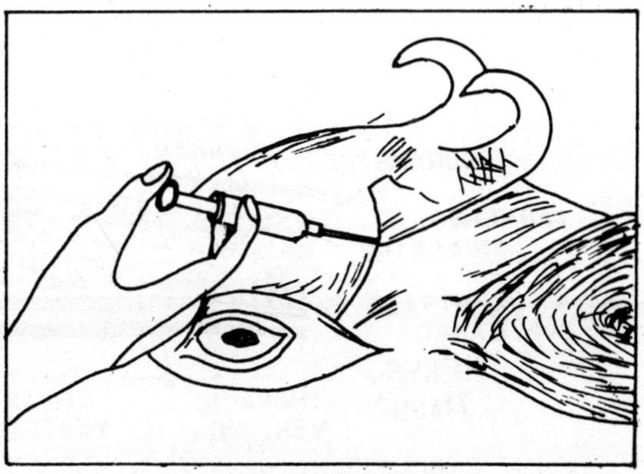

Fig. 3.2 Cornual nerve block

Extradural (Epidural) Anaesthesia

Local anaesthetics are injected into the extradural space. In large animals the drug can be injected between thoracic and coccygeal vertebrae (Fig. 3.3).

Types of extradural anaesthesia	Injection site (between)	Purpose	Amount of anaesthetics
Thoracolumber (Segmental)	13th thoracic and lumber or 1st & 2nd lumber vertebrae.	Laparotomy	5-10 ml
Lumbosacral (Lumber)	Last lumber and Sacral vertebrae	Operation on hind quarters, castration	20-30 ml
Sacrococcygeal (Sacral)	Last sacral and coccygeal or first two coccygeal vertebrae	All types of operation on hind limbs, fetotomy, laparotomy etc.	Minor sacral anaesthesia: 5-15 Major:20-100 ml

Techniques

Sacral Anaesthesia: Restrain the animal in standing position. The site between last sacrum and first coccygeal vertebra is shaved and dressed aseptically. A 3" x 15 gauge needle is inserted at 45° angle and pushed downward. Any obstruction or blood flow indicates wrong place. Reattempt, and as soon as the needle reaches at right place, the drug is deposited comfortably. For laparotomy, the injection is made on recumbent animal. The head must be kept raised. Animals must be prevented from injury while getting up.

Lumber Anaesthesia: The site between last lumber and sacrum is shaved and dressed with antiseptic. For adult cattle, buffalo and horse, a needle of 3-6" x 15 gauge is inserted at 90° till it reaches the extradural space. It is about 1-1.5" deep from skin penetration. Suck with syringe to check vessel penetration. Inject the required amount of anaesthetics.

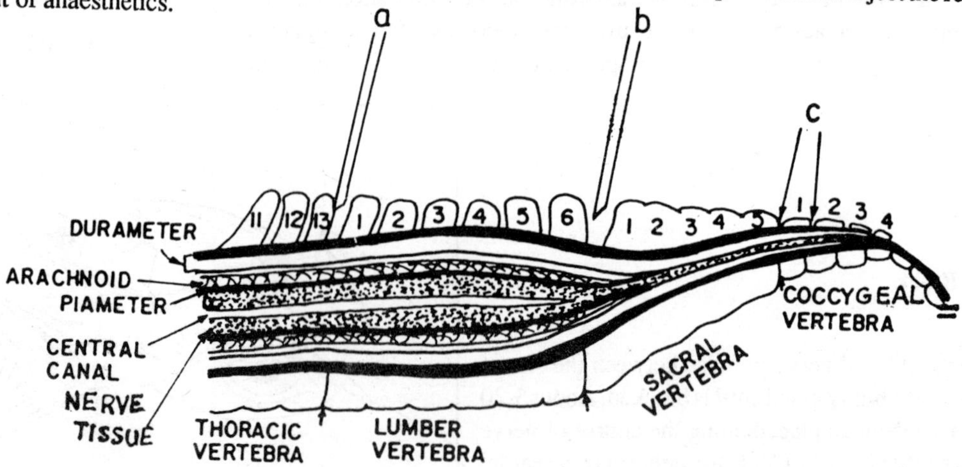

Fig. 3.3 Sites for extradural anaesthesia. (a) Thoracolumbar (b) Lumbosacral (d) Sacrococcygeal

Segmental Anaesthesia : Prepare the site as above between first and second lumber vertebrae. About 2-3 cm away from mid line, 5-10 ml anaesthetic is deposited at middle transverse process of second lumber vertebra (on the right for left flank anaesthesia and vice-versa). After that a 6" long needle is inserted at the first site anteriorly and medially till it reaches the internal diameter indicated by resistance shown by the animal. The stylet is removed. Absence of blood or CSF points right place. About 10-12 ml of drug is injected smoothly. The procedure needs special care in the introduction of needle.

General anaesthesia: There are three routes for the induction of general anaesthesia. The students are required to consult book on anaesthesia.

Inhalation Anaesthesia: Volatile or gaseous anaesthetics are administered through mask. Special instruments are available for large and small animals.

Ether: For good general anaesthesia, ether consumption rate is 700 g/hr for adult cattle. The after sleep is 1-1.5 time more than the duration of anaesthesia.

Chloroform: Gauze soaked in chloroform is placed within the mask. About 30-50 ml is required for induction and 10-30 ml for continuation. Prior injection of thiopental @ 500 mg/50 kg b.wt. controls excitement. Animals recover soon after withdrawal. It is suitable for beef animals.

Halothane: Being a good inhalation anaesthetic, it is generally used after induction of anaesthesia with thiopental administration. About 30 ml is required for induction in adult cattle and 35 ml/hr for continuation. The recovery period varies from 1-1.5 hour.

Parentral Anaesthetics: Are administered with injection.

Chloral Hydrate: Suitable for large animals. Chloral hydrate @ 10g/100kg b.wt. as 5-10 per cent aqueous solution is injected intravenouly till full anaesthesia is obtained. It takes 10-15 minutes which lasts for 2-3 hours. A mixture of 10 g chloral hydrate and 10 g of pentobarbital dissolved in 100 ml water is injected @ 20-30 ml per 100 kg b.wt.

Pentobarbital: It is injected @ 2-3 g/100kg b.wt. The anaesthesia lasts for about 30 minutes and the recovery period is 1.5-3 hours.

Thiopental sodium: It is short acting general anaesthetic. Injection is made rapidly @ 1-1.5 g/100 kg b.wt. Anaesthesia lasts for 5-10 minutes and the recovery period varies from 45-120 minutes.

In dog intramuscular injections of atropine sulphate @ 0.02 mg/kg b.wt. followed by chlorpromazine HCI @ 1 mg/kg b.wt. and 15-30 minutes later, thiopental sodium @ 20-30 mg/kg b.wt. are given intravenously to produce general anaesthesia.

Oral Anaesthetics

Chloral hydrate: Aqueous solution is given orally @ 10 g/100 kg body wt in cattle and buffaloes. Anaesthesia starts 20-30 minutes later.

Ethyl alcohol: Oral administration of 50 per cent ethyl alcohol @ 2.5 ml/kg body wt. is needed. The disadvantages are excitement and even death in certain cases.

4

BASIC MEDICATION TECHNIQUES

Medication: The proper application of medicaments on animals is essential. Fundamentally the medication methods can be grouped into these three categories:

1. Surface medication (topical application).
2. Internal medication (through natural orifices)
3. Parentral medication

Surface Medication

The therapeutic agents in proper concentration are applied directly on the body by hand. It may include a part of the body or the whole body. Similary application can be made particularly on the back with impregnated rope fixed between two poles at low level. When the animals are forced to move, the drug adheres on the back. Ointment is applied directly on the prepucial mucosa and the penis.

Spray: For generalised application, as for the control of ectoparasites (mange, mite, ticksetc.), the medicaments are diluted to desired concentration and sprayed with a sprayer. Instillation of liquid preparation into ear, nose and eye, is done with suitable dropper. Swabing is done with a piece of cotton or gauze.

Internal Medication (through Orifices)

Oral: Oral medication is the most common route. Either tablets, bolus or liquid can be administered easily. Help of a balling gun can be taken for the administration of tablets or boluses. For liquid, a drenching bottle (metallic) or glass bottle with long neck is used. The head of the animal is held slightly raised (not too high). The mouth is opened with left hand leaving the tongue mobile. Fluid is allowed to trickle slowly from the opposite side with the help of right hand. Care is to be taken to avoid liquid entry into the lungs, which will be marked by cough instantaneously. For large volume, pass the stomach tube.

Rectal: Administration of medicated liquid or buffer water or soap water (enema) may be carried out. The fluid is kept at higher level and the lubericated (with glycerine, soap or paraffin) free end of the tube carrying fluid is introduced into the rectum. The anal sphincter is kept closed with fingers to avoid back flow. The required amount is introduced.

Uterus: Intrauterine medication is done with a long metallic or glass pipette attached to a syrine. The cervix is held through rectal wall and the tube is directed through the cervix deep enough and the drug is discharged applying pressure on the piston

Intranasal: Liquid is instilled drop by drop into the nasal cavity.

Inhalation: Medicated vapour, produced by heat or water bath or so, is allowed for inhalation. The particles of the vapour may reach to upper respiratory tract only.

Vaginal route: Ointment is applied in the vagina using suitable vaginal speculum.

Intracystic: Administration of liquid medicaments into the urinary bladder is done in females following introduction of suitable rubber or polythene catheter. Prior to drug infusion, the urine must be sucked with syringe or by syphoning.

Parentral Administration

The method requires use of syringe and needle. The drug is deposited in the muscles, subcutaneous tissue, intradermal (intracutaneous), veins or into the organs, directly.

Subcutaneous Injection

A fold of skin, preferably of neck, anterior to the shoulder in cattle, buffalo and horse, while of back in dog and cat is lifted. Suitable sized needle is swiftly pricked at right angle of skin. The medicine is deposited under the skin.Following withdrawal of needle, the site is pressed (10 seconds) or massaged to prevent escape of injected fluid. Continuous infusion should not exceed 60 drops per minute. Irritant and large volume of fluid should not be injected. Drug absorption is slower than intramuscular route.

Intradermal (Intracutaneous)

The drug is deposited in the dermis. A needle of 28 gauge x 1/2" long, is suitable. Direct the needle at 30 degree with the skin. Injection leaves a beady elevation at the site of inoculation. For tuberculin, Johnin and drug sensitivity tests, this route is used.

Intramuscular Injection

The injection is made in the gluteal muscle, neck, back or in hind quarter muscle. Prick the needle deep into the muscle. Attach the syringe and pull back the piston to assure that it is beyond the vein. If blood is not appearing, inject the drug. A maximum of 25-30 ml is to be injected at one site in large animals. It takes about half hour for its action. For wild or zoo animals, a self emptying syringe, attached to a long pole, can be used.

Intravenous Injection

The drug is poured directly into the vein for quickest action. The more amount of drug can be infused @ 60-150 drops per minute easily. Preferably jugular, ear or milk or sub-cutaneous abdominal vein (cattle, buffalo, horse, pig, camel, sheep and goat) and cephalic or tarsal vein in dogs and cats, should be selected. Suitable needle is pricked first into skin, then into the vein forwardly. A jet flow of blood through needle indicates proper injection. In dog and cat, back pulling of piston is required to assess if the needle is in vein. These possibilities must be ruled out if blood is not coming: (i) needle is not in the vein, (ii) crossing of needle through the vein, (iii) tip of the needle is blocked with tissue material. Reattempt is made anterior to the first one. As soon as the blood emerges, the infusion set or syringe is attached to the needle. The doubt of escape of needle from the vein is ruled out by lowering the infusion set or back pull of piston. If blood comes into the tube or barrel, indicates correct position. Following infusion, the needle is withdrawn and the site is pressed for 1-2 minutes with spirit soaked cotton swab. Ear vein gets prominent by applying tourniquet around its base and massage on the pinna. This site is preferred for continuous fluid drip as the needle is comfortably fixed on ear with adhesive tape. The subcutaneous abdominal vein or milk vein is attempted when other veins are not easily approachable.

Intraperitoneal Injection

Electrolyte solutions, glucose saline, calcium preparation and whole blood infusion is indicated by this route.

Irritant material should not be infused intraperitoneally. Right flank in ruminants and left flank in horses, while both sides of the linea alba in dog and cat are the sites for injection. The site must be prepared properly. The needle (3-4" x 15 gauge) is inserted at 6-8" below the transverse process of lumber vertebrae on the right flank in cattle and buffaloes. Skin penetration is followed by abdominal muscle reaching well into the peritoneal cavity. Care should be taken to avoid intesine and kidney puncture. As soon as the needle enters the cavity, it sucks air which can be appreciated carefully Carefulbackpressurecreatedbysyringes should draw nothing being the needle properly in the cavity. Some times the needle gets blocked by cut skin,which can be cleared with stylet. The advantage is that the technique does not restrict the rate of infusion. In pups and youngs where intavenous injection is not feasible, this route is advised.

Intrathecal Injection

It is indicated when CNS involvement is suspected. The technique is employed as for extradural anaesthesia. The preferable site is lumbo-sacral junction in cattle and buffalo.

Intra-articular Injection

The medicaments are directly injected into the joints. The anatomical appreciation is must for selecting the site for needling. Strict aseptic precautions are emphasised to avoid introduction of infection.

Intra-ovarian Injection

Chorionic gonadotrophin is injected for the treatment of cystic ovaries in large animals. The ovary is held between thumb and forefinger through rectum. A long, thin and hollow needle is introduced through cleaned vagina. The point of the needle, passing through vaginal fornix enters the cyst. The cystic fluid is withdrawn and the drug is injected.

Intra-testicular Injection

It is indicated during castration in bulls. The testicles are grasped at the lower end of the scrotum with one hand and the needle is inserted in the middle of the testis and the anaesthetic is injected.

Intra-tracheal

This route is not generally preferred but wherever it is required, the lower third of the neck is selected as site. Taking all the aseptic steps, needle is introduced between two tracheal rings. A maximum volume of 100 ml is advisible for large cattle and buffalo.

Intramammary Injection

It is advised for the treatment and prevention of mastitis. The teat tips are washed properly, disinfected and evacuated completely. The tube nozzle is lubricated and introduced carefully in the streak canal of the teat held in one hand and the tube is squeezed out with other hand. Following drug administration, the teat opening is kept closed and massaged vertically. Aseptic cares are necessary to avoid introduction of infection.

Intra-ruminal Injection

Anti-bloating and anti-foaming agents need intraruminal administration. A 15 gauge x 4.5 to 6" long needle is introduced carefully at dorso-cranial level in left para lumber fossa. The ruminal fluid or gas comes out of the needle. Using suitable syringe, the drug is deposited directly in to the rumen.

Intra-abomasal

The technique is very similar to that of abomasal fluid collection in cattle and buffaloes. The needle (3-4" long) is introduced midway between the umbilicus and caudal point of the xiphoid cartilage (Fig. 4.1). .

As soon it reaches the abomasum, fluid comes out and with the help of syringe the drug is introduced.

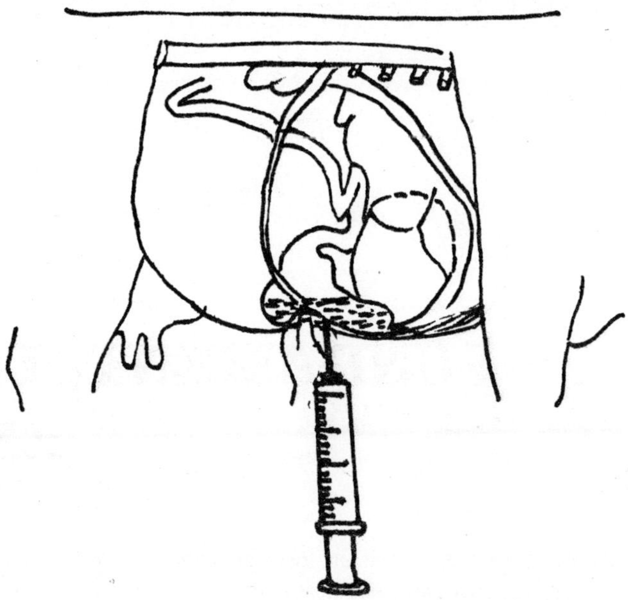

Fig. 4.1 Intra-abomasal injection

REFERENCE

Rosenberger, G (1979) *Clinical Examination of Cattle*. Verlag Paul Parey, Berlin and Hamberg.

5

FUNDAMENTALS IN ANIMAL EXAMINATION

The senses of sight, hearing, smell and touch are applied by the clinician during clinical examination of animals. This is performed under two basic headings:

1. Inspection
2. Physical examination

Inspection of the animal is carried out by the clinician being at a distance from the animal. He is to utilize principally the sense of sight. Preferably, the inspection should be done in day-light. The outer bodily condition of the animal is recorded, so also the general behaviour of the animal is recorded. The inspection should be done, while history is being undertaken.

The physical examination of the animals is performed with or without the help of some instruments. Under physical examination, the animal has to be examined very closely. Thus, it is imperative that the animal should be well restrained, unexcited and the room should be calm and quiet. The following techniques are used.

Palpation

The sense of touch is used for this. The fingers of one or both hands are put in the direct contact of body tissues. The abnormal tissue changes, like increase in size, shape, the consistency, pain and temperature may be appreciated. The area palpated may be doughy, firm, hard, fluctuating or emphysematous (presence of gas under the skin). For judging the consistency of the organ, the clinician must be apprised of feeling of normal organs.

Percussion

Information on the condition of deeper organ or tissue is obtained by this method. The part of the body is struck by means of fingers or instruments. Audible sound is being produced by the tissue struck. However, the sound varies according to the density of tissues. Percussion is used for the organs of thorax (heart, lungs), abdominal cavity (rumen, reticulum, abomasum, liver, uterus),paranasal sinuses and the underlying structure of skin. However, its diagnostic application varies according to species and is limited in large animals. The percussions are of two types.

Immediate Percussion

Striking the part directly with finger tips, is called immediate percussion.

Mediate Percussion

In this method a circular or oval plastic plate (pleximeter) and a firm rubber-hammer (plexor) are used. The pleximeter is placed in direct contact of the body surface and the stroke is applied with plexor (Fig. 5.1).

In thin and small animals, mediate percussion can be performed using hand fingers. The middle finger of the left hand (as pleximeter) is placed on the area to be percussed, and the finger (middle) of the right hand (as plexor) is struck. This is also known as finger-finger percussion.

The information obtainable by this method is very limited in buffalo and fatty animals. However, experience may be helpful in using this technique. In order to obtain best percussion sound, the following principles are to be adopted:

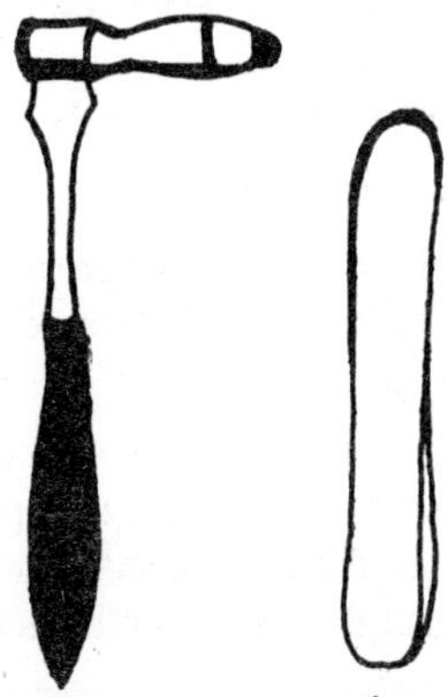

Fig. 5.1 (a) Plexor (hammer)
(b) Pleximeter

1. The pleximeter/finger should be in close contact with skin.
2. The handle of the hammer should move loosely between the thumb and first two fingers.
3. The hammer hand should be higher than the hand holding pleximeter.
4. Each stroke should be perpendicular to the pleximeter.
5. Whole area should be percussed and repeated if necessary.

Very gentle percussion (threshold percussion) gives accurate information while strong percussion is used for deeply placed organs.

Modified Percussion

The technique in which both percussion and palpation are applied together. eg ballottement and fluid percussion.

Ballottement

The method of percussion in which repeated, firm push is applied to a needed part of the body to propel away the underlying organ and the rebound of that organ is felt with the finger tips. Detection of foetal ball can be achieved in pregnant cow and buffalo by this technique.

Fluid Percussion

The abdominal wall of one side is precussed and the fluid wave (as in ascites) is perceived by palpation on the other side of the abdomen.

Auscultation

The process of listening the sound of internal organs in order to assess their functional status is called auscultation. For example, the appraisal of heart, lungs or intestinal sounds. The technique is applied either directly or indirectly.

Direct Method

When the organic sound is listened without the help of instrument. The ear is placed directly on the lung or cardiac area and the sound is noted. A piece of fine cloth may be placed if the skin is soiled. This method is not useful in unco-operative animals..

Indirect Method (Stethoscopy)

The sound is heard with the help of instrument. Either stethoscope (Steth=chest, scope=examination) or phonendoscope (phone=modified sound; scope=examination) is used for the purpose. The instrument contains a chest-piece, rubber tubes and ear piece (Fig. 5.2). The chest-piece with diaphragm is termed as phonendoscope.

The bell shaped chest piece is applied on the part to be auscultated. Friction sound produced by hairs is minimised if the chest-piece has a rubber rim. This method is superior than the direct method. Pertinent informations about the organ can be derived by stethoscopy.

(a) Phonendoscope

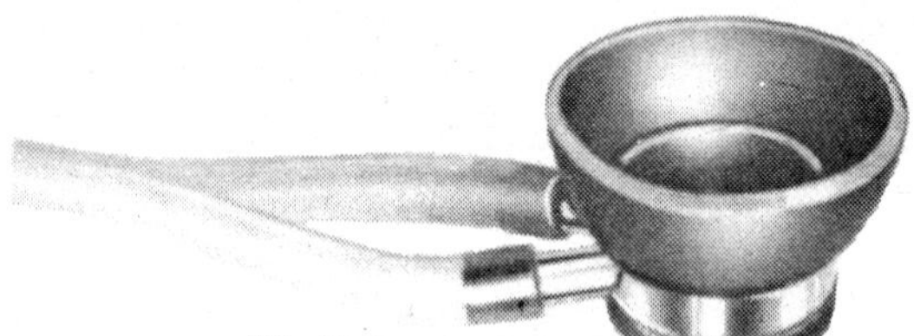

(b) Bell stethoscope

Fig. 5.2

REFERENCE

Kelly, W.R. (1984) *Veterinary Clinical Diagnosis, 3rd ed. Bailliere, Tindall, London.*

6

ROUTINE EXAMINATION OF THE PATIENT

The procedure is termed also as general examination or preliminary general examination. The fundamental steps in carrying out the preliminary general examination are to record the following things:

1. Indentification of the patient
2. History or anamnesis
3. Routine clinical examination
   A. General Inspection
   B. General Clinical Examination

1. Identification of the Patient

In order to establish the identity of the animal, it is imperative to note the description of the animal. This not only helps in narrowing the field of diseases to which that patient is susceptible but does help in certification of the cases of litigation and vetro-legal evidences.

In case of horse, the height, colour-marks, brand marks on the hip or the number marked with tatooing machine on the ear and the pedigree number are to be recorded.

Species of the Animal

There is marked species difference in the susceptibility to a particular disease. The horses and mules are highly Susceptible to glander but the cattle and buffalo are totally immune.Traumatic pericarditis is most common in cattle and buffalo because of their unselective habit of feed intake Cattle and buffalo are most vulnerable to foot and mouth disease while the horses are immune to this disease.

Breed of the Animal

High milch dairy breed of animals suffer more commonly from production diseases. Jersey cows suffer more from milk fever. Photosensitization occurs mostly in light coloured horses.

Sex

Certain diseases pertain to either sex only. Metritis is a disease of female while phimosis and paraphimosis are the problems of males.

Age

New-borns are more susceptible to diseases than the adults. Calf-scour, ascariasis, umbilical disease and joint-ill are the diseases of youngs primarily.Adult cattle are less susceptible to paratuberculosis. Distemper is more common in young dogs while circulatory and renal diseases are more common in older dogs.

2. History (Anamnesis)

In veterinary practice, the disease problem is presented indirectly in the form of complaint by the owners or the attendants. Thus it is necessary to have all the information very intelligently from the owner. Accurate information may be expected from an educated owner or otherwise most of the time, the attendant fails to provide pertinent history. Inaccurate history may lead to mis-diagnosis. The clinician must substantiate these with rational questions utilizing professional acumen. The history taking can be achieved under three headings.

(i) Immediate History

It comprises recording of sequential events from the start of the sickness. Questions about physiological functions such as appetite for feed or water, urination, defaecation, rumination, respiration, sweating, milk production, hearing ability, gait, posture, voice, odour, working ability etc. should be put.

(ii) Past History

If number of animals are sick in one herd, the feed specimen must be examined. The treatment given, if any and the period of medication are also to be recorded. Prolonged use of some medicine creats symptoms other than primary disease, which is known as **iatrogenic** disease. Wrong medication techniques cause diseases in animals e.g. mastitis, metritis, cystitis etc.

(iii) Environmental or Nutritional History.

Acquaintance of environment and state of nutrition are some time helpful in the diagnosis of disease. Geographical factor and season help in the incidence of a particular disease.

Animals grazed on pastures irrigated with sewerage water or municipality waste may suffer from nitrate or nitrite toxicosis. Wilted plants may cause cyanide toxicosis. Sudden change from roughage to rich carbohydrate diet may lead to acid indigestion. Similarly, inadequate supply of minerals leads to deficiency diseases. Calves fed exclusively on milk may suffer from hypomagnesaemic tetany. Parasitic diseases are more common in animals grazed on marshy and canalised areas where water logging is present. Recent application of insecticides or weedicides may poison the grazing animals. Evidence of recent painting on wood works may provide valuable clue in relation to lead poisoning.

Both hygiene and climatic factors also have influence on the incidence of disease. Poor hygiene causes mastitis in dairy herd while warmth and humidity are conducive for parasitic diseases. Disease associated with vector, for example trypanosomiasis in animals, is more common in summer season, when the flies are abundant.

3. Routine Clinical Examination

A. General Inspection: Routine examination of the patient starts from inspection of the animals from some distance. The animals should be examined from all the angles. A thorough appraisal must be made in respect of the followings:

Physical Condition: Simple inspection can assess the body condition of the animal. However, the presence of long hair and wool masks the physical status. Well nourished animals have rounded appearance and the bones are covered with flesh. Animals in poor condition appear hide-bound. The bones are prominent, supraorbital fossae are deep and the body coat is lusterless, starring, dry and loss of elasticity. Chronic diseases like tuberculosis, Johne's disease, parasitic diseases, malnutrition and copper deficiency cause emaciation of the animals.

Appearance: Abnormal conformations of the body are suggestive of certain disease. Stunted growth is suggestive of parasitism while bending of legs of ricketic animals.

Expression: Peculiar facial expression attracts the attention of clinician. Anxious expression of a dog is seen in rabies and dilation of nostrils in horse suffering from tetanus.

Behaviour: Behavioural changes often help in establishing the disease from which the animals is suffering e.g. apparent blindness in cattle in lead poisoning dummy syndrome in horse suffering from cirrhosis of liver, comatose state in cow suffering from milk fever and aggressive behaviour in rabid animal(Colour PlateNO.A.)

Hair: The hair coat of the healthy animal appears shining, which however, depends on the management and grooming. In cattle, presence of lick marks on the skin speak good health. Erection of hairs occurs in febrile condition. Loss of hairs at places of body may be due to fungal infection. Generalised alopecia is noted in pigs suffering from iodine deficiency. Shedding of hair of tail and around coronary band of the feet is seen in buffalo suffering from degnala disease. Chronic indigestion also causes loss of hair in this species. Diffuse blotching is seen in pigs suffering from swine fever. Pregnant as well as lactating bitch lose hairs significantly.

Posture: Abnormal presentation of the body during disease condition helps in diagnosis. Buffalo suffering from traumatic pericarditis keeps the elbow abducted, Cow suffering from milk fever sits on its sternum and keeps her head flexed on one side. Wry-neck is seen in cervical vertebra dislocation (Colour Plate No.A.).

Typical rigid (wooden horse)posture is characteristic of tetanus in horse. In acute laminitis, horse keeps hind legs well forward under the body. Prolonged standing is seen in cattle and buffalo suffering from pneumonia in order to alleviate respiratory embarrassment.

Gait: Evidence of disease is recognized when the animal is forced to move. No doubt, tetanus is suspected in horse moving stiffly. Similarly jerky lift and forced touch to the ground by hind leg (s) in horse suggest presence of stringhalt.. Horses suffering from shivering shows inability in backing. Pigs suffering from pantothenic acid deficiency have peculier goose-stepping. Shortening of medial patellar ligament causes dragging of hind legs in cattle and buffaloes.

Cattle, buffalo, sheep and goat suffering from hydatidosis (*Taenia multiceps)* may move in circle, turning the head on affected side or they may move in straight direction till they strike against some object.

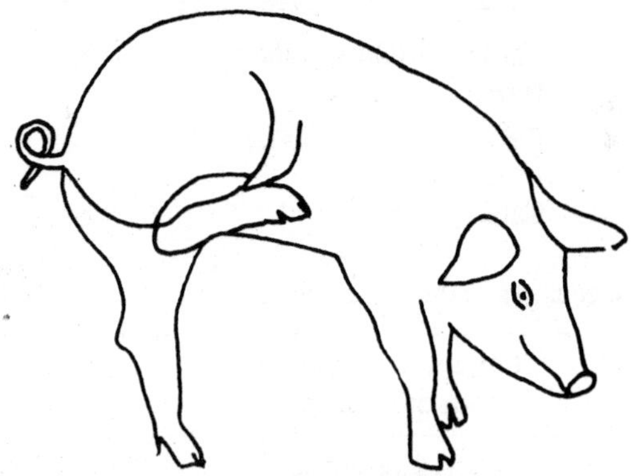

Fig. 6.1 Goose-stepping in pig-pantothenic acid deficiency.

Abnormal Action

Abnormal actions attract the attention of clinician, which help in reaching the diagnosis. Straining (tenesmus) is seen in dog suffering from constipation. Frequent lifting of tail in order to defaecate, is seen in cattle and buffalo having intestinal obstruction or fecoliths. Kicking at the belly is seen in horse suffering from colic and in bullocks having overdistension of urinary bladder due to urethral calculi.

Striking of horns against wall or manger is seen in buffalo with horn-sinus infection. Frequent micturition is characteristic of urethral obstruction in male dogs, bullocks and male buffaloes. Both frequency as well as volume of urine are increased in patients suffering from diabetes mellitus. Similarly yawning gives evidence of digestive disturbance in animals, while coughing is indicative of respiratory problem.

Abdomen: The state of abdomen speaks certain pathological conditions. Distension of rumen is seen in bloat while tucked-up belly is seen in horse suffering from grass sickness. The abdomen becomes pendulous and distended in dogs with ascites.

Rumination: Rumination is the fundamental exercise of the ruminants in normal health. Suspension of rumination invariably be considered as an evidence of abnormality in the digestion.

Respiration: Normal respiratory rate varies according to the size and age of the animal. Accelerated respiration is observed in fever. Animals suffering from respiratory disease have marked changes in respiratory rate. e.g. pneumonia.

Thoracic respiration is prominent in animals suffering from acute peritonitis and opposite to this, abdominal respiration is marked when there is presence of pleurisy. Double expiratory lifts of abdomen are seen in horse suffering with heaves (broken-wind).

B. General Clinical Examination

Following general inspection, a thorough general clinical examination is performed on the patient. This requires a close visualization of the patient with eyes and also with the use of clinical tools (e.g. thermometry, stethoscopy etc). For accurate examination, the animal must relatively be calm and quiet, as nervousness not only enhances the pulse rate and respiration, the haematological norms are also influenced markedly.

Visible Mucous Membrane

Examinations of visible mucous membranes, namelyconjunctival, nasal, buccal, vaginal, urethral and rectal, are helpful in diagnosing the diseases. The tissues around the orifice by which particular mucosa extends, should be inspected. The changes in these membranes closely relate the pathological condition on the membrane or its contiguity. The examination must be done in day-light, as artificial light masks the colour of mucous membranes (colour plate-A).

The normal appearance of conjunctiva in different species of animals:

Animals	Conjunctival colour
Cattle, buffalo and sheep	Light pink
Horse	Pale pink/roseate
Pigs	Reddish
Dogs	Pale pink
Cats	Pale

The changes in the conjunctival mucous membrane are indicative of diseases in general

Changes in conjunctival mucous membrane	Associated disease
• Pale and watery	Anaemia, blood loss.
• Blanched	Acute haemorrhage, shock
• Injected (intense), congested	Encephalitis, enteritis, pneumonia.
• Cyanosed (bluish grey)	Nitrite toxicosis, defective oxygenation of blood, pneumonia, over dosing with methylene blue.
• Yellow colouration	Jaundice, haemolytic crisis, hepatitis.
• Bright pink	Equine influenza (pink eye)
• Petecheal haemorrhage	Haemorrhagic septicaemia in cattle and buffalo, glanders and perpura haemorrhagica in horses.

Presence of eye discharge is also to be recorded as it is of significance in conditions like malignant catarrh in cattle, canine distemper and swine fever. Changes in one mucous membrane should be correlated with the others. Congested vaginal mucous membrane in female may be during heat, which must not be considered as systemic involvement.

Nasal Mucosa

The possibility of inspection of nasal mucosa is limited in cattle and buffalo and very little in dog, cat and pig. The changes like pallor, discolouration, congestion and petechiasis should be noticed. Ulceration of nasal mucosa of horse in glander is of particular importance. A rusty foetid nasal discharge is characteristic of pulmonary gangrene.

Mouth

Inspection of mouth is carried out in respect of the appearance of buccal mucous membrane, the odour of the mouth and the condition of teeth. The examination is facilitated by use of mouth gags in different animals. (Plate No. 3,4,5).

Excess salivation is an important symptom of foot and mouth disease in cattle and buffalo but in general it may arise in stomatitis caused by number of factors like chemicals, fungi, bacteria or viruses etc.

Changes in oral cavity	Possible diseases
• Hypersalivation	Stomatitis (chemical, bacterial, viral), foot and mouth disease, mouldy feed, hard feed.
• Acetone smell	Ketosis (post-parturient dyspepsia).
• Sour sticky smell	Chronic digestive upset.
• Offensive smell	Lungs gangrene, teeth decay.
• Ulcers	FMD, mucosal disease, bad teeth, actinomycosis.
• Vesication	Foot and mouth disease, irritant chemicals or drugs.
• Dirty brown discolouration	Toxaemia of gastro-intestinal and teeth origin.
Appearance of Tongue:	
• Wooden	Actinobacillosis.
• Velvety	Fungal infection.
• Whitish film	Indigestion (dog).
• Copper coloured	Toxaemia/uraemia.

Eye

Following examination of oral cavity, the eyes are to be examined. It is essential to examine both the eyes and any deviation from the normal is to be recorded. Normal eyes are moist and shining. Breed variation is not uncommon but excess bulging or sunkening should be taken as pathological condition. Dryness of eye surface and sunkening in the socket occur in dehydration. For detail, see examination of the eyes.

Ear

The shape and size of the ears vary in different species of animals. The ear of cattle, buffalo, sheep, pig and cat is erect. In dog, some breed have erect ear (Alsatian) and some have flat (Spaniel). Grossly the ear should be looked for injury, swelling, ectoparasites and the discharge.

Direct examination of ear drum is not possible owing to large external meatus. A right angle turn at the bottom makes practically difficult. Waxy glandular secretion is present on the external meatus of all the animals, which should be cleaned with the help of cotton swab held in artery forceps.

For inspection of the ear, an electric torch or suitable auroscope is used. It projects light into the external ear. The inspector's eye is placed behind a lens of the apparatus, which provides magnified field of vision. Ulceration or inflammation of the ear membrane is recognised.

Any abnormal secretion in the ear is noted. Inflammation of lower part of the external meatus is well appreciated as palpation of ear provokes pain. The ear debris with waxy material must be examined for mange or mite. Direct trauma or suppuration may lead to rupture of tympanum, which is characterised by severe pain and the animal keeps head tilted towards affected side.

Ear Function Test

The proper function of ear is tested by clapping with hands, drum sound or canister beating. Turning of head and looking towards the direction of sound indicate normal function of the ear. The test is of not much help in mild deafness.

Skin and Body Surface

The different body surfaces are palpated in order to appreciate the temperature and also to determine the inflammatory swelling in localised parts of the body. If there is localised inflammation, the other parts of the body will be colder comparatively. In hyperthermia (sunstroke) the whole skin surface feels hot. In healthy cattle and buffalo, ears and the lower parts of the limbs feel colder. The muzzle is cool and moist. The nose is the best indication of body temperature. Presence of dry and hot nose in dog indicates febrile condition. Normally it is cool and moist.

In chronic diseases and poor nutrition, the hairs are pulled out very easily without pain. In certain disease (e.g. Johne's disease) it becomes difficult to raise the skin fold due to depletion of subcutaneous fat. The condition is called as "hide-bound". The skin fold is lifted (tenting) for assessing the degree of dehydration and also to know the adherence to the adjacent tissue. The skin of neck, back and behind elbow can be lifted for the purpose in cattle, bufalo, horse and sheep.

Clinical assessment of degree of dehydration in animals:

Body wt loss(%)	Sunken eyes	Tenting of skin fold (sec)	Haematocrit (%)	Fluid required to meet the loss (ml/kg. b.wt)
4-6	Not detected	- -	40-50	20-25
6-8	+	2-4	50	30-50
8-10	++	6-10	55	50-80
10-12	+++	20-45	60	80-120

Superficial Lymph Nodes

The superficial lymph nodes are examined for its size, (Fig. 6.2). Swelling of these nodes often occur in diseases like theileriasis, tuberculosis, leukemia and the dieases of lymphatics.

Rumen Movement

The churning movement of the rumen is an index of normal digestive function of the ruminant. The frequency varies from 2-3 per min in cattle and buffaloes. The motility ceases in acute acidosis/alkalosis. In the early stage of tympany, there is hypermotility of rumen. Both the frequency and force of contraction must be noted for grading the rumen movement. It may be either weak, feeble or forceful.

Animals	Rumen motility every 5 minutes
Cattle	8-10
Buffalo	10-12
Sheep	7-8
Goat	7-8

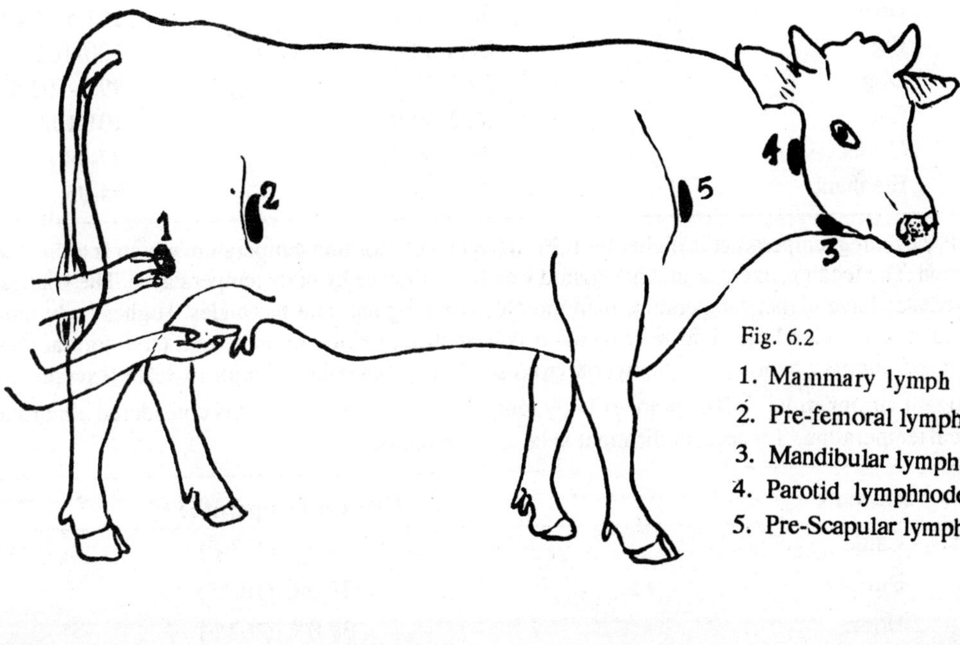

Fig. 6.2
1. Mammary lymph node.
2. Pre-femoral lymphnode
3. Mandibular lymphnode
4. Parotid lymphnode
5. Pre-Scapular lymphnode

Temperature

The oxidative processes in liver and skeletal muscle of animal generate heat which is measured as body temperature. The thermoregulatory centre, the hypothalamus, maintains a balanced between heat production and heat loss, keeping the body temperature independant to the environment. The body heat is lost by radiation, conduction, convection, evaporation, sweating, respiration, defaecation and urination.

Thermometry

The body temperature is recorded with the help of a clinical thermometer,graduated between95 110° F with round bulb. The thermometer should be lubricated with soap or jelly before insertion into the rectum. In female, the temperature can be recorded in vagina, where the value is approximately 1°F higher than the rectum.

Precautions in Thermometry:

- Allow the animal to rest in shade for at least 20-30 minutes.
- Avoid intake of cold water before thermometry
- The bulb of the thermometer must touch the rectal or vaginal mucosa.
- Hot-humid or chilled weather and the physiological states must be considered while interpretation of temperature.

Normal Body Temperatures (Average)

Animals	°C	°F
Cattle (adult)	37.8-39.2	100-102.5
Buffalo (adult)	37.5-38.5	99.5-101.3
Horse (adult)	37.2-38.0	99-100.5
Sheep	38.9-40.0	102-104
Goat	38.6-40.2	101.5-104.5
Pig	37.8-38.9	100-102
Dog	37.5-39.2	99.5-102.5
Cat	38.2-39.0	101-102
Camel	36.1-36.7	97-98
Elephant	34.6-35.0	94-95

The evening temperature is higher by 1.5°F from that of morning temperature which is termed **as diurnal** variation. The feeding, exercise and hot-humid weather influence by body temperataure. The youngs, pregnants and females have higher temperature than the old, non-pregnant and the males. Higher body temperature is indicative of increased metabolism (exception is heat-stroke) while hypothermia (sub-normal temperature is seen in old animals, debility, shock, hypothyroidism, hypocalcaemia and prior to death (exception in tetanus).

Critical Temperature: The point of body temperature beyond which it is considered abnormal is called critical temperature. It varies in different species of animals.

Animals	Critical Temperatue °C
Cattle	39.5°C (103°F)
Buffalo	39.0°C (102°F)
Horse	39.0°C (102°F)
Goat	40.0°C (104°F)
Sheep	40.0°C (104°F)
Pig	40.0°C (104°F)
Dog	39.5°C (103.1°F)

The variation in body temperature is dependent on the type of fever. Fever produces a symptom complex like rise in temperature, shivering, increased pulse and respiration, firm faeces and less and concentrated urine. The degree of fever is judged based on the body temperature as mild (low), moderate- severe and severe,if the temperature is above normal by 2°F, 3-4°F and 5-6°F respectively.

Types of fever

Based on the elevation of body temperature and its periodicity of occurrence, the fever has been typed as below:

- **Simple Fever:** The raised temperature varies less than 2°F (1°C) which remains for several days and it falls as the animal recovers e.g. pneumonia, surgical fever and ephemeral fever.
- **Atypical Fever:** It runs an irregular course. It is very common type of fever in animal. e.g.swine erysipelas, strangles in horse.
- **Continuous Fever:** The elevated temperature runs for a longer period than simple fever. e.g.tic Traumatic pericarditis, tick-borne fever.
- **Intermittent Fever:** Short attacks of fever for 2-3- days accompanied with non-febrile stage at regular intervals e.g. distemper in dogs.
- **Recurrent Fever:** There is relatively prolonged attack of fever with long afebrile interval of equal duration.
- **Relapsing Fever:** Slow rise in body temperature to a peak level which falls rapidly and rises again. The cycle continues several times.
- **Remittent Fever:** There are rise and fall in temperature by more than 20F at short and irregular intervals e.g. septicaemia and U.T.I.

Undulant Fever: Occurrence of high and less severe fever for long period at irregular intervals. The lowering of body temperature occurs either by crisis (rapid lowering) or by lysis (slow lowering). (slow lowering

Pulse

Proper appreciation of pulse in the domestic animals provides idea about the circulatory as well as systemic states. The frequency as well as the characters of the pulse change following structural or functional alterations either in the heart or by other secondary conditions within the body. For taking pulse, the animal must be quiet, otherwise the clinician may feel difficulty in perceiving it.

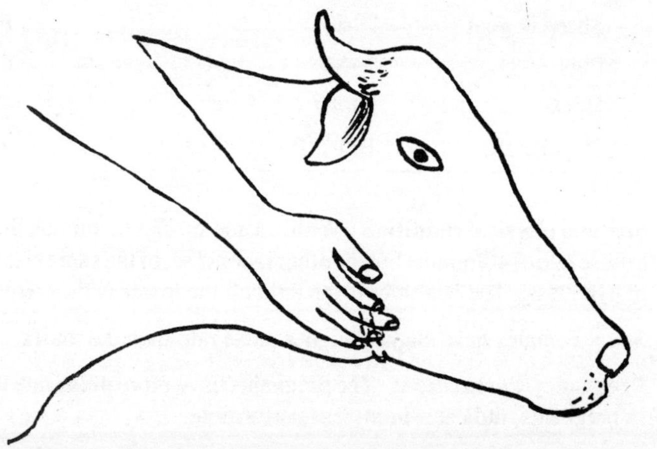

Fig. 6.3 Maxillary artery pulsation

The site of pulsation varies in different species of animals and any one site is selected as per convenience. In cattle, buffalo and horses, the external maxillary artery on the lateral aspect of mandible (Fig. 6.3) is used for taking the pulse. The median artery at the upper extremity in fore limb is also used. The coccygeal artery at the base of the tail (Fig 1 Colour Plate) may be used but switching movement of the tail by the animal and feeble blood pressure pose difficulty in judging both the frequency and the quality of the pulse.

The femoral artery on the medial side of the thigh is used in sheep, goat, pig, calf, dog and cat. However, in adult pigs, the ventral coccygeal artery can be used for pulse recording. Whenever the pulse is not felt properly, as in generalised muscle tremors, the cardiac rate is noted. The frequency of pulse rate is equal to the cardiac rate with exception in conditions like extrasystolic arrhythmia, where the beat fails to induce pulse wave sometimes.

The counting of pulse must be either for 30 seconds and the value is multiplied by two or for 1 minute to escape error. The middle finger tip should be placed on the artery gently. The undesirable pressure of the finger may block the pulse wave. For judging the quality of pulse, finger tip pressure is applied on the artery till the wave is not felt. However, it requires practical experience to appreciate the quality of pulse. The practitioners are advised to gain experience first on normal animals and then to apply on the patient, in order to appreciate the frequency, rhythm and quality of pulse.

Factors Affecting Normal Pulsation in Animals:

Age: The pulse rate of youngs is much higher than the adults. The new - born calf has a pulse beat of 90-110 per minute in comparison to 50-70 per minute of the adult cattle and buffaloes.

Species: The pulse rate varies according to the species of the animals (described in the table)

Normal Pulse Rate in Animals (per minute)

Animal	Pulse rate	Animal	Pulse rate
Cattle	50-70	Dog (large)	70-90
Buffalo	48-65	Cat	110-130
Sheep & goat	70-80	Poultry	150-200
Pigs	70-80	Camel	30-50
Horse	30-40	Elephant	30-40
Dog (small)	100-110		

Size and physical condition : Within same species of animal, the pulse rate varies. A normal horse may have a pulse rate of 40/minute but the other race horse, of the same size and physical condition, may have 30, minute or even less. The healthier is the animal, the lesser is the frequency of the pulse.

Sex : Females have slightly higher pulse rate than the males.

Pregnancy/Parturition: The pregnants have more pulse rate than non-pregnants and if it further increases in pregnants, indicates imminent parturition.

Lactation : The high yielders have more pulse rate than the non-lactating animals.

Excitements: A strange person's approach may cause 10 per cent increase in the pulse rate in dairy animals. Similarly the nervous animals have more pulse rate.

Feed intake: The frequency of pulsation is more soon after intake of feed in animals.

Rumination: Ruminants have an increased pulse rate upto 3 per cent at the time of rumination.

Exercise: The exertion of exercise increases the pulse rate. The elevated rate normalise comparatively sooner (within 10 minutes) in healthy animals in comparison to sick animals.

Climate: During hot-humid weather, the frequency of pulse increases significantly.

The rythm is noted, whether there is missing of some pulse or not. If it is missing, whether it is at regular interval or irregular interval.

Respiration

Recording of respiration assists in assessing the involvement of respiratory tract. The respiratory action is achieved by both abdominal and thoracic movements. The contraction and expansion of diaphragm play major role in the process of respiration. The respiration must be recorded when the animal is in standing position, as recumbency alters the rate and character of respiration. The observations on both the sides are advised to judge uniform bilateral expansion of the abdomen. The rate and rhythm of respiration are appreciated by keeping hand on the lower part of the flank or placing the palm infront of the nostrils. This is also achieved by auscultation of the thorax. The rate, type, rhythm and quality of respiration are to be recorded.

Animals	Normal Respiration Rate (per minute)
Cattle	20-30
Buffalo	20-28
Sheep & Goats	20-30
Horse	10-14
Pig	12-18
Dog	15-30
Cat	20-30
Camel	5-12
Elephant	6-9

Rate: The frequency of respiration is increased (polypnoea) in excitation, fear, high environmental temperature and after exercise. It is also increased in fever, diseases of respiratory tract, diseases of heart, peritonitis, pleurisy, anaemia and methaemoglobinaemia.

Decreased respiratory rate (oligopnoea) is noted in uraemia, stenosis of upper respiratory tract, space occupying lesion in brain and respiration failure.

Type: The type of respiration changes based on the disease affecting the different organ. The abdominal respiration is prominent, which is characterised by forceful lifting of the abdomen, as seen in case of pleurisy. There is the least movement of the thoracic wall to alleviate the pain. Similarly, when there is painful lesion in the abdominal cavity, for example acute peritonitis or ascites, the thoracic respiration is prominent. For general inference, the cattle, buffalo, sheep and goat have mainly abdominal, the horse costo-chondral, while the dog and cat have thoracic respiration.

Rhythm: One cycle of normal respiration comprises inspiration, expiration and a pause. The inspiratory period is shorter than expiratory period. The pause is dependant on whether the animal is resting or not. The sniffing habit of dog and pig makes the normal respiration irregular. Prolongation of inspiration is met with in condition causing obstruction of upper respiratory tract e.g. nasal polyp or nasal granuloma. The expiratory period longs in pulmonary emphysema, characterised by double movement of the flank. Respiratory pause does not occur when the lungs are involved e.g. pneumonia. Irregular respiration is seen during recumbency.

Depth: The quality of respiration alters according to the disease conditions. The depth of respiration increases (laboured breathing) in acute methaemoglobinaemia and anoxia. In this, thoracic as well as abdominal movements are clearly appreciated. Shallow respiration is seen in pneumonic patient. Unilateral movement or asymmetrical respiratory movement is noted when either one lung is consolidated.

Difficult respiration (dyspnoea) may be either inspiratory, as in pneumonia, lung oedema, pleurisy, hydro-cyanic poisoning or expiratory as in pulmonary emphysema, where expulsion of air out of the lungs is impeded.

References

Boddie, G.F. (1969) *Diagnostic Methods in Veterinary Medicine*, 6th ed. Oliver and Boyd, Edinburgh.

Gibbons, W.J. (1966) *Clinical Diagnosis of Diseases of Large Animals*. Lea and Febiger, Philadelphia.

Kelly, W.R. (1984) *Veterinary Clinical Diagnosis, 3rd ed.* Bailliere, Tindall London.

Rosenberger, G. (1979) *Clincal Examination of Cattle*. Verlag Paul Parey, Berlin and Hamberg

7

BODY COAT (SKIN)

The body coat of the animals reflects their health status. A shiny coat speaks good health while the dull one points some ailment, either within or without. Thus examination of skin is necessary to ascertain lesions present or infestation by external parasites. Primarily, inspection and palpation help diagnose a number of conditions. Care must be paid in respect of following:

1. Hair coat
2. Colour of skin
3. Elasticity of skin
4. Sweat secretion
5. Primary lesions
6. Microscopic examination for parasitic, bacterial and mycotic infections.
7. Skin biopsy for histopathological studies.

Hair Coat: The hairs become lusterless, dry and starring in malnurished animals. The texture also depends on species, grooming and housing of animals. Presence of lick marks on the hair coat indicate good health. Uncared hairs appear dull, dirty and rough and finally become matted or locked. Erection of hairs occurs in shivering, excitement, fear, anger and in urticaria.

Shedding of hairs (moulting), particularly in summer, is normal in most species of animals. Generalised loss of hair occurs in iodine deficiency (in pigs) and hyperkeratosis, while localised in conditions like eczema, ringworm and mange. Alopecia (loss of hair without structural change in skin) is seen in slenium, thallium, mercury and potato poisoning in horse, copper deficiency, hypothyroidism and sertoli cell testicular tumour in dogs. Inherited as well as senile alopecia has been recorded in cattle. Prolonged illness and peripheral nerve injury lead to generalised loss of hair.

Table Showing Discolouration of Skin of Animals Associated with Diseases

Nature of Discolouration	Disease Conditions
• Depigmentation (Vitiligo)	Albinism, chronic eyes or nasal discharge, Dourine (Dollar plaque)
• Reddening of skin	Congestion/haemorrhage
• Petecheal or echymotic haemorrhage	Swine fever
• Red and raised rectangular skin (diamond skin)	Swine erysipelas
• Purplish red/cyanotic colour	Heat stroke, photosensitization
• Purple udder/teat skin	Gangrenous mastitis
• Yellow discolouration	Jaundice, anaplasmosis, leptospirosis, babesiosis
• Pallor (pale)	Anaemia, parasitic diesease, cardiac insufficiency
• Bluish discolouration	Pneumonia, lung collapse, hydropneumothorax
• Hyperpigmentation (acanthosis)	Chronic dermatits, thyroid hypoplasia (dog)

Over-growth of hairs (hypertrichosis) is a hereditary rather being a pathological condition. White hair patches are seen at the harness site in horses. Brittleness (trichorrhexis nodosa) is characteristics of interruption in normal hair growth. In old age, the hairs become greyish. Depigmentation of hair occurs in copper deficiency, molybdenum toxicosis and chronic disease like Johne's disease in cattle.

Colour: Appreciation of pigmented skin of most species of animals is of limited value. Discolouration of skin is well appreciated in white pigs or colourless area of the skin in other animals.

Haemorrhage causes reddening of skin. Petecheal and echymotic haemorrhages are seen on the ear and vulval margin in hog cholera. Haemorrhagic spots on the abdomen and inside the thigh are also seen. Raised red areas (diamond shape) on the skin of neck and back indicate swine erysipelas.

Purple red discolouration of skin takes place in sunstroke and photosensitization. Purplish discolouration of skin of udder and teats of cattle and buffalo takes place in gangrenous mastitis.

Elasticity of Skin: Adequate blood and lymph supply makes the skin elastic in normal health. Skin is loose at neck, ribs, elbow, axilla and flank. Normal skin fold when lifted, regains its position immediately after release. In dehydration, tenting of skin remains for varying duration depending on the degree of fluid loss. Opposite to this, skin gets adhered to subcutaneous tissue and it is difficult to lift up. The condition is known as hidebound, which is seen in chronic wasting diseases like Johne's disease, diabetes mellitus, malnutrition, chronic parasitism and tuberculosis.

Sweat Secretion: Certain breeds of cattle and horse have true and functional sweat glands which secrete watery secretions on the body surface. In exotic cattle, buffalo, sheep, goat, pig and dog, the sweat glands are limited and poorly developed. In cattle, buffalo, dogs and pigs, the muzzle or snout sweats generally. Profuse sweating (hyperidrosis) occurs in horses during exercise, hot-humid stable, during remission of fever, pneumonia, acute colic, laminitis, equine viral arteritis, poor health, encephalomyelitis, rabies etc.

Hot Sweat: Profuse sweating with warm skin is seen in normal horses.

Cold Sweat: Usually seen in terminal stage of diseases like generalised peritonitis and intestinal rupture. The cold skin indicates unfavourable prognosis.

Decreased sweat secretion is noted in severe diarrhoea and continuous fever in cattle, buffalo and pigs. The muzzle becomes dry. Absence of sweating (anhydrosis) is seen in horse with sodium chloride deficiency and sudden and prolonged exposure to hot climate. Sweating in any particular place or side of the body may be associated with nervous origin. Patchy sweating in neck, flank and buttock area is observed in horses suffering from colic or pneumonia.

Haematidrosis (bloody sweat) occurs in horse when parasite *Filaria haemorrhagica* invades the sweat gland, equine babesiosis and warfarin, sweet clover and bracken fern toxicoses in cattle.

Urethral obstruction or cystic rupture gives urine like smell of sweat. Animals with acetonaemia and advanced diabetes have acetone like smell of skin. Generalised dermatitis, advanced demodectic mange and canine distemper give strong unpleasant smell.

Sebacious Glands: Its secretion lubricates the growing hairs and makes the hairs soft, oily and tensile. Pityriasis or excess secretion produces dandruff (scales) or seborrhea nodosa (greasy skin). The condition is seen in eczema, mange infestation, greasy heels in horses, chronic gastric upset, malnutrition and iodide toxicosis.

Skin Lesions

Spots (macules) are flat, circumscribed skin discolouration owing to disturbed blood circulation. Hyperaemic spots appear red or pink.

Roseolas are small hyperaemic macules while *erythema* are larger macules. Pin-point skin haemorrhages are termed as petechiae and larger haemorrhages are known as *echymoses*.

Papules are firm elevated skin of size between pin-head to a pea, due to cellular infiltration. Larger papules are termed as nodules and larger nodules are called **phyma**. Such eruptions are met in the early stage of acne, eczema, pox, pustular dermatitis in sheep and lumpy skin disease in cattle.

Vesicles are raised pockets of superficial epithelium containing serous fluid or lymph between epidermal or dermal layers (e.g. in foot and mouth disease). A large vesicle is termed as blister or bleb. *Pustules* are the vesicles containing pus.

Wheals or Urticaria are flat swellings on the skin caused by serous infiltration and erythema. The affected areas have bristled hairs.

Dandruffs (Scurf) are denuded epithelium on the skin. Normal epithelial proliferation leads to dandruff formation. The amount is more in pityriasis due to parasitic, nutritional and toxicological agents. Bran-like deposits are noted in chronic iodism and hyperkeratosis.

Crusts or Scabs are the hard masses of exudate and epithelium, being black in appearance.

Chaps are cracks or fissures on the skin surface reaching to subcutaneous tissues.

Ulcers are the localised lesions owing to breakdown of tissues. The margins of ulcers are elevated and have a delay healing tendency e.g. cutaneous ulcers in glanders (floor appears beaded) and equine epizootic lymphangitis (the margins are inverted)

Scars are plain, depressed or raised areas following healing of lesions. This is due to formation of fibrous tissue. Initially the colour may be red, purple or white with or without hair, depending on the sites.

Eczema is characterised by sequential formation of erythema, papules, vesicles and pustules as a result of inflammatory reaction of epidermal cells to either exogenous or endogenous substances. It may be dry or moist, itching and covered with scales. Moist eczema is most common in dog and cats and the usual sites are the back, croup, base of the tail, loins or any parts of the body. Such eczemas are less common in large animals. Both external and internal parasites, ingestion of foreign proteins, application of some chemicals, industrial effluents and keeping of animals in dump are responsible for the genesis of eczema in animals.

Hyperkeratosis is the thickening of skin due to excess keratinization of epithelial cells. Exposure of cattle with chlorinated naphthalene, arsenic or creosote alters the metabolism of fat soluble vit. A and cell division in granular layer of epidermis, resulting into hypertrophy of stratum corneum and formation of scales. The affected areas of skin becomes wrinkled and thickened. Hyperkeratinization gives rise to hard-pad condition in dogs suffering from distemper. Icthyosis (fish scales disease) in calves, is congenital hyperkeratosis.

Parakeratosis is localised or generalised skin condition in which there is incomplete keratinization of surface epithelium. The cells are soft and remain adhering to the underlying tissues. Excess calcium intake, dry feeding and deficiency of zinc in pig are known to cause parakeratosis.

Cracked Skin: Cracks and fissures on the skin of the pastern are usually the outcome of constant contact with mud or wet litter. Fissures on the back of the knee are called mallenders while infront of the hock are known as *sallenders.*

Dermatitis is the inflammation of both epidermis and dermis which may be due to bacterial, fungal, metazoal, chemicals and allergens contacts. Clinically it may be acute, chronic, exudative, ulcerative or necrotic. Erythema and itching are characteristics of dermatitis.

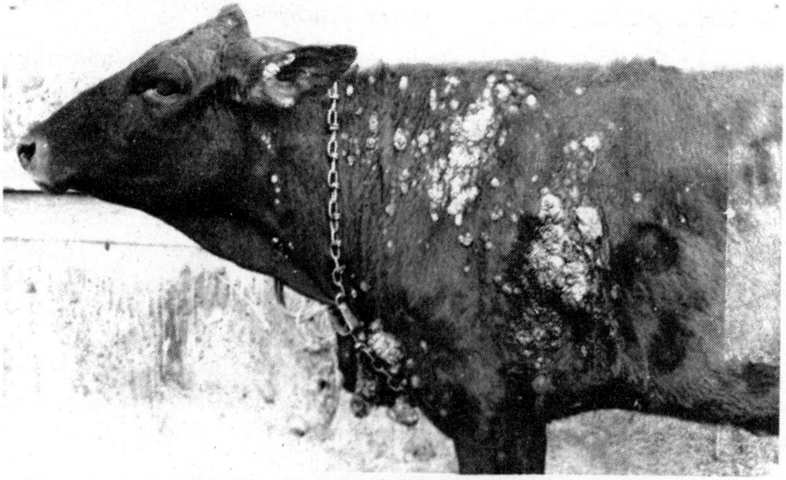

Fig. 7.1 Cutaneous warts in a heifer.

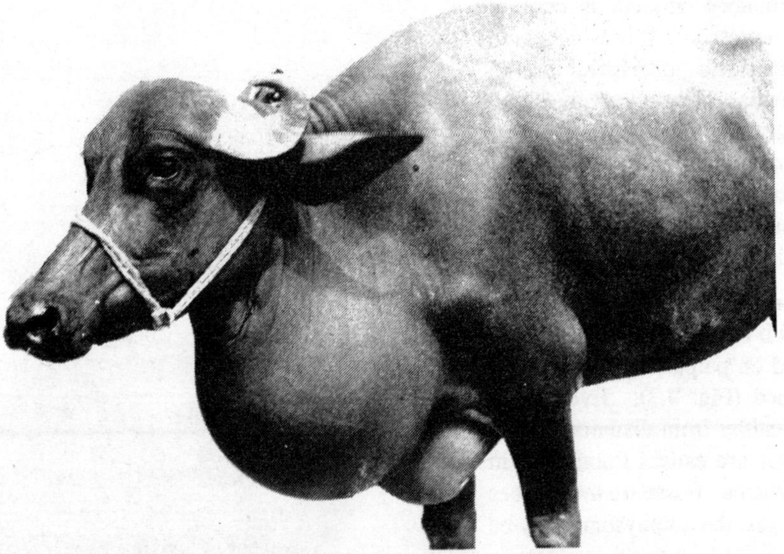

Fig. 7.2 Tumour in the lower neck of a she buffalo.

Tumours are elevation on the skin due to abnormal cells growth. Papillomas (warts), lipomas, fibromas (Fig. 7.1 & 7.2) are benign skin tumours, usually present on the head, neck, abdomen, oral commissure and mammary glands. Warts may be present in the oral cavity of dogs and oesophagus and in the rumen of cattle.

Skin tuberculosis: There is formation of tuberculous nodules on the lateral aspect of fore arms and laterocaudal aspect of hock joint of cattle. They are of varying size of pea to amla fruit. They may rupture and heal or may contain caseous material. Acid-fast bacteria are demonstrated from the nodule smears, not the tuberculous bacilli.

Warble nodules are the swellings (nodules) along the back of cattle and buffalo, usually seen in summer. The migrating larvae of *Hypoderma lineata* are responsible for it.

Pruritis (itching): The act of rubbing the body against object, pawing, biting, licking and scratching, generally speak skin disease. Itching may be either peripheral in origin (mange/mite infestation) or central-origin (scrapie in sheep, pseudorabies, hepatitis, nephritis and acetonaemia). However, presence of itching is not always associated with skin diseases. Cattle and buffalo prefer when itching is made at the dorsum of the tail and the base of the horns. Similarly, horses appreciate itching anterior to the wither. Animals drive away the body when scratching is painful.

Otodectic mange causes pawing at the ear with hind legs in dogs. Presence of foreign objects in mouth also cause pawing in dogs. Infestation with *Oxyuris equi* provokes rubbing of anus against the wall. Tape-worm infestation and obstruction of anal gland force the dogs to rub the anus on ground.

Swelling (oedema): The swellings may be either local or general, General swelling of whole body is termed as *anasarca*. In general, the swelling is due to excess accumulation of fluid in to the tissue spaces of the skin. Oedema may be inflammatory or non- inflammatory. The former oedema is associated with damage of small blood vessels by toxins or other infectious agents e.g. abscesses, anthrax and malignant oedema. Such oedema bears the cardinal signs of inflammation like redness, hot, swelling, pain and loss of function. Insect bites, plant stings, tuberculin test (positive) etc. produce such local oedema.

Non-inflammatory oedema is cool in touch and pits on pressure. It is a sequela to increased hydrostatic pressure, as in obstructive oedema, cirrhosis of liver and passive congestion of the heart. Hypoproteinaemia due to malnutrition (Vit. A deficiency), parasitic diseases (fascioliasis, strongylosis) and other metabolic diseases lead to such oedema.

Subcutaneous emphysema: Accumulated gas under the sub-cutaneous tissue space is well appreciated on palpation. The animal appears ballooned (Fig. 7.3). Even weak animal seems healthy from distance, if it is generalised. Pressure causes fluctuation in subcutaneous oedema. Based on the sources of accumulated gas, the emphysema may be of two types.

(i) **Endogenous emphysema :** Accumulated gas is produced locally e.g. black quarter in cattle and buffalo and malignant oedema in sheep and horses.

(ii) **Exogenous emphysema:** The gas leaks from other organs like lungs, oesophagus, rumen, intestine and surgical incisions and accumulates in the subcutaneous tissue spaces.

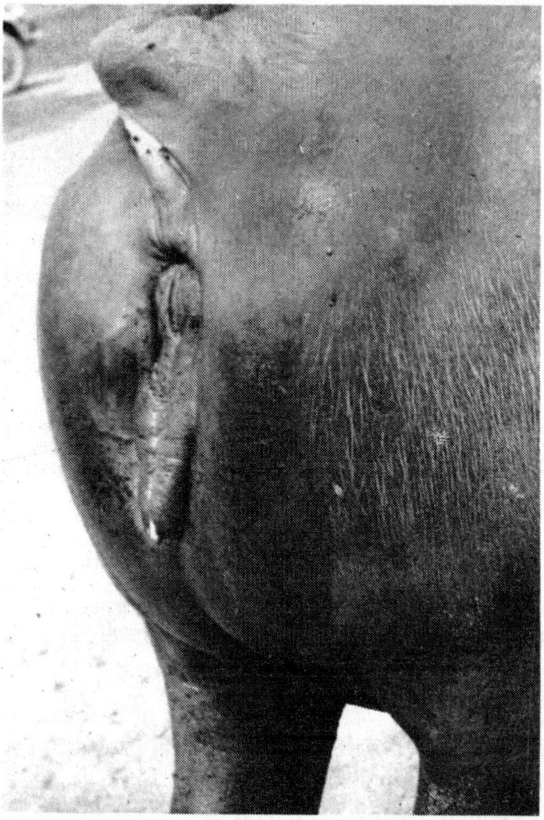

Fig. 7.3. Sub-cutaneous emphysema in a buffalo (leakage of gas from rumen).

Examination for ectoparasites

External parasites like ticks, keds, fleas and lice cause marked uneasiness and skin problems. These are recognised on visual inspection.

Examination of skin scraping

Scrapings of skin are examined microscopically for identification of mange, mite and fungal infection. Sarcoptic, psoroptic and chorioptic mites infest cattle, buffalo, horse, sheep, goats and pigs, while demodectic mange affects mostly the dogs and cats.

Collection: The scraping is obtained from the periphery of active lesion with a sharp blade till skin bleeds slightly. Preferably, the scales are removed by applying 5 per cent potassium hydroxide or water on the lesion. Scraping may be examined using the techniques as mentioned.

Direct Smear Technique

The material, triturated with few drops of 10 per cent potassium hydroxide for 10-15 minutes, is placed on a glass slide. Gentle heating the slide on low heat helps better softening of the crusts. The cover glass is placed on the scraping, avoiding traping of gas bubble under it. Alternatively, the scraping may be heated slowly in a test tube containing 10 per cent sodium or potassium hydroxide solution. Following centrifugation, the sediment is examined on a slide under low power microscope. Recognition of mange and mite is done based on the presence of their portion or the eggs. The absence does not rule out infection. Repeat examination is essential from other lesions for final diagnosis.

The adult mites have eight legs, while the larvae have six legs. The ova are oval and large and may be with or without the larvae. Recognition of different species of mite and their host specificity are essential for diagnosis.

Sarcoptes affect the skin of head in cattle, buffalo and horse, while in dog behind the muzzle, elbow, sternum, thigh region and tail. In sheep, goats and rabbits, the mites affect head and ears, while in pigs the legs and inner pinna.

Psoroptic mange produces sheep scab, affects back, shoulder and base of the tail of sheep. In horse, mane and saddle area are involved. Ears of goats and rabbits are affected.

Chorioptic mange can affect any part of the body of cattle and buffalo. In horse is produces itchy legs.

Demodectic Mange

Deep scraping is essential to locate this mange. Pusy material is suitable for it. They are small and enlongated mites with four pairs of legs. The larvae have only three pairs of legs. Demodecosis occurs in either scaly form, mostly around head, neck or eyes in dogs or pustular form affecting any part of the body. A third eczematous type affecting the skin of head and abdomen is also seen.

Dermatophytosis/Dermatomycosis (Ringworm)

Species belonging to two genera of fungi i.e. Trichophyton and Microsporum affect the domestic animals. *T. verrucosum* affects all most all species of animals while microsporum affects horse and small animals. Dogs and cats are usually affected by *M. canis*. Young animals are usually affected by *T. verrucosum* around head, neck, perineum or the whole body. The lesions are being circular and covered with thick white-greyish crusts. In horse, the lesions develop on trunk, croup, head, neck or limb. In dog and cat, the lesions are on head and forelimbs. Circular areas covered with thick crusts project on the skin.

Microscopic examination is necessary for identification of ringworm. The scraping is collected from the periphery of active lesion and is placed on the slide with 5-6 drops of sodium hydroxide solution (10%) and warmed gently. Under a coverslip, the smear is examined. Trichophyton appears like chains while microsporum looks like irregular mosiac. Under high power, often sheath of arthrospores are visual around hair-shaft.

Wood's Lamp Examination

Only microsporum infection is diagnosed with the help of Wood's lamp in dark room. Infected hairs give bright pale-green fluorescence on exposure to Wood's lamp light (i.e. ultraviolet light passing through nickel oxide glass). The only limitation is that all affected hairs do not fluoresce and oily applications also give bluish-white fluorescence.

Cutaneous Nematodal Infection

Stephanofilaria stilesi produces lesions of 1-6 inch diameter on ventral abdomen in cattle. Dermatitis is produced by *Rhabditis strongyloides* nematodes in cattle and dog. *Parafilaria multipapillosa* produces urticarial lesions in European horses.

Bacterial Infection

A variety of bacteria, like strpetococci, staphylococci and diphtheroids are associated in pyogenic dermatitis in animals. These organisms are usually secondary in order. Microscopic examination of stained smear made from the lesions, helps in diagnosis.

8

DIGESTIVE SYSTEM

The diseases of digestive tract influence the appetite of the animals, which is characterised either by partial loss of appetite (inappetence) or complete loss of appetite (anorexia). Opposite to this, certain digestive conditions provoke unsatiable appetite (hyperoxia), as in parasitism, Johne's disease, chronic diarrhoea etc.

Topography (Cattle, Buffalo, Sheep and Goat)

The space between two lips is the enterance of the digestive system. The central area of the upper lip (the muzzle) is devoid of hairs which remains moist in healthy animals. Adult cattle/buffalo has 32 teeth, without upper incisors, the place is taken by dental pad. The anterior hard palate has transverse ridges, while it is smooth posteriorly. The mouth can be explored with hand and so also the pharynx and the enterance of oesophagus. The approximate length of oesophagus in adult cattle and buffalo is 90 cm to 105 cm. The oesophagus has marked dilatation capacity, owing to its thin wall. It terminates in the oesophageal groove which opens into the joint cavity of rumen and reticulum. From the oesophageal groove, runs a groove ventral to omasum which terminates in the true stomach (abomasum).

The ruminant's stomach consists of four compartments; the rumen, reticulum, omasum and abomasum (Fig. 8.1) which fill nearly half of the left abdominal cavity.

The relative sizes of the compartments vary in different species of animals.

Per cent Capacity of Forestomachs of Ruminants

Animals	Rumen	Reticulum	Omasum	Abomasum
Cattle and buffalo	55	5-7	26-30	13-14
Sheep and goat	62	11	5	22-23

Rumen

At birth, the rumen is half of the abomasum and at the age of two months it becomes twice to that of abomasum. A fully developed rumen of cattle and buffalo has a capacity of 120-150 litres. It occupies almost the entire left side of the abdominal cavity.

Reticulum

The reticulum lies between the diaphragm and cranial part of the rumen, mostly on the left to the median plane, at the level of 6th-7th rib. A vertical ridge (rumeno-reticular fold) separates reticulum from rumen. Direct contact of reticulum with diaphragm is of importance as foreign bodies, often swallowed by cattle and buffalo perforate the diaphragm. The inner lining of reticulum resembles honeycomb. The reticulum of sheep and goat is larger than cattle.

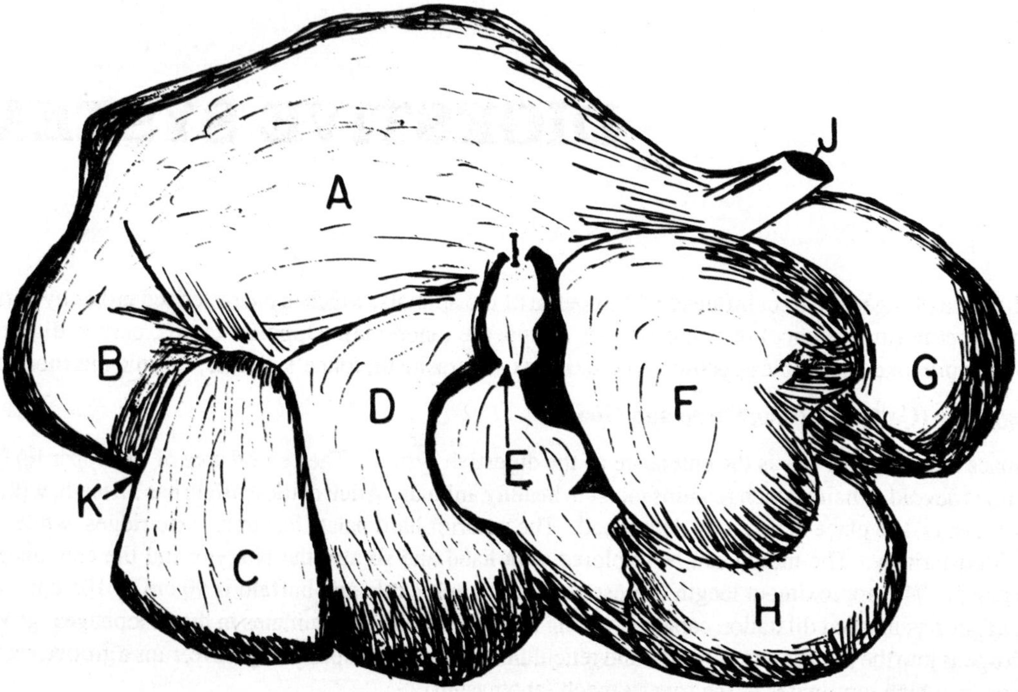

Fig. 8.1 Fore-stomachs of ox, right side. A. Dorsal sac of rumen, B. Caudo-dorsal sac of rumen, C. Caudo-ventral sac of rumen, D. Ventral sac of rumen, E. Pylorus, F. Omasum, G. Reticulum, H. Abomasum, I. Duodenum, J. Oesophagus, K. Caudal groove of rumen. jaws, caudal

Omasum

The topographical position of omasum is almost on the right side of the median line, above abomasum. It is in contact with rumen and reticulum on its left. The right surface touches the abdominal wall at the level of lower third of 7th to 9th intercostal space. There are strong muscular folds interior of the omasum. The omasum of sheep and goat is much smaller than reticulum.

Abomasum

The abomasum lies chiefly on the abdominal floor, more on the left than on the right median plane. The visceral surface is incontact with rumen and omasum and the fundus lies near the xiphoid. It is glandular and joins duodenum at pylorus.

Small and Large Intestine

The small intestine has an average length of 40 m in cattle and 25 m in sheep and goat. The diameter is approximately 5-6 cm in ox and 2-3 cm in sheep and goat. Owing to bulky rumen on the left, the intestine lies entirely on the right side of the abdomen. The small intestine comprises duodenum, jejunum and ileum.

Most part of the large intestine resembles small intestine in diameter and composed of caecum and colon which terminates in rectum. But for larger size of abomasum, the alimentary canal of sheep and goat is very similar to the cattle.

Horse: The oral cavity of horse is comparatively large and cylindrical as compared to cattle. The highly developed soft palate extends upto the epiglottis posteriorly. Owing to the presence of musculo-membranes veils, the pharynx can not be inspected directly. The oesophagus (125-150 cm long) begins on the mid-line initially. It turns to the left at middle-third of the neck and finally terminates in the stomach.

The stomach of horse is J-shaped sac and relatively small. It lies high up in the abdominal cavity on left side of the median plane, just behind the diaphragm and liver. It is glandular in structure. The small intestine lies on the left side mostly but for the presence of some coils on the right abdominal floor. The large intestine is more developed and comprises of caecum, large and small colon and the rectum. Caecum is very large. It is being 1.25 m long and has a capacity of 15-30 litres; the round border of which lies in the right *iliac* and sublumber region and the pointed end (apex) lies a hand's length caudal to the xiphoid cartilage. The termination of ileum and origin of colon are 5-7.5 cm apart on its concave curveture.

The great colon is about 3-3.37 m long with an average diameter of 20-25 cm. It has double capacity to that of caecum. It has three flexures. The first, right ventral colon begins near the base of the caecum at the level of ventral part of last rib. The initial curve is incontact with upper right flank. Subsequently it moves cranially along the floor of abdomen and bends sharply to the left (sternal flexure). The left ventral colon runs caudally on abdominal floor and turns dorso-cranially at the level of pelvic inlet (pelvic flexure) forming left dorsal colon. The left colon passes cranially and reaching the diaphragm, it turns to right (diaphragmatic flexure) forming the right dorsal colon which passes caudo-dorsally. It turns to left and at the level of base of the caecum forming transverse colon, joins the small colon, below the left kidney.

Rectum is the terminal part of the bowel. It is about 30 cm in length. It extends from the pelvic inlet to the anus.

Dogs and cats: Variation in the shape of the mouth of dog depends on their breed. The examination of oral cavity needs different techniques. The cardiac part of the stomach lies on the left side while the pyloric part on the right side of the abdomen. The fully distended abdomen reaches the floor of the abdomen caudally to the *xiphoid cartilage*. The duodenum begins from the pylorus in the right side of the abdomen, which touches the right flank. As it reaches to 6th or 7th lumber vertebrae, it turns medially and the jejunum starts at the level of left kidney. It is arranged in loops attached to long mesentry reaching the abdominal floor. The terminal part is the ileum. It forwards in the right sub-lumber region, contiguous medially to caecum and opens into colon, opposite to the lower extremity of the last rib.

The internal diameter of large intestine is slightly more and it is shorter than small intestine. The caecum has spiral flexures held together by the peritoneal covering, situated midway between flank and median plane in right sub-lumber region. The colon contains three segments held in short mesentry to the sub-lumber region. The dorsal segment extends forward from the ileocolic orifice opposite the last rib on the medial aspect of duodenum. It turns left behind the stomach, near pyloric region forming the second part. The last segment extends caudally, reaching the vicinity of the left kidney and it turns medially and continues as rectum. The rectum is covered with peritoneum almost. The opening of two lateral anal sacs are situated between internal and external sphincters. Around the sacs are apocrine and sebacious glands, the secretion of which is collected in the sacs.

The abdomen of cat is more rounded than dog. The abdominal portion of the alimentary tract simulates the anatomical pattern of dog in most respects.

Examination Techniques

Oral Cavity: The labial mucous membrane can be examined by lifting the upper and lower lips. For examination of interior mucous membrane of buccal cavity in large animals, the tongue is grasped by inserting the hand through interdental space. The tongue is drawn to one side of the mouth and area of the opposite side is examined. In order to examine the other side, the tongue is drawn to the opposite side.

For examining the mouth of dog, the upper jaw is held with one hand and the lower jaw with the other hand, pushing the labial skin fold inside. In furious dog, the mouth is opened by means of tape. Two tapes are tied around both upper and the lower jaws,caudal to the canine teeth. The tapes are held firmly and pulled them apart to open the mouth. For thorough examination of oral cavity and the pharynx of large animals, different types of gags are used (Plate - 3).

The animals showing resentment, use of narcotics prior to examination is advised. In dog, chlorpromazine @ 1-2 mg/kg body i/m will serve the purpose.

The buccal cavity should be examined in respect of inflammation, necrosis, foreign bodies, awns or other lesions. The quantity as well as the quality of saliva are to be recorded. Blood or pus mixed saliva indicates presence of haemorrhagic inflammation. Normally the odour of the mouth is not unpleasant but in cases of teeth decay and gangrene of the lungs, evoke offensive odour. Ketotic cows and buffaloes have fruity sweet smell of the mouth.

Tongue: The surface of the tongue is examined for the presence of lesion. Presence of vesicles on the dorsal surface of the tongue in foot and mouth disease and ulcers on the volar surface in case of rinderpest in ruminants are usual. The tongue hardens in actinobacillosis. The tongue of dog becomes copper coloured in uraemia or toxaemia.

Teeth: The deformities like malapposition of incisor (parrot - mouth) and displacement of lower molars due to deformed mandible are recognised easily. Enlarged and irregular molar teeth cause indigestion. The condition is common in old cattle and buffaloes, which is characterized by sudden cessation of the process of rumination, infrequent and careful chewing movement and the presence of coarse, undigested feed materials in the faeces. The ailment can be cured by rasping or cutting the projected molars. The deposit of tar-tar on teeth gives not only the bad appearance but it is injurious for the teeth and labial mucosa. It can be removed using a rasp (Plate-3.).

Pharynx: The pharyngeal cavity of cattle and bufallo can be explored smoothly with hands using suitable mouth - gag. In horse, general anaesthesia is advised for the desired results. The whole pharynx is explored for the presence of foreign bodies, abscess, enlargement of pharyngeal lymph nodes and the presence of tumour. Palpation induce pain in pharyngitis, while in pharyngeal paralysis there is failure of swallowing and retching movements.

Gutteral Pouch: The pouch is present only in equine. Inflammation causes swelling (uni or bilateral) of the anterior cervical region adjacent to parotid salivary glands. Severe swelling causes pain, dysphagia and difficult respiration. The pouch can be viewed with laryngoscope (Fig. 8.2) or X-ray examination will provide definite information of the gutteral pouch.

Sputum: Often microscopic examination of properly stained sputum smear is helpful in diagnosing pulmonary tuberculosis (open tuberculosis) in animals with clinical manifestations of the disease. Microscopic examination of sputum also reveals parasitic infestation with species of Dictyocaulus, Spirocerca, Filaroides and Capillaria. The absence of both tuberculous bacteria and parasitic eggs/larvae does not rule out the existence of infection.

Fig. 8.3 Sputum cup

The sputum can be collected by introducing sterile cotton swab in the pharynx immediately after the animal coughs. Keeping a brown paper on floor below the animal head will also help in harvesting the sputum.

The introduction of sputum - cup (Fig. 8.3) into the oesophagus collects sputum when the animal tries to swallow the coughed sputum. The coughing in animals may be induced by pressing the pharyngeal region externally. Alternatively, a trocar of suitable calibre may be introduced directly into the trachea and through it sterile swab is introduced for collection of sputum. This procedure requires pre-medication with sedative drugs. Fungi causing respiratory diseases are also detected in the sputum.

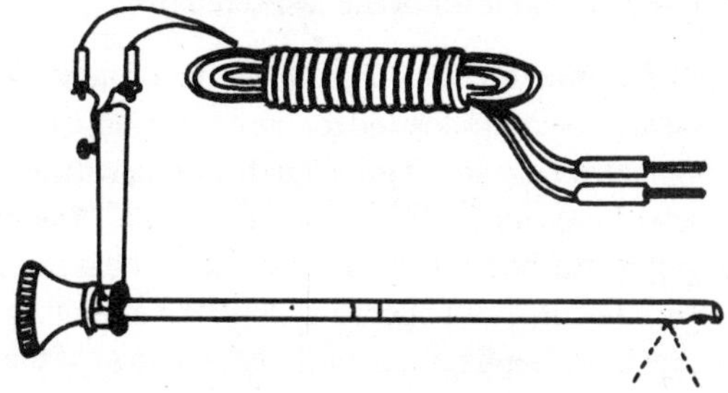

Fig. 8.2 Laryngoscope

Oesophagus: The oesophagus of adult cattle and buffalo measures 90-105 cm in length and 3-4 cm in diameter. The cervical portion is palpable on the left jugular furrow. Presence of foreign bodies or neoplasm either in the pharynx or oesophagus leads dysphagia. Diverticulum in the oesophagus causes difficulty in ingestion of feed. Such animal takes abnormally excess time to consume normal feed. Regurgitation of semi chewed feed (quidding) is suggestive of pain in the buccal cavity.

Oesophageal obstruction can be palpated externally e.g. the presence of foreign body. To know the patency of oesophageal lumen in large animals, a stomach tube made of plastic or probang can be introduced. In tuberculosis, actinobacillosis or lymphomatosis, the posterior mediastinal lymph nodes get swollen, which cause compression stenosis to the oesophagus.

An illuminated oesophagoscope can be used for examination of oesophagus of dog and cat. The examination must be carried out under general anaesthesia. In addition, contrast radiography and fluoroscopy are advised if the clinician feels these necessary.

Forestomachs of Ruminants

Rumen: Ruminal movement is the index of digestive function in ruminants. The status of rumen is appreciated by inspection, palpation, percussion and auscultation. In selected cases, introduction of stomach tube, in order to evacuate the gas or rumen content and for evaluation of rumen liquor, is needed. In addition, rumenotomy is also required in emergent cases and for manual exploration of reticulum for the search of metallic or foreign objects.

Inspection of rumen from a distance may reveal gaseous balooning of the left paralumber fossa. The consistency of rumen is appreciated by palpating the rumen. Rumen feels firm in touch in impaction. The rumen movement can be recorded by pressing the fist of right hand. The force and frequency are to be noted for a period of 5 minutes. In cattle and buffalo, the frequency of rumen movement ranges 8-10 per five minutes. It may either decrease or increase in atony and hypermotility of rumen respectively. Percussion of rumen reveals presence of free gas giving drum like sound while impaction and overloading of rumen provides dull sound. By putting stethoscope on the rumen, the gurgling (churning) sound produced by the rumen contents, can be appreciated distinctly. Atony of rumen is characterised by decrease in the frequency and volume of the sound. In the left displacement of abomasum, tinkling sound is audible at the centre of left para-lumber fossa, at the ventral level of the last three ribs.

Passage of Stomach Tube: The tube is being passed into the rumen for the release of free gas as in secondary bloat, washing of the rumen and for the collection, examination and transplantation of rumen liquor. A suitable sized stomach tube made of good quality of plastic or rubber tube is used for adult cattle and buffalo. It needs 2.5-3 meter long and 20-25 mm diameter tube. The tube is well lubricated with paraffin or glycerine. The mouth gag is attached with a spring and the tube is introduced. As the tube end reaches the level of epiglottis, a resistance is felt. It is better to wait till the animal tries to swallow it. This takes only few seconds. As the tube enters the oesophagus, the forward passage of the tube becomes easier. Perchance if the tube enters the trachea, the animal coughs immediately. The tube is withdrawn and reattempted. Presence of the tube in the rumen is judged by appreciating rumen liquor smell or the gurgling sound in the tube.

Rumen lavage: For washing the rumen, preferably large calibred tube is advised. The required amount (8-10 litres or more) of normal saline or diluted potassium permanganate solution (1:10,000) or water is introduced and then sucked up with the help of suction pump. The tube may act as a syphon.

Examination of rumen liquor: In order to examine the rumen liquor, the required amount (300-500 ml) is being collected and examined as below. Some amount may be collected directly from rumen with hypodermic needle (6-8" long) and syringe.

Rumen liquor is examined physically, chemically, microscopically and microbially. Collected liquor should be examined soon if possible, otherwise changes are likely to occur. At room temperature (20-22°C) sample should be examined within 9 hours while at 4-5°C it may be extended upto 24 hours.

Consistency: Normal rumen liquor is slightly viscous. Presence of small gas bubbles suggests frothy bloat and watery appearence indicates inactive liquor.

Colour: Depends on the type of feed. Cattle fed on green pastures have green or olive green colour and yllowish-brown when fed on straws. In wheat flour engorgement, it turns milky.

Odour: Normally it is not repellent but have peculiar aroma of particular feed like grass, roots or silage etc.

Foul odour is noted in protein decomposition, acid odour in acute lactic acidosis and bitter almond in cyanogenetic glycosides rich plants intake.

Rumen pH: Normal rumen pH varies between 5.5 to 7.5. In concentrate fed animals, it is towards lower side while in cattle fed largely on roughages, it ranges towards higher side. The pH paper (BDH) is generally suitable for clinical purpose or otherwise it can be measured with electrodes. Rumen becomes alkaline (pH 8.5 or more) in urea toxicosis, termed as alkalosis while a rumen pH 5.0 or below, as in grain over-load, is termed as acidosis. Rumen pH is lower in abomasal obstruction, pyloric stenosis and abomasitis.

Microscopic examination: Rumen fluid is examined microscopically for its microbial fauna.

Protozoa: Various species of Holotricha and Spirotricha (Entodeniumorph) are present in the rumen liquor. Their presence enables ruminants to digest polysaccharides like cellulose, hemicellulose, starch, xylan and pectin. The main end products of protozoal carbohydrate digestion are lower fatty acids, carbon dioxide lactate, hydrogen and methane. Rumen bacteria thrive on these end products thus the distribution pattern of protoza furnishes information on bacterial activity in the forestomachs. The protozoal concentration varies according to composition of ration, feeding time and the part of rumen from where sample has been collected.

Examination of a drop of rumen liquor on a slide covered with cover - glass under low power (X 100) is very informative. An approximate density of protozoa ranging 30, or more, below 30, between 10-20 and nil is termed as abundant, moderate, few and none respectively. They are classified as motile and non-motile based on their movement.

Protozoa counting: Freshly collected rumen liquor is filtered through double layers of muslin cloth or gauze. With the help of pipette, it is diluted in 1:5 (1 ml rumen fluid + 4 ml distilled water) or 1:10 ratio together with few drops of methylene blue solution. Abnormally high and low rumen pH lead to poor population of protozoa. A normal rumen protozoal count varies between 10^5-10^6 per ml in cattle and buffaloes maintained on mixed ration.

Total Protozoa Count Reagents: Glycerine 30%, Methyl green (0.5%) in glacial acetic acid and Formalin 50%.

Procedure: One ml filtered rumen flud is mixed with 0.8 ml formalin and 0.2 ml methyl green (dilution 1:1). For higher dilution add 3 or 8 ml glycerine to give 1:5 and 1:10 dilution respectively. Diluted rumen fluid (0.1ml) is spread on a counting chamber or calibrated glass slide. Count the protozoa in at least 50 microscopic field (x 400). Total number of protozoa per ml = average protozoa in one microscopic field x dilution x 10 x microscopic factor (9600 or so).

Rumen bacteria: They play a major role in the digestion of ruminants. The total count ranges between 10^7-10^{12} per ml of rumen fluid. There are large number of species with diverse functions. Some break down propionic, butyric or lactic acids, some are methanogenic and some are proteolytic.

Bacterial pattern: At normal pH range, the Gram negative bacteria are dominant. Cattle fed on hay ration have higher proportion of Gram negative cocci. And cattle maintained on carbohydrate rich diet show Gram positive bacteria dominating.

Indirect microbial activity test : The digestive abilities of rumen microbes are judged indirectly by estimating their end products or by their actions on the substrate provided.

Sedimentation floatation test: Fresh rumen liquor is filtered with a gauze and about 30-50 ml is placed in a small beaker. Note the time and incubate at 39°C. The small feed particles first clump and settle down at the bottom. Small gas bubbles produced by fermenting bacteria get adhered to these particles. Such particles become lighter and float on the surface of beaker. Note the time when the sediment floats. Normal rumen liquor takes about 4-8 minutes for this. The sedimentation floatation time is abnormally increased in rumen microbes dysfunction.

Cellulose digestion test: The filtered rumen liquor is kept in a beaker. An unmercerised thread is hung in the centre of beaker tying a glass bead at the lower end. Note the time. The beaker is incubated at 39°C. The microbes act on the thread (cellulose) and lastly it breaks. Normal rumen liquor takes about 30-48 hours for the digestion of the thread. The technique is time consuming and proper standardisation of thread is required. Now a days, a number of good tests have replaced it.

Glucose fermentation test: Glucose is fermented by the microflora and the gas so produced is measured. In a saccharometer tube (Fig. 8.4) 0.5 ml of 16 per cent glucose and 10 ml of filtered rumen liquor are placed. Incubate the tube at 39°C and the amount of gas produced is measured after half and one hour. Normally 1-2 ml gas is being formed in one hour. Less gas formation suggests diminished or abnormal microbial function.

Volatile fatty acids and lactic acid: The microbial fermentation products of carbohydrates are the chief source of energy for the ruminants. Total volatile fatty acids measure about 60-120 mol per litre of rumen liquor. Per cent molar concentrations of different acids are being 20-25 propionic acid, 50-65 acetic acid, 10-20 butyric acid and 5 each of formic, valerianic, caproic and the higher fatty acids. Lactic acid concentration is 20-30 mg per cent. Rumen fluid, to be analysed chromatographically, is preserved by putting 1 ml saturated solution of mercuric chloride per 20 ml. In alkalosis, the concentration of volatile fatty acids decreases significantly. In severe lactic acidosis, lactic acid rises upto 3 g per cent.

Redox potential: Variation in the oxidation-reduction power speaks about the activity of rumen anaerobes. Redox potential is measured with potentiometer. One ml of 0.03 per cent methylene blue and 20 ml of fresh rumen fluid is mixed in a test tube. The time taken for decolourisation of fluid is noted. For comparison, plain rumen liquor is placed in other tube. Methylene blue is reduced within 3 minutes by highly active microflora. Reduction is more quick in cattle fed on concentrate ration while on exclusive hay ration, it takes 3-6 minutes. In both alkalosis and acidosis, the reduction is abnormally delayed.

Fig. 8.4 Glucose fermentation test

Titrable acidity: It is measured by putting 1-2 drops of phenolphthalein in 10 ml of rumen fluid. The mixture is titrated with N/ 10 NaOH till the colour turns fleshy. Total unit of acidity is obtained after multiplying the ml of NaOH needed by 10. Normal rumen liquor has 8-25 units of acid while it touches to 70 units in rumen lactic acidosis or reflux of HCl from abomasum in pyloric obstruction.

Chloride content of rumen liquor increases in conditions like abomasitis, abomasal ulcer, abomasal displacement, pyloric stenosis, intestinal obstruction and paralytic ileus. Determination of chloride helps in distinguishing between hydrochloric acid and lactic acidosis. Normal chloride content of rumen fluid of cattle ranges 15-25 ml per litre.

Reticulum: Direct palpation of reticulum is not feasible. Percussion on the left side at the ventral level of 6th, 7th ribs, is of some value. Adhesion gives dull sound while tympanic sound is heard in early metallic penetration. Auscultation of reticulum provides good information as it contracts every 40-60 seconds biphasically. The contraction is strong and most frequent soon after feeding and during rumination. In traumatic reticulitis the cattle grunts as it contracts. In case of right herniation, which is very common in buffalo, the reticular sound is clearly audible on the opposite (right) ventral side. The fluid sound of the reticulum follows the rumen contraction which can be appreciated by putting right hand on the rumen and placing the phonendoscope at the reticular area.

Tests for metallic objects: Some physical tests are applied. In traumatic reticuloperitonitis, the peritoneum around it becomes more tender. The animal expresses pain when strong pressure is applied with the fist or the thumb at the reticular area.

Down hill movement: If the animal is allowed to move down hill, the reticulum emits grunt sound in painful lesion.

Back grip test: The animal's back is lowered suddenly by pulling the fold of skin of the wither. Sudden displacement of reticulum causes pain if there is adhesion or penetration.

Pole test: A 1.5-2 metres long bamboo pole is crossed below the reticular area. With the help of two assistants, the pole is lifted up and released suddenly. The animal keeps the back and abdomen arched upward incase of foreign bodies penetration or increased tenderness.

Metal Detector (Ferroscopy): The instrument is applied at the ventro-lateral aspect of chest and the abdomen of animal. It is capable to detect iron, steel and nickel particles. Some non-iron metals like aluminium and copper are also detectable with high frequency instrument. Appreciable ringing sound and the deflection of the needle of the meter are recorded in the presence of metals. The disadvantage in the technique is that it gives positive indication even with innocuous metals and fails to identify penetrating non-metallic objects e.g. sharp wood and bone piece.

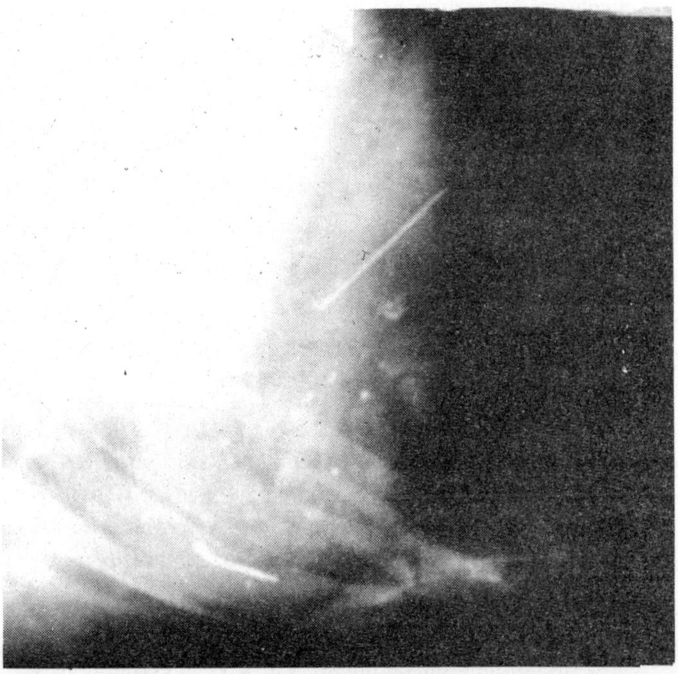

Fig. 8.5 Nail in the reticulum

Radiography: X-ray of the reticular area reveals presence of both foreign bodies and its position. Thus it helps in determining the shape, size and the location of the objects (Fig. 8.5) and also provides information if there is diaphragmatic herniation of the reticulum.

Omasum: Direct examination of omasum is not feasible. Its functional status is usually determined by assessing the function of other forestomachs. Impaction of omasum occurs due to accumulation of soil and hard feed materials, which may be characterised clinically by irregular dyspepsia. Firm palpation at the right costal arch or at the 7th-9th intercostal spaces causes pain reaction. Omasum is affected in certain specific diseases like rinderpest, mucosal disease complex, bovine malignant head catarrh and naphthaline toxicosis.

Abomasum: It is the true stomach of ruminants. In unweaned calf it is about twice the size of rumen, becomes half the size of rumen at 3 months age and remains one-ninth of rumen in adult. In calf-hood, abomasum secretes chymosin or renin which converts milk into paracasein by hydrolysis. Paracasein combines with calcium forming insoluble coagulation of milk. Later, digestion of protein takes place by pepsin secreted which is activated by hydrochloric acid. Reflux of lipase from intestine commences lipid hydrolysis in the abomasum. Carbohydrates pass unchanged. The pH of abomasum ranges between 2-4.5 owing to hydrochloric acid secretion.

The functional activity of rumen is directly related to the status of the abomasum. Inflammation of abomasum leads to atony of rumen and suspension of rumination. The diagnosis of conditions like displacement, tortion and impaction is made by palpation, percussion and stethoscopy.

Forceful palpation on the right side behind xiphoid cartilage evokes pain in abomasitis. Displacement of abomasum may be either on the left or right side, which is usually associated with late pregnancy. On left deviation, it is essential to push the left paralumber fossa to feel the rumen. Sometimes, there appears a bulging mass between rumen and abdominal wall, just under the margin of last rib. A splashing tinkling sound is audible on auscultation over last two ribs. For confirmation, laparotomy is advised.

Impaction of abomasum is commonly noted in young calves due to coagulated milk. There is distension of abdomen and animal remains completely off feed. On deep palpation to the right side of the abdomen, a large firm mass may be felt.

Torsion of abomasum cuases great pain characterised by rapid and weak pulse. The right abdomen is distended and on auscultation splashing sound is audible. On rectal examination, distended abomasum is felt in the posterior abdomen.

Ulcers in abomasum are seen in parasitic gastritis, theileriasis, fungal infections, rinderpest, malignant catarrh and hyperkeratosis. The animals have indifferent appetite, loose motion with intermittent occult blood in faeces. Parasitic gastritis is a serious problem in calves causing diarrhoea, anaemia and weakness. Examination of faeces confirms the type of parasitism.

Abomasal puncture: The abomasum of both young and adult animals can be punctured for the collection of abomasal fluid and its examination. A 4-8 cm long and 15 gauge needle is inserted midway between the xiphoid cartilage and umbilicus (Fig. 4.1). A syringe can be used for sucking the fluid. In suspected left side displacement, a long needle (10-12 cm) is inserted cranio-ventrally on the lower area giving tympanic sound.

Intestinal Examination

On the right side of the abdomen, the intestine can be examined physically but is not much informative. In hypermotility of inflammatory origin, diarrhoea is characteristic, while in hypomotility of intestine, constipation is present invariably. Hypomotility of intestine is characterised by hard mucous coated faecal ball. There is absence of faecal passage in intestinal obstruction, volvulus, intussusception and strangulation. In such conditions only blood stained mucous is passed and the animal shows abdominal pain and shock. Intussusception in adult cattle and torsion of mesentry, causing intestinal obstruction in calves are most common.

Sudden and complete obstruction of intestine is characterised by acute abdominal pain. The animal feels restlessness, kicks at the belly, depresses its back and emits pain grunt. The pulse rate is increased but the body temperature and respiration remain usually unaffected. When this phase passes, the development of shock is evident by depression, anorexia and cessation of gut movement. When the obstruction is incomplete or the development is slow, the abdominal pain is not so marked. The animal passes small quantity of faeces containing mucous or blood. The animal may linger a week or so. Rectal exploration reveals presence of only mucous and blood.

For confirmation of specific disease condition, e.g. bacterial (colibacillosis, vibriosis, anthrax, paratuberculosis), viral (rinderpest, viral diarrhoea, mucosal disease), protozoal or parasitic, (coccidiosis, liver flukes and others,) the faecal culture, staining or microscopic examination is required.

Common Diseases of Cattle and Buffalo Characterised by Diarrhoea

---

A. **Primary diarrhoea:** There is enteritis and the faeces is bad smelling.

(a) Specific enteritis:

Bacterial	—	Colibacillosis, salmonellosis, vibriosis, paratuberculosis, anthrax.
Viral	—	Rinderpest, viral diarrhoea, mucosal disease.
Fungal	—	Intestinal mycoses.
Parasitic	—	Strongyloides, neoscariasis and coccidia.
Toxicosis	—	Mercury, lead, copper, molybdenum, croton oil, nitrate, magnesium sulphate and aflatoxicosis.

(b) Non-specifc enteritis: Decomposed or mouldy feed, exclusive greens feeding, drinking of excess cold water.

(c) Symptomatic enteritis: The functioning of intestine is affected due to diseases at other places e.g., Lactic acidosis, alkalosis, malignant catarrhal fever, tuberculosis.

B. **Secondary diarrhoea:** Without enteritis and absence of foul smelling faeces e.g. in Pericarditis, ascites, endocarditis, congestive oedema, traumatic reticulitis, renal insufficiency, intrathoracic lesions.

The loose faeces of cattle suffering from paratuberculosis is just like pea-soup, contains gas bubbles and without much offensive smell. Demonstration of *M. paratuberculosis* in faecal smear or rectal pinch smear confirms the diagnosis.

Foul smelling and blood mixed stool is characteristic of coccidiosis in calves. The oocysts are demonstrable under microscope. Chronic diarrhoea is seen in fluke infestation. Faecal examination confirms the presence of eggs.

The chemical agents which are responsible for severe diarrhoea are arsenic, mercury, molybdenum, phosphorus, nitrates and copper. The diagnosis is confirmed by establishing the level of these elements either in soil, forages or in blood/serum.

Intestinal puncture: It is performed to remove accumulated gas in the caecum. A 5-6" long needle is inserted into the tympanic area on the right flank. Needling can be done also through rectum after washing the rectum with potassium permanganate solution (1:1000).

X-ray examination of intestine is useful in calves. Obstruction of rectum can be appreciated by infusing contrast medium through anus.

Rectal Manouvring

Rectal examination is performed to assess the organs of pelvic as well as abdominal cavity. The fingers' nails are to be well trimmed and a full sleeve glove is desirable. Lubrication of external side of glove is done either with soap or other lubricating oils. The hand is introduced in cone-shape of rectal sphincter contracts and waiting is required till the wave has passed. Following introduction of hand, animal usually defaecates the faeces present in the rectum or otherwise it is scooped out, so as rectum becomes empty, providing easy exploration. The organs, which can be palpated through the wall of the rectum, are the loops of intestine, rumen, displaced abomasum, left kidney, pelvic brim, cervix, uterus, ovary, urinary bladder, liver, colon, and ileofemoral lymph nodes. These are some common findings on rectal examination.

Rectal wall: It is checked for its thickness by pulling a fold inwards. Normally it is soft and slippery which glides past the fingers.

Enteritis: In acute enteritis, the mesenteric lymph nodes are swollen and the mesentery is thickened. In chronic enteritis, the lymph nodes are markedly enlarged and the wall of intestine is thickened e.g. in paratuberculosis.

Intestinal obstruction: The loop of intestine feels tense and swollen.

Strangulation of intestine: Tense band of mesentery feels alongside the distended intestine.

Dilatation of caecum: Tense dome shaped mass is felt just infront of the pelvis.

Overload of rumen: The posterior-ventral blind sac of the rumen crosses the midline to the right ventral abdominal cavity, immediately cranial to the pelvic brim.

Abomasal displacement: Feels like a balloon on the left dorsal sac of rumen, if it is displaced to the left. In right displacement, the abomasum occupies the right dorsal quadrant of peritoneal cavity, reaching as far as pelvis.

Kidneys: In hydronephrosis, they feel soft and enlarged while in case of amyloidosis, the kidneys are firm and enlarged.

Urinary bladder: In urinary calculi, the bladder feels tense and filled with urine. It presses the rectum dorsally and the animal may show difficulty in defaecation.

Faecal examination: Examination of faeces provides good information about the condition of digestive tract easily. Sometimes the gastrointestinal functions get upset when the lesion is somewhere else. Faeces should be either collected directly from the rectum or freshly voided. It should be kept in plastic envelop or any tight container. It is examined physically for its colour, consistency and smell. Examination for parasites, bacteria, virus, and toxins, is sought when there is diarrhoea or in special circumstances.

Colour: Depends on type of the feed. The colours of faeces in different conditions have been summarised.

Variations in the colour of faeces

Animals	Conditions	Colour
Calves	• Unweaned (normal)	Yellowish-brown to grey
	• Diarrhoea	Whitish or yellowish
Adult	• Grazing on pasture	Dark green (loose)
Cattle/buffalo	• Stall feeding	Brownish
	• Constriction of bile duct	Pale to grey
	• Acute acidosis (Grains overload)	Yellowish-brown
	• Excess bile	Yellowish
	• Poor ration, ketosis	Brown-black surface
	• Occult blood	Dark brown or tarry
	• Blood from caudal intestine	Dark red

Consistency: It depends on the water content of faeces which inturn depends on water intake and stay of ingesta in large intestine where the absorption of fluid takes place mostly. Faeces of calves fed on milk or milk substitute become pasty or greasy. Normal faeces are semi-solid and do not scatter when passed out. It becomes tightly packed, coated with mucous when sojourn is increased. Greasy or pasty faeces are seen in adults suffering from left displacement of abomasum. Diarrhoeic faeces contain more than 90 per cent water (80-90 %) and spread on the ground when defaecated e.g. in paratuberculosis and rinderpest.

Smell: Normal faeces of healthy cattle and buffalo are not offensive in smell. Foul smelling dung is indicative of enteritis. A penetrating smell is noticed in salmonellosis in calves. Acid smell of stool speaks over administration of glucose in calves. In adult, chronic diarrhoea without foul odour is noted in renal insufficiency, traumatic pericarditis, endocarditis and leucosis of the heart.

Size of feed particles: Presence of particles larger than 5 mm indicates rapid passage of ingesta. And if it measures more than 10-20 mm or match-stick size, confirms involvement of abnormal mastication owing to teeth defects. Occurrence of very fine particles suggests delayed passage of ingesta, as in abomasal displacement.

Abnormal materials : *Mucus* a viscous coating on the faecal balls is seen in intestinal obstruction, *fibrin* as a long thread, present in severe catarrhal enteritis and *blood* in haemorrhagic enteritis. *Occult blood* is detected with the help of benzidine test. Faecal dilutions of 1:100, 1:1000, 1:3000, 1:4000 are made. Two-Three drops of each dilution are taken in test tubes and a pinch of benzidine and few drops of glacial acetic acid are added to each. To these, 2 ml hydrogen peroxide (3%) is added. Development of blue-green colour over dilution 1:3000, speaks positive for blood.

Presence of gas bubbles in faeces is characteristic of Johne's disease. Ingestion of sand coated leaves may cause colic. Sometimes, segment of tapeworm and whole ascaris are seen with the faeces.

Microscopic Eamination of Faeces

Direct Smear: A small portion of the faeces is mixed uniformly with 1-2 drops of water. Large particles are removed. The smear is covered with coverslip and examined under low power. The technique is very easy and quick but it fails to detect light infestations. However, eggs of ascaris and liver fluke are detectable by this method often.

Sedimentation method: About one gram or more faeces is mixed with water in a porcelain container and is passed through a plastic seive into a cylinder. The cylinder is filled with more water and mixed properly. Half an hour is allowed to settle. The supernatent fluid is poured off. The process is repeated 2-3 times. With the help of a pipette, 1-2 drops of sediment are placed on a clean glass slide. A coverslip is put and examined under low or high power of the microscope. The method is best suited for flukes eggs.

Floatation method: In this method the parasitic eggs are allowed to float on the dense fluid surface. For this purpose, saturated solution of sodium chloride or sugar (1g per ml) or magnesium sulphate may be used. About 1g of faeces is mixed with 10 ml of fluid and is transferred to a centrifuge tube till the miniscus protrudes the rim. Carefully, a coverslip is placed on the rim of the tube avoiding gas bubbles. About 10-15 minutes are allowed. The coverslip is removed gently so as a drop of fluid hangs the slide and is examined microscopically. The method is very useful for strongyle, light infestation of ascaris and strongyloides (Fig. 8.6)

Egg counting: In order to assess the severity of infection and to judge the efficacy of anthelmintics, egg counting is needed.

McMaster Slide technique: One gram of faeces is mixed with 30 ml of salt solution in a mortar and is filtered with seive. The chambers of both the sides are charged with filtered fluid and a cover slip is placed. Eggs are being counted on both the sides with the help of microscope. The fluid volume on each side is 0.15 ml. Thus the counts of eggs have been made in 0.3 ml. of suspension.

Calculation: 0.3 ml of faecal suspension contains X number of eggs.

Thus 30 ml of faecal suspension contain $= X \times 30/0.3 = X \times 100$ per gram of faeces.

Stoll technique: One gram of faeces is dissolved in 10 ml of water and mixed properly in a mortar. The suspension is passed through a nylon seive. With the help of a pipette, 0.1 ml of suspension is placed on a clean glas slide and is examined under microscope after putting a coverslip avoiding air bubbles under it. Whole area of the coverslip is scanned and eggs are counted.

COMMON PARASITIC EGGS OF ANIMALS

1. Ascaris equorum

2. Oxyuris equi,

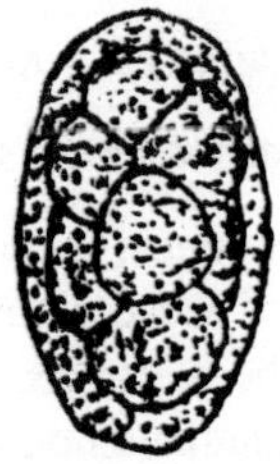

3. Strongylus sp.

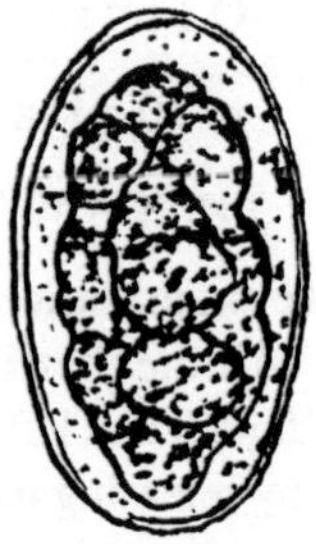

4. Trichonema sp.

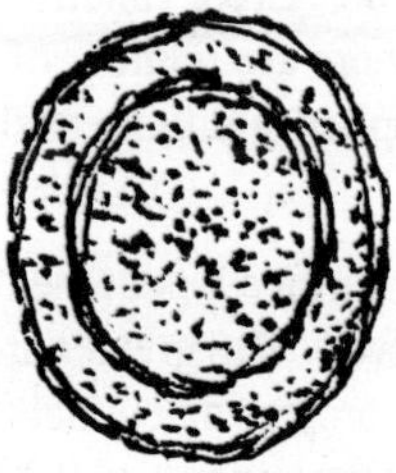

5. Toxocara canis

6. Taenia sp.

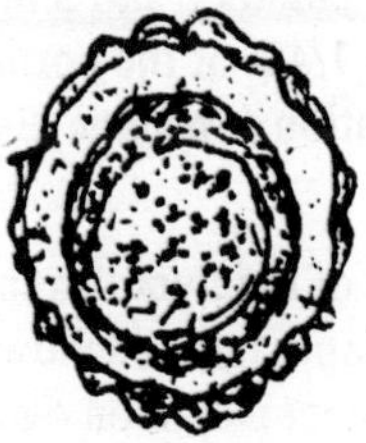

7. Ascaris lumbricoides

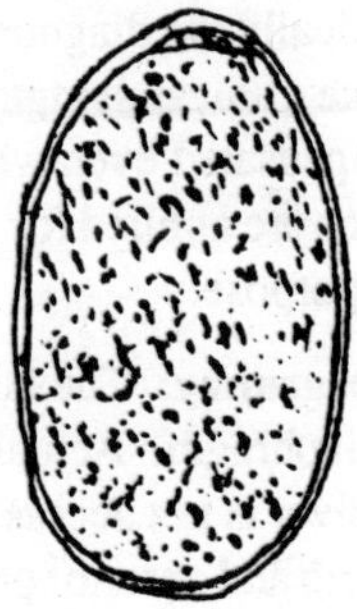

8. Fasciola hepatica

9. Trichuris sp.

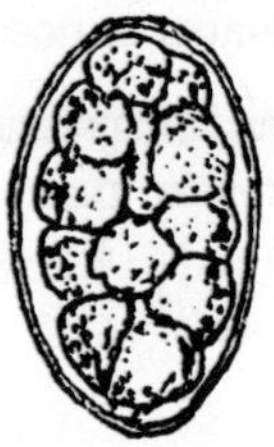

10. Chabertia ovina

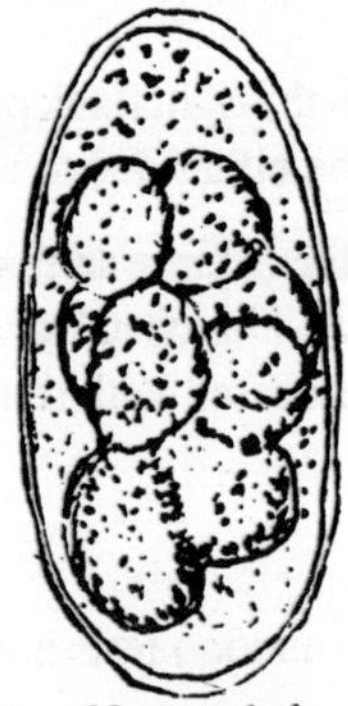

11. Nematoderius sp.

12. Moniezia expansa

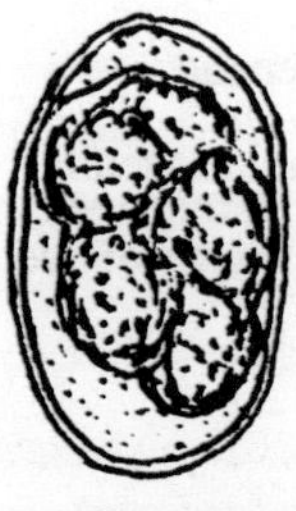

13. Bunostomum sp.

14. Ostertagia sp.

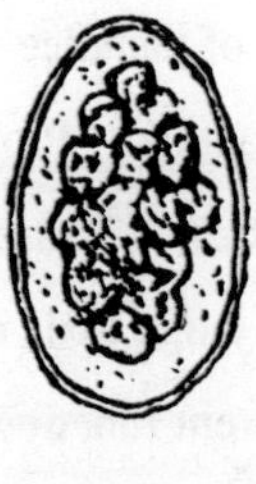

15. Trichostrongylus sp.

Calculation:

O.1 ml suspension contains X number of eggs

so 10 ml suspension contains 10 × X/0.1= X × 100

i.e. X X 100 eggs per g of the faecal sample.

Larvae examination: A glass funnel is used. The tip is fitted with rubber tube and clip. A wire mesh is placed in the chest of the funnel. The faecal sample is placed on the mesh. Now warm water (40°C) is poured in the funnel and left for 3 hrs. The larvae become active and sink down in the tip of the funel. The fluid is taken by releasing the clip and examined microscopically for the larvae.

The Liver

Clinically the diagnosis of hepatic diseases is difficult in cattle and buffalo. Even extensive damage fails to evoke clinical symptoms like jaundice and tenderness on palpation in large animals. Liver functions are compensated even when 1/3 - 1/4th of the normal parenchyma are functioning. There are number of tests which are applied for confirmation of hepatic disorders. Usually a set of tests are applied simultaneously for the purpose.

Topography: The larger part of the liver lies to the right median plane. Its perital surface lies in the dome of diaphragm. Actually the diaphragm is sandwiched between the right lung and liver. The greater area of the liver is not accessible to direct palpation owing to lung except a palm size area, projecting caudal to the last rib and anterior point of the right paralumber fossa. The weight of normal liver approximates 1/100th of the body weight of the animal.

Clinical Examination

Inspection: Gross swelling on the right flank posterior to the dorsal angle of last rib is indicative of abnormal enlargement of liver. It may be either due to abscess or tumour or posterior displacement of liver.

Palpation: It is of limited value in large animals. However, firm pressure with finger tips or use of hammer on liver site, on the right last two intercostal spaces, may provoke pain sensation. For comparison, the same area on the opposite side is percussed with same force.

Liver Function Tests:

The basic indications of liver function tests are to assess:

(a) Primary liver diseases e.g. infectious hepatitis, hepatic fibrosis, toxic necrosis, hepatoma etc.

(b) Secondary liver dysfunctions: Fatty liver, diabetes mellitus, pancreatic atrophy, starvation.

(c) Determination of type of jaundice (icterus): Hepatic, pre-hepatic or post-hepatic.

(d) To acertain type of anaemia: Prothrombin, deficiency causes haemorrhagic anaemia.

(e) Prognosis of liver diseases: To assess residual damage and to evaluate the efficacy of liver therapy.

(f) Specific research: To judge toxic effects of drugs, parasitic migration etc.

The tests are based on the different functions of the liver.

(i) **Tests based on excretory and secretory functions:**

Bile pigment in urine: Presence of increased amount of bilirubin or its metabolites in urine indicates liver damage. The urine becomes yellowish and there is formation of stable yellow foam when it is shaken.

Bile pigment in serum: Both qualitative and quantitative tests, are applied to assess the presence of bilirubin in serum.

Vanden Bergh test: With the help of this test, both conjugated and unconjugated bilirubin are appreciated.

Reagents :

Solution A	Sulphanilic acid	1g
	Concentrated HCl	15 ml
	Distilled water	1000 ml

The solution can be kept indefinitely.

Solution B	Sodium nitrite	0.5g
	Distilled water	100 ml

The solution is to be prepared fresh at week interval.

Working solution: Mix 0.3 ml solution -B with 10 ml of solution A. In a centrifuge tube, take 1 ml non-haemolysed serum and pour 0.5 ml working solution along the wall of the tube. If a reddish-purple ring develops within 30 seconds at the level of contact, indicates direct reaction positive. In the absence of ring, two minutes later add 3 ml 95 per cent alcohol and shake. Pinkish turning of solution indicates indirect reacion positive. Postive direct reaction is seen in post-hepatic obstruction (conjugated bilirubin) while the indirect reaction indicates haemolytic (free bilirubin), whereas the biphasic reaction speaks hepatic involvement.

Classification of Jaundice Based on Vanden Bergh Test

Type of Reaction	Location of Lesion	Type of Jaundice
(a) Direct	Bile duct obstruction	Post-hepatic
(b) Indirect	Haemolytic	Pre-hepatic
(c) Direct and Indirect (biphagic)	Hepatitis	Hepatic

The quantitative amount of bilirubin in serum is estimated colorimetrically. Normal bilirubin in serum is given below:

Serum total bilirubin in different species of animals:

Animals	Normal (mg%)	Hepatopathy (mg%)
Cattle	0.2-0.5	> 0.5
Buffalo	0.3-0.4	3.17-4.5
Horse	1.3	—
Sheep	0-0.4	—
Dog	0.5-1	—
Pig	0-0.4	—

Dye excretion test: Aqueous solution (50 mg/ml) of bromsulfophthalein (BSP, sulfobromophthalein) is infused intravenously@ 1 mg/kg. b.wt. for cattle and buffalo and 5 mg/kg b.wt. for dog. Two samples of blood, at 4 and 9 minutes post-infusion are collected from the opposite vein. The plasma is separated by centrifugation. To one ml non-haemolysed plasma, 3 ml of 0.1N NaOH is added, while in blank 1 ml plasma and 3 ml of O.INHCI is added. The colour is measured at 365 nm against blank and the concentration/optical density is plotted on a semilogrithmic paper. The t 1/2, the time (min) taken to become the plasma dye concentration half, is calculated. Fractional clearance (k%), per cent dye excreted per minute is determined by the formula K=In 2/t 1/2 (Where In 2=0.69). In hepatic disorders the t 1/2 increases while K decreases. The values also change when there is structural change in liver without presence active lesions.

BSP half time (t 1/2 min.) in Animals

Animals	Normal	Hepatopathy
Cattle	2.5-4.1(3.3)	11.7-69.3 (Acute hepatosis)
Buffalo	0.8-4.5 (2.28)	15.78 (Carbontetrachloride poisoning)
Horse	2.8	62.0 (Herring meal poisoning)
Goat	2.13	4.4-16.5 (Carbontetrachloride poisoning
Sheep	1.6-2.7	3.2-46.2

In dog, per cent retention of dye is calculated. If the retention per cent is more than 5, liver abnormality is suspected.

(ii) Based on enzymes activity of liver: Enzymes like aspartate aminotransferase (AST, formerly GOT), alanine aminotransferase (ALT, formerly GPT), sorbitol dehydrogenase (SDH), glutamate dehydrogenase (GD), gamma glutamyl transferase (GGT), prothrombin, arginase and ornithine carbamoyl transferase (OCT) are estimated. Out of these, AST, OCT, GGT and prothrombin are sensitive indicators of liver status. The elevated concentrations of these enzymes indicate presence of active lesion in the liver.

(iii) Tests based on protein, carbohydrate and lipid metabolism by liver

Serum protein: Electrophroretic analysis of serum protein is very sensitive. In general albumin decreases and relatively the globulin content increases. Over all total protein is decreased in hepatopathy.

Blood glucose : The blood glucose level decreases in hepatic abnormality. The normal blood glucose ranges in cattle and buffalo 50-60 mg%, horse 80 mg% and in dog-80-120 mg%.

Cholesterol: Owing to wide variation, the use of total serum cholesterol is of limited value. Generally-cholesterol content falls during acute inflammatory and degenerative liver diseases. However, it rises in bile duct obstruction, fascioliasis, fatty degeneration of liver and lymphatic leukosis.

(iv) Liver biopsy: A small sample of liver tissue from live animal is required for histological evaluation, toxicological analysis and determination of Vit. E and copper. Vim-Silverman needle is required for the purpose. In cattle and buffalo, at the level of 11th or 12th intercostal space, about 20-30 cm right to the median plane, the needle is inserted.

Technique: After clipping and cleaning the proper site, stylet fixed biopsy instrument is introduced through the skin in a twisting action till it passes the intercostal muscles, peritoneum and the liver capsule. It is halted at the skin with the help of side-screw . The stylet is withdrawn and needle is pushed down about 1-1.5 cm into the liver parenchyma. A peculiar sound is heard when the needle enters the liver. The needle is inserted till the halting screw comes in contact with the skin which is at about 5-6 cm in length. For histological examinations, the tissue should be collected in 10 per cent formaldehyde or other suitable fixative.

Laparoscopy: This method can be used in large animals. The limitation is that it can view only the right half of the liver and the gall bladder. Left half is not visualised. Endoscope is inserted into the hollow of the right flank for the purpose.

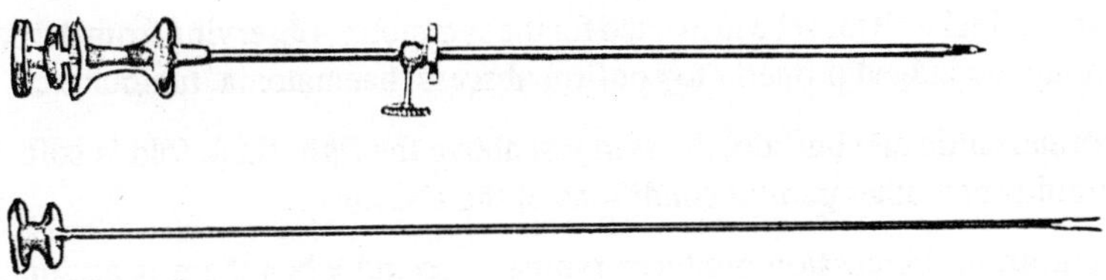

Fig. 8.7 Vim-silverman liver biopsy needle

Cholecystography: A contrast medium is injected intravenously which reaches the gall bladder. The bladder is X-rayed and interpretation is made. The method is suitable for small animals and calves. In adult cattle, it remains of limited use.

REFERENCES

Boddie, G.F.(1969) Diagnostic Methods in Veterinary Medicine 6th ed. Oliver and Boyd, Edinburgh.

Rosenberger, G (1979) Clinical Examination of Cattle. Verlag Paul Parey, Berlin and Hamberg.

Getty, Robert, (1975) The Anatomy of the Domestic Animals. 5th ed. W.B. Saunders company, West Washington Square, Philadelphia, U.S.A.

9

ABDOMINAL CAVITY

Inspection of the outline of abdominal wall, testing its tension, percussion and auscultation help in the diagnosis of abdominal ailments. Some times puncture or laparotomy is required. X-ray is of value in dogs, cats and the calves in particular.

Inspection : Abdominal wall must be inspected for the symmetry, observing from the behind. Any swelling or asymmetry should be judged properly to confirm abscess, haematoma, tumour etc.

Tension: In normal cattle and buffalo, the skin just above the right flank fold is soft. It becomes tense in generalised peritonitis and other painful conditions of the abdomen.

Percussion/auscultation: Percussion produces tympanic sound when there is accumulation of gas in the peritoneal cavity. It occurs as a complication of trocarization, rumenotomy or laparotomy. Grossly the flank gets distended out. Enough pressure on the flank is required to feel the rumen wall.

When there is accumulation of fluid in the peritoneal cavity, the lower abdomen bulges out. By percussing on one side and auscultating on the other side, fluid movement or splashing is heard. Rectal exploration down towards right flank reveals presence of fluid. It can be further confirmed by abdominal paracentesis.

Abdominal puncture: For the escape of intraperitoneal gas, a strong needle, about 3 .5" to 4.5" long of 15-18 gauge is required. After shaving and cleaning the area, about 4-6" below the transverse process of lumber vertebrae of right or left flank, the needle is inserted. The gas often smell bad, particularly when there is intraperitoneal abscess. The best sites for tapping the intraperitoneal fluid are about 4" right to the umbilicus or just behind the xiphoid cartilage and between udder and flank fold. The area is shaved and disinfected. A strong needle (4.5" x 15 gauge) with stylet is inserted. In case fluid does not flow, it can be sucked by attaching a syringe and needle and moving obliquely in different positions. The presence of fibrin or clots, sometimes plug the small bored needle. For this, a wide calibred needle is required. The fluid obtained may be examined for leucocytes, bacterial culture and other biochemical constituents, particularly bilirubin and urea nitrogen.

Laparoscopy: Suitable endoscope is inserted into either flank or in the belly. According to the need, the animal may be kept standing or on its back. Creation of artificial pneumoperitoneum by pumping air, provides better details.

Laparotomy: In cattle and buffalo, this technique is preferable. Approach through left flank is advisible when disease is suspected in reticulum, omasum and the spleen. The right flank is selected when probable abnormalities lie in abomasum, liver and the intestine.

Radiograph of abdominal cavity is suggested only in small animals and the calves.

10

URINARY SYSTEM

A pair, each of kidneys and ureters, urinary bladder and urethra comprise urinary system. The kidneys play important role in the excretion of metabolic waste products and absorption of essential metabolites selectively. They also help in the maintenance of body water by reabsorption of water from the glomerular filtrate under the influence of antidiuretic hormone of the pituitary gland.

Diseases of urinary bladder and urethra are more common in large animals, while that of kidneys in dogs and cats. The partial loss of function of kidney is termed as renal insufficiency and complete loss as renal failure. Whenever there is doubt of urinary diseases, the urine must be analysed.

Topographic Outline

Cattle and buffalo: The kidneys of cattle and buffalo have 20-25 superficially divided lobes. The right kidney lies under the transverse process of first 2-3 lumber vertebrae. The position of left kidney varies as per the fullness of rumen. In partially filled rumen, the kidney lies to the left of the median plane. The full rumen displaces it to the right side below and caudal to right kidney under 3-5th lumber vertebrae. The ureters originating from the kidney pelvises, terminate on the bladder. The bladder is placed just anterior to the pelvic bridge and touches the abdominal floor, when filled with urine. The male pelvic urethra measures about 5" in length. The extrapelvic urethra continues as sigmoid flexure behind the scrotum and ending at the terminal opening of penis. In female, the urethra measures 2-3", which opens on the vulvar floor, about 4" from the ventral vulvar commissure and just above the suburethral diverticulum.

Horse: The right kidney lies under the last three ribs and the transverse process of Ist lumber vertebra and is adhered firmly. The ventral surface is in touch with liver, pancreas and caecum. The left kindney is variable in its position. It lies a bit more caudal to a level of the transverse process of 3rd lumber vertebra. The origin of ureters and its termination on the dorsal surface of bladder, just cranial to the neck of the bladder, simulate to that of cattle. In male, the dorsal surface of the bladder is in contact with rectum, while in mare it is in contact with the anterior part of vagina and the body of the uterus. In male, pelvic urethra measures about 4-5." Extra-pelvic urethra commencing at the level of ischial arch, passes through the ventral penis under the corpus cavernosus and terminates at glans penis. The mare's urethra is about 2-3" long and opens at the anterior floor of vulva. The opening allows one finger.

Sheep and goat: Morphologically the kidneys of sheep and goats are bean shaped, smooth and are located as in cattle and buffalo. The male extrapelvic urethra has a twisted urethral process projecting beyond the glans penis. The female urethra relatively simulates the urethra of cows and female buffalo.

Pig: The kidneys are bean shaped, elongated and smooth and usually symmetrically situated ventral to the transverse process of 1-4th lumber vertebrae. Some times the left kidney is situated a bit anteriorly than the right. The distended bladder lies in abdominal cavity. The pelvic urethra measures 6-8" which continues as sigmoid flexure in boars. The terminal orifice is located on the ventro-lateral aspect of pointed penis. In female, the urethral orifice is walled by a thick fold, extending caudally, giving an assumption of projection in the vulva.

Dog: Bean shaped and smooth kidneys are convex on both the surfaces. The right is fixed ventral to sub-lumber muscle opposite to 1 to 3rd lumber vertebrae. The left kidney is movable according to the fullness of stomach. When stomach is full, it may lie under the transverse process of 3rd-5th lumber vertebrae. The ureters are alike horse. Empty bladder lies on the pelvic cavity but when distended, the vertex extends to umbilicus. The pelvic urethra is surrounded by large prostate. The extra-pelvic urethra is, situated in the ventral groove of penis, where its lumen is fixed owing to os-penis. The urethra ends beneath the pointed end of glans-penis. In bitch, the urethra bulge opens on the vulvar floor, about 1-2" from the ventral commissure.

Cat: The kidneys are relatively large and variable in location owing to loose attachment with the peritoneum. When the stomach is empty, they hang down the middle plane, which may be mistaken for tumour or foreign bodies. The bladder is similar to that of dog. The vertex of fully distended bladder may extend beyond umbilicus. The extrapelvic urethra of male is comparatively narrow because the penis is composed of connective tissues.

Clinical Appreciation

The problems of urinary tract are manifested clinically by pain, change in the act of urination and later development of toxaemia affecting digestive tract, cardiovascular system and the nervous system.

Posture of urination: The normal posture of voiding urine varies in different species. The cow and female buffalo extend hind legs, thus make the back arched and lift their tail at the time of urination. The male urinates while ploughing, moving or feeding. The sheep and goats urinate as cattle.

The postures in both female and male horses are typical. They urinate on rest by advancing their forelegs and lowering the abdomen. Male protrudes penis of varying degree. Bitches lower perineum by flexing hind limbs while the males raise either of the rear legs and prefer to ejaculate urine against a wall or any object.

Deviation from normal posture should be suspected for abnormality. Cystitis in male dog evokes squatting posture. Involvement of spinal cord causes the dog to urinate while standing.

Frequency: The frequency depends largely on water intake, weather and work. The cattle, buffalo and horses micturate 5-6 times a day, pigs 2-3 times, while sheep and goats 1-3 times. The male dog urinates voluntarily at indefinite intervals.

Frequent urination may occur in diabetes mellitus, chronic interstitial nephritis, under the influence of diuretics, excess intake of water, cold weather, urethritis and partial occlusion of urethra. Complete absence of urine (anurea) occurs in complete urethral obstruction in bullocks.

Oligurea (partial decrease in volume of urine) is seen in diarrhoea, haemorrhage, dehydration, shock, febrile conditions, nephritis and congestive heart failure. In continence of urine flow develops due to paralysis of sphincter.

Pain: The animal feels discomfort while urination (dysurea) and when the back is depressed. Paddling with hind legs and kicking at the belly are observed in urinary tract affections. Some times defaecation is also difficult in some urinary tract diseases.

Physical examination

In cattle and buffalo, the left kidney is palpable through rectum. Only in some medium sized animal, the caudal part of right kidney is felt. In acute nephritis, pain reaction is shown by the animal. Similarly, in horse only posterior part of left kidney is palpable. In sheep, goat and pigs, direct physical examination of kidney is not possible. But in dogs, the left kidney and in cats both kidneys are easily palpable through the abdominal wall. The kidney gets enlarged in hydronephrosis and neoplasia. Reduction in size occurs in advanced interstitial nephritis. The swollen ureters are also appreciated by careful examination, in particular in hydronephrosis.

Urinary bladder should be examined carefully for distension which occurs in urethral obstruction or in initial paralysis of bladder sphincter. Palpation may reveal pain in cystitis and when the bladder is empty, the calculi and thickening of bladder wall may be felt. Complete obstruction of urethra due to calculi in male cattle and buffalo invariably causes rupture of bladder, which appears small and atonic. Digital exploration helps recognition of enlargement of prostate due to hyperplasia or neoplasm. The point of obstruction with calculus can be detected by palpation of the urethra and the penis, particularly in male cattle and buffalo. At the site of calculus, it feels hard and animal shows pain on pressure application.

In males, the prepuce must be examined. Prepucial tumour gives hanging appearance (coloure plate-B). Urethral rupture leads to swelling of ventral abdomen and the prepuce. In male horse, excess deposition of smegmas in the coronal fossa of the glans penis compresses the urethra interfering urination. Purulent discharge from the prepuce is seen in male dog suffering from balanitis.

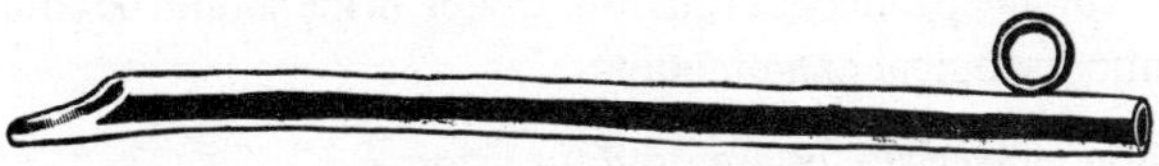

Cow Catheter Dawson, single channel

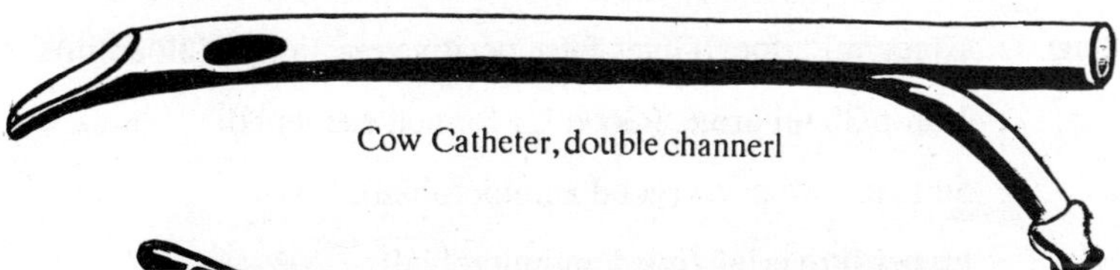

Cow Catheter, double channerl

Catheter Mare, Metal, jointed, with stillette.

Horse and Mare Catheter, combined, metal, Horse Catheter, red rubber.

10.1 Catheters for animals

Catheterization: The purpose of catheterization is to collect urine, to locate the position of calculus or to assess the lumen of urethra.

Cows, she buffaloes, mares and bitches can be catheterized with ease. Different sized sterile catheters (Fig. 10.1) are to be used for different species of animals. In cow and buffalo one finger is inserted into the suburethral diverticulum and the catheter is passed into immediately cranial to the diverticulum. In mares and bitches, the use of proper vaginal speculum is required.

Catheterization in male cattle and buffalo requires pudental nerve block or ataractic drugs to loosen the sigmoid flexure. A 114" long (0.1-0.12"dia) plastic tube may be introduced following proper lubrication with vaseline. The male horse also needs protrusion of penis which can only be achieved by ataractic drugs. A good quality, flexible tube is tried after lubrication. Catheterization in boars and rams is not feasible owing to inaccessibility of penis in former and urethral process in latter. The penis of dog is easily accessible and hence catheterization is easy. In male cats, rigid metallic catheter of 0.1-1 mm diameter is used after exposing the penis. Utmost care should be given to avoid rupture or injury of urethra during catheterization, as it will alter both chemical and microscopic examination of urine.

Urinalysis

Urine, the easiest body fluid, gives enormous diagnostic information. Thus, it should invariably be examined when the general health of the animal is disturbed. It should be examined physically, chemically, microscopically and microbially.

Collection: Urine can be collected from the animals voiding spontaneously. Urination can be induced by gentle strikes on vulvar lips in females and prepucial stimulation in males. Per-rectal stimulation of bladder induces urination in large animals. Pouring of cold water on the back or head stimulates urination in cattle and buffalo. Closing of nostrils in sheep induces urination. Better, urine should be collected by catheterization for bacterial, chemical and microscopical examination.

Preservation: The following preservatives are used for urine:

(i) Toluene : Overlay the urine sample. (Very good of chemical analysis.)

(ii) Thymol crystal : 10 mg/ml urine. (Gives false positive reaction for albumin).

(iii) Formalin : 1 drop/30 ml urine. (Good for formed elements).

(iv) Chloroform : 5ml per litre urine (good antimicrobial).

(v) Boric acid : lg. per litre urine (good antimicrobial).

Physical Examination

Colour: Normally bovine urine is light or straw coloured. Light yellow to intense yellow coloured urine is seen in febrile conditions, red in haematuria and coffee coloured in haemoglobinuria or myoglobinuria. Therapeutic or diagnostic use of phenothiazine, phenol red and bromsulfophthalein causes red colouration of urine, temporarily.

Transparency: Normal urine is transparent and clear. Varying degree of cloudiness appears in the presence of blood cells, salt crystals, protein and epithelial cells.

Odour: Urine has normally slight ammoniacal smell. It becomes penetrating ammoniacal in bacterial infection of urinary tract. The urine of ketotic animal is fruitish in smell. Species specific odour is present in urine of buck, tom cat and boar.

Viscosity: Fresh urine of cattle and buffalo is watery. The viscosity increases in pyelonephritis, due to presence of pus, blood and epithelial cells.

Specific gravity: Specific gravity of urine increases in the presence of more solute e.g. sugar, cells etc. and it decreases when there is polyurea (diabetes insipidus). It is determined with the help of urinometer. About 2/3 of the cylinder is filled with urine. The urinometer is dipped vertically in the cylinder. The lower miniscus of urine is recorded. The calibration of urinometer is being made at 15°C. A correction factor of 0.001 is added to the measured specific gravity for every 3°C above 15°C atmospheric temperature and 0.001 is substracted for every 3°C below 15°C.

Normal Specific Gravity of Urine

Species	Range	Average
Cattle	1.005-1.040	1.035
Buffalo	1.011-1.035	1.031
Horse	1.020-1.050	1.035
Sheep	1.015-1.045	1.030
Dog	1.150-1.045	1.025
Cat	1.020-1.045	1.030
Pig	1.005-1.025	1.015
Goat	1.010-1.035	1.030

pH : Reaction of urine varies species to species. In gernal, herbivora have alkaline pH, while that of carnivora have acidic urine.

Normal pH of Urine in Different Species of Animals

Cattle	7.5-8.00
Buffalo	7.8-8.17
Horse	8.0-8.20
Pig	6.5-7.50
Sheep and goat	8.0-8.20
Dog	6.0-7.00
Cat	6.0-7.00

Approximate pH of urine is measured with the help of BDH pH paper and accurately with electrically operated pH meter. The urine becomes acidic in grain engorgement, acute nephritis and ketosis. In bacterial infection it becomes more alkaline.

Chemical examination

Protein: Turbid urine should be filtered for protien test.

(a) Heat-acetic acid test: A test tube containing 3-5 ml urine is boiled at the upper column. Coagulation of protein turns the urine cloudy which can be easily compared with unboiled lower urine. Put a few drop of acetic acid (3%) and reboil. Disappearance of turbidity indicates presence of phosphate and persisting cloudiness indicates proteinurea.

(b) Sulfosalicylic acid test: To 5 ml urine, about 0.5 ml sulfosalicylic acid (25%) is added and mixed. Development of white turbidity indicates proteinurea.

(c) Heller's ring test: Along the wall of the test tube containing 3-4 ml urine, concentrated nitric acid is overlayed. Development of white ring between urine and acid is seen if protein is present.

Albumin in urine is present in nephritis, febrile conditions, poisoning with copper, mercury, lead, urinary calculi, epilepsy, brain tumour etc.

Sugar:

Benedict test: The reagent contains:

Copper sulphate	17.3g (Dissolved in 100ml water)
Sodium citrate	173.0g
Sodium carbonate (anhydrous)	100.0g (Dissolved in 500 ml water, alkaline solution)

Mix copper sulphate solution in alkaline solution and make volume to 1000 ml with water.

To a test tube containing 5 ml benedict reagent, add 8 drops of urine and boil for 5-8 minutes. Development of red, yellow or green colour reflects presence of reducing sugar. On cooling, there is precipitate deposit in the test tube.

Clinstix: Commercial paper strips are impregnated with glucose oxidase, orthotolidine and peroxidase. The strip is dipped in urine and taken out. Glucose present in urine, is oxidised in air in presence of enzyme glucose oxidase producing gluconic acid and hydrogen peroxide. In presence of peroxidase, hydrogen peroxide releases nascent oxygen which reacts with orthotolidine giving blue colour. It is more sensitive than Benedict's test.

Presence of glucose in urine usually indicates abnormal high blood glucose level exceeding renal threshold. In diabetic dog, both sugar and ketone are present in urine. If only sugar is present, investigation is required before confirming the case as diabetic. Soon after glucose intake, infusion and in advance pregnancy, glycosurea is present.

Bile pigment:

(a) **Foam Test:** About 3-4 ml urine is shaken vigorously. Formation of stable yellow foam indicates presence of bilc pigment.

(b) Methylene blue test: To 5 ml urine in a test tube, add one drop of methylene blue (0.25%) which turns urine green. Now add drop by drop methylene blue and shake it. If it takes more than 4 drops to change green to definite blue colour, the urine is positive for bile pigment.

(c) Fouchet's test: Reagent (i) Barium chloride 10 per cent solution, (ii) trichloroacetic acid 25g, ferric chloride (10%) 10 ml, distilled water 100 ml. To 10 ml acidified urine (with acetic acid), 5 ml barium chloride solution is added, mixed and filtered. Unfolded filter paper is placed on a dry filter paper and one drop Fouchet reagent (ii) is put on the precipitate. Development of green or blue colour indicates presence of bile pigments.

Bile Salts

Hay's sulphur test: A pinch of sulphur powder is poured on the surface of urine. If it sinks down indicates presence of bile salts. Bile salts lower the surface tension which allows the sulphur powder to sink. The tube must be free from detergents as it may give false positive reaction.

The tests of urine for bile pigment and bile salts are not so useful in cattle and buffalo as in case of dogs and cats. In latter species, the presence of both bile pigment and bile salts is suggestive of hepatic involvement. To confirm type of jaundice, Vanden Bergh test must be applied.

Blood

Traces of blood can be detected by the following test. In addition, intact red blood cells may be seen microscopically.

Benzidine test: In a test tube, 3 ml benzidine solution (saturated) in glacial acetic acid is mixed with 3 ml hydrogen peroxide (3%). Few drops of urine are added and mixed. Development of green to blue colour indicates blood in urine.

Ketone:

(a) Rothera's test

Reagents: Sodium nitroprusside-3g
Sodium carbonate anhydrous 50 g
Ammonium sulphate 100g

Make fine powder and mix. About 5g reagent powder is taken in a dry test tube. Carefully urine is poured along the wall of the tube to form a layer over the reagent. Observe for few minutes. Appearance of permanganate colour indicates presence of ketone in urine. This test is more applicable on milk as compared to urine.

(b) Gerhardt's test: Dilute solution of iron perchloride is added drop by drop to urine in a test tube till precipitation of iron phosphate continues. The urine is filtered and one or two drops of ferric chloride solution (10%) is added to the filtrate. Raddish-brown colour develops in the presence of ketone bodies.

Presence of ketone indicates faulty metabolism of fat. It is seen in frank hypoglycaemia, diabetes, displacement of abomasum, pregnancy toxaemia (in sheep)and starvation.

Indican: **Obermeyer's test:** The reagent comprises

Ferric chloride	2g
Hydrochloric acid (concentrated)	1000 ml

To a test tube, put 5 ml each of urine and Obermeyer reagent and mix. Add 2ml chloroform and allow it to settle at the bottom. Development of blue colour in the chloroform layer indicates presence of indican.

The indican is a product of protein digestion. Excess amount of it is being excreted in urine when there is intestinal stasis, blockade and other allied condition. The test is more applicable on dogs and cats than cattle and buffaloes.

Calcium: **Sulkowitch test**

Reagent:

Ammonium oxalate	5g
Oxalic acid	5g
Glacial acetic acid	5g
Distilled water q.s.	150 ml

In a test tube, take equal amount of the reagent and urine and mix. In the presence of calcium, urine develops turbidity and the degree of turbidity is directly proportional to the amount of calcium present in urine. For comparision, a control urine should be tested. In cow and buffalo, suffering from milk fever, the urine calcium is greatly reduced.

Microscopic Examination

Urine is examined microscopically for the evaluation of urinary sediments including some parasitic eggs e.g. *Capillaria plica* (the bladder worm of dog, cat and fox), *Stephanurus dentatus* (swine kidney worm) and *Dioctophyma renale* (kidney worm of dog).

The urine sample is centrifuged at 1500 rpm for 5 minutes. Discard the upper urine and take one drop of sediment on a clean slide. Put a coverslip and examine for urinary sediment indicated below.

Urinary sediments

Organised (derived from the organ): Casts (hyaline, blood, epithelial), epithelial cells, rbcs, wbcs, spermatozoa, parasitic eggs etc.

Unorganised (non-organic): Crystals, ammonium oxalate, triple phoshate, uric acid, cholesterol, tyrosine and urates

Organised sediments: Presence of RBCs indicates leakage of blood from injured tissues, while leucocytes and pus cells indicate suppuration. Characterization of cells helps in locating the lesion in the urinary tract. Polygonal cells of the kidney, columnar of renal tubules and squamous cells from ureters, bladder and urethra help in ascertaining the foci of trouble easily. Cellular casts (epithelial or blood) suggest acute inflammatory condition. The other forms of cast but for hyalines (long standing urinary disease) are not commonly met with.

Unorganised sediments: Presence of calcium-magnesium phosphate is not uncommon in bovine urine, as these are derived from their diet, while calcium oxalate is relatively rare. The excretion of these are not warranting but may help in the formation of calculi incombination with necrosed cells. Acidic urine of dogs and cats reveals deposits of uric acid and urates. Presence of carbonate produces carbon dioxide after addition of acetic acid.

Radiological examination: Generally applied in small animals. The presence of tumour in kidneys or bladder is well appreciated. Air may be used as contrast media. X-ray may reveal non -radiopaque calculi. The common sites of calculi are the renal-pelvis, ureter, bladder or the urethra.

Kidney Function Tests:

There are number of cumbersome tests to assess the function of kidney. Out of which estimation of blood urea nitrogen (BUN) is easy and good. Normally BUN level lies between 8-18 mg%. Increase in the level of BUN speaks kidney damage. The other tests are:

(a) **Creatinine clearance test:** Creatinine is excreted chiefly by kidneys. Elevation in the level of blood creatinine (normal 1-2 mg%) directs kidney dysfunction.

(b) **Dye clearance test:** (i) Phenol red @ 4 mg/10 kg. bwt is injected intravenously. Blood is collected 30 minutes later and the concentration of dye is measured colorimetrically. Normal concentration of dye should be 50 μg/100 ml of plasma by this time.

(c) **Methylene blue excretion test:** Methylene blue (2%) @ 0.4 ml/kg body wt. is injected intramuscularly. Cent per cent dye is excreted out within 24 hours normally. Dysfunction of kedneys delayed its excretion.

Kidney biopsy: The technique seldomly used in routine practice for histological and histochemical studies. However, sample can be obtained using 10" to 12" long punch needle. Specimen from left kidney can be had through rectal approach. Otherwise, laparotomy is essential. Blind needling through skin is not without danger.

Glucose Tolerance Test (GTT)

In order to assess the type of diabetes mellitus, either oral glucose tolerance test (OGTT) in non-ruminants or intravenous glucose tolerance test (IVGTT) can be applied.

Intravenous Glucose Tolerance Test (IVGTT)

Procedure: The animal is kept on fast for 16-24 hrs (except adult ruminants). Obtain blood in heparin before glucose injection. Inject glucose (50%) @ 0.5 g/kg bwt. within 2-3 minutes or as quick as possible. Collect blood in heparin or sodium fluoride at 5,15,25,35,45 and 60 minutes post-injection. Determine the glucose concentration or optical density colorimetrically at 420 nm. Plot the results on semilogrithmic ordinates and obtain T 1/2 (the time required for glucose to become half) , between 15 and 45 minutes post-infusion.

Intravenous Glucose T 1/2 in Animals

Animals	Normal	Diabetes mellitus
Cow	35 min.	182 min.
Buffalo	43-60 min.	142 min
Dog	17-33	

Reference

Oser, B.L. (1971). Hawk's Physiological Chemistry. 14th ed. Tata Mc Graw Hill Publishing Company Ltd, New Delhi.

11

RESPIRATORY SYSTEM

The system of respiration begins with the nostrils and ends in alveoli. In between constitutes the nasal passage, pharynx, trachea and the bronchi. The examination of entire course is essential to appreciate the trouble.

Topography of lungs: Major area of the thoracic cavity is occupied by the lungs. Both lungs are in close contact with the boundry of the chest cavity and other organs lying in it. The visceral pleura covers both the lungs and are separated by a longitudinal septum, the mediastinum.

The trachea of cattle and buffalo measures about 80-90 cm which is relatively shorter than the horse. The right lung is slightly larger than the left in most of the animals. The ventral border of the lungs runs dorsocaudally from the lower extremity of 6th rib to the 11th intercostal space.

The trachea of horse is longer than cattle. It bifurcates at the level of 5th rib. The dorsal border runs caudally upto 16th intercostal space. The lower borders of the lungs are thin and ventrally convexed (Fig. 11.1). In dog, the trachea bifurcates at the level of 5th rib forming a wide angle. The costal surface is more convex. Opposite the cardiac notch of the right lung, the pericardium is in touch with the thoracic wall at ventral 4th and 5th intercostal space. The pigs have shorter trachea. There is a special bronchus to the apical lobe of right lung. The lungs extend caudally to 11th or 12th intercostal space and the ventral border line, from the level of 6th rib, is almost straight posteriorly.

Clinical Examination of Lungs

Abnormal sounds like coughing, whistling, grunting, snoring, roaring, growling, wheezing and sneezing are indicators of respiratory involvement. Information of the condition can be obtained by systematic examination of the lungs' area. The methods are to be applied constitute palpation, percussion, auscultation and radiography. It must be borne in mind that the inferences drawn by these techniques vary greatly in different species of animals.

Percussion : Variation in percussion sound is of great help in diagnostic follow-up. Both normal and abnormal lung areas can be demarketed with the help of change in percussion sound (resonance). The sound varies according to the consistency of lungs and the air or the gas within it. The following types of percussion sound may be appreciated clinically.

Ringing sound: Audible when gas or air is present beneath the site of percussion. Normal lungs give ringing sound, which is intensified when excess quantity of air or gas is accumulated e.g. in pulmonary emphysema, pneumothorax and subcutaneous emphysema.

Dull Sound: In the absence of gas, lungs give dull sound which definitely points the presence of disease. Dull sound indicates consolidation of the area of the lung. Only superficial consolidation of area measuring about 4" X 4" is appreciated. Dull sound is heard in congestion, tumours growth, collapse, hydrothorax, wet-pleurisy and thickening of the subcutaneous layer.

Tympanic sound: This sound simulates kettle-drum like sound. It appears in conjunction with the above two types of percussion sound. In early and late stages of pneumonia, pneumothorax, subcutaneous emphysema, pulmonary cavitation and herniation of gas-filled-intestine in the thoracic cavity, give tympanic sound.

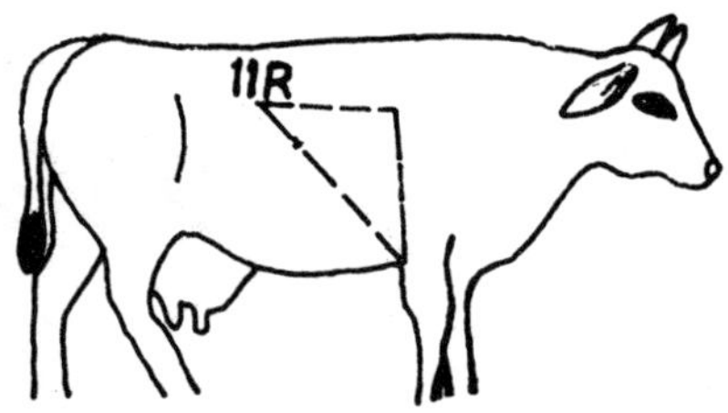

Fig. 11.1 (a) Cow

Metallic ringing: It is more intense in character from that of tympanic sound. It simulates the sound produced on strking a metallic jug. Such sound indicates presence gas under tension.

Crack-pot sound: It resembles the sound produced by strking a cracked pot. Gas passing through a narrow opening produces such sound, as in sub-cutaneous emphysema and some tracts in pneumonia when gas-filled portion of lung is isolated.

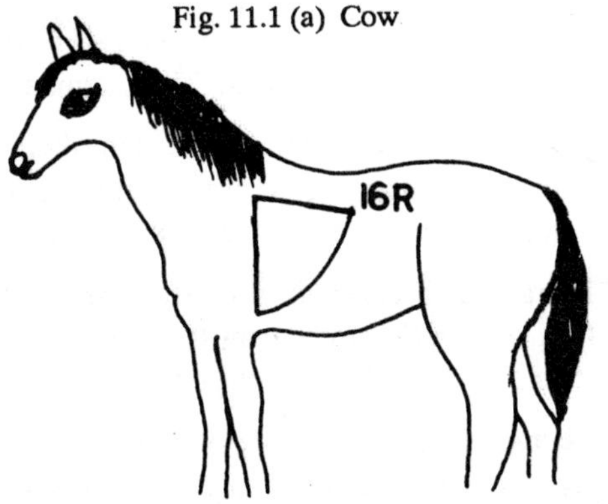

Fig. 11.1 (b) Horse Auscultation area for lungs

Area of Percussion of Lungs

The area of percussion of lungs in different species of animals are given below:

Percussion area in Animals in terms of Intercostal Spaces

Animals	Pairs of ribs	At the level of external angle of ileum	Mid Thorax	Ventral border
Cattle, buffalo	13	11	9	5
Sheep, goat	13	11	7	6
Horse	18	16	11	6
Dog,cat	13	11	9	6
Pig	14	11	9	6

Percussion of healthy lungs evokes ringing sound in most species of animals, while in dogs and cats, the sound is tympanic one. However, such percussion in buffalo is of limited use owing to thick skin.

Percussion Technique

Percussion of the lung area should first be made in horizontal and then vertical line, starting behind the posterior border of scapula. The scanning must be done carefully to delineate the normal respiratory boundary. The percussion area increases in pneumothorax and pulmonary emphysema. Clinically, in pneumothorax, both inspiratory and expiratory dyspnoea exist while in pulmonary emphysema, only expiratory dyspnoea. Reduced respiratory area is seen in conditions like advance pregnancy, ruminal or intestinal tympany and ascites. These conditions restrict full expansion of lungs due to increased intra-abdominal pressure. Hydropericardium and hypertrophy of heart also reduce lung area.

Resonance of percussion sound is diminished in pneumonia, severe congestion, consolidation, collapse and chronic tuberculosis of the lungs in general, whereas local diminution occurs in bronchopneumonia and congestion of dependant portion of the lung. Hypostatic congestion of lung gives unilateral reduction in the resonance. Due to small area of dullness in dogs and cats, percussion provides not much help. Deep percussion may elicit pain which is appreciated if the animal coils the body, becomes uneasy, kicks or tries to bite, as in case of pleurisy and fracture of ribs. In pleurisy, bronchitis and pneumonia, percussion produces coughs. Usually tympanic sound is audible when the gas filled loop of herniated intestine is present in the thoracic cavity.

These are the differentiating features between increased density of the lungs and fluid in pleural sac causing reduction in resonance.

Increased density	Fluid in the Pleura
(a) Pneumonia: area of dullness with regular outline.	(a) Hydrothroax: Percussion dullness has horizontal delineation.
(b) Clear and audible heart sound.	(b) Change in posture alters dullness area, as the fluid moves
(c) Abnormal broncheal sound on auscultation.	(c) Cardiac impulse indistinct.
(d) Tracheal percussion produces loud sound, which is audible by auscultation of thorax.	d) Absence of rales/friction on auscultation.
(e) No fluid.	e) Fluid escapes on exploratory puncture.

Auscultation of the lung

The area of auscultation is similar to that of percussion. Chest piece is applied on the thorax firmly to avoid friction sound of the hairs. Whole lungs area is auscultated beginning at the dorsal cranial part and moving caudally. The clinician must appreciate one complete respiratory cycle (inspiration and expiration) at one point. Any deviation in sound in one lung must be compared with other lung at the same level. Thickness in the chest wall minimises the respiratory sound e.g. subcutaneous oedema or emphysema.

Respiratory Sounds

The normal vesicular repiratory sound: The sound produced simulates softly whispered letter 'V' sound. It indicates presence of patent alveoli containing air. The vesicular sound is comparatively more audible during inspiration and well appreciated in small animals. In buffalo, it is not much clear.

Hyperpnoea: When the respiratory rate is enhanced.

Dyspnoea: When the respiration is difficult.

Cog wheel respiration: Interrupted vesicular clicking sound is audible when there is partial blockade of lumen of the bronchioles or irregular expansion of lungs.

Localized Interrupted Vesicular Sound: The sound is appreciated in tuberculous bronchopneumonia and fibrosis of lung.

Bronchial Respiratory Sound: The sound is audible near larynx and trachea resembling long drawn guttural "Ch" which starts and finishes abruptly. Bronchial sound is very clear in the anterior part of the lung. However, in healthy lungs only vesicular sound is audible. In conditions like pneumonia, wet pleurisy and hydrothorax, the bronchial sound is heard beyond its normal area owing to increased structural density of the lung, acting as better conductor of sound.

Indistinguishable respiratory sound: When the respiratory sound is masked by external noise or strong bronchial rale.

Abnormal (adventitious) respiratory sound: The diseases of bronchi, lungs, pleura and other associated organs give rise to such sounds.

Rales: Presence of exudate, fluid or blood in bronchi produces rale sound. It is of two types.

Moist rale: Characterized by bubbling in nature, which is due to fluid motion produced by passing air.

Dry rale: It is produced when the air current vibrates thready tenacious secretion present in the bronchi. The rale depends on the lumen of the bronchi. It may be humming, rattling, whistling or squeaking type. This type of rale is seen in chronic or acute bronchitis and pulmonary tuberculosis.

Crepitant rales: Are audible when the mucosa of alveoli get adhered due to inflammation and air current forces them apart. Sudden separation of walls emits crackling sound simulating the sound produced by rubbing hair tuft between fingers near the ear. Friction sound produced between body coat and the chest piece of stethoscope must be taken care. Crackling sound is heard in early pneumonia and pulmonary oedema

Emphysematous sounds: Seen in alveolar emphysema. The sound simulates crushing a sheet of soft paper into a ball, which is harsh and crackling.

Friction sound: Audible in dry pleurisy and early stage of pericarditis. The sound is produced by visceral and costal pleural glide over each other in absence of lubricating lymph-like fluid. The friction sound is very similar to the sound produced by rubbing two pieces of dry leather. Pericardial friction sound can be differentiated as it does not coincides with respiratory cycles.

Often the dry rales and friction sound are confusing. They differ from each other as below:

Dry rales	Friction sound
Not constant	Constant
Change of places (usually inspiration)	Audible at definite phase of respiration
Not painful on coughing but strong	Painful on coughing

During auscultation, care must be taken to rule out the various sounds produced in groaning, trembling, contraction of muscles and intestinal borborygm. These do not coincide the respiratory cycles in general.

X-ray examination: It is helpful in establishing ailments of a number of thoracic organs including the lungs. Patchy radiograph is seen in bronchopneumonia. Presence of fluid, neoplasia, abscess and cysts is well appreciated by this technique.

REFERENCE

Kelly, W.R. (1984) *Veterinary Clinical Diagnosis. 3rd ed.* Bailliere, Tindall, London.

12

CIRCULATORY SYSTEM

Haemodynamic system, comprising the heart, blood vessels and blood, helps supply of tissue oxygen, electrolytes and other nutrients and excretes the waste products like carbondioxide. To regulate this system, the nervous system plays an indispensable role. One must try to explore the system of circulation first in order to acertain its status.

Topography

In all species of animals, the heart is suspended by the base of big vessels in the thoracic cavity. The apex of the heart lies on the middle line just above the sternum.

In cattle and buffalo, the base on the heart lies apposite the 3rd to 6th rib. The apex lies an inch cranial to the diaphragm opposite to 6th costal cartilage and sternal articulation. The heart is in contact with left chest wall at the level of 3rd rib to 4th intercostal space.

More than half heart of the horse lies left of the mid line. The base lies opposite the 2nd to 6th intercostal space. The apex is situated about 1/2 inch above the sternum and one inch cranial to the sternal diaphragm.

The heart of dog is placed so obliquely that the base faces mainly in anterior direction. The apex, being blunt is positioned near diaphragm. The area of contact between heart and the left chest wall extends from 3rd to 6th rib. On right side, it is limited between 4th and 5th ribs.

The heart comprises four chambers, dorsally the right and left auricles and ventrally the right and left ventricles. The right atrioventricular orifice is controlled by tricuspid valve while the left atrioventricular orifice is guarded by bicuspid valve. The pulmonary orifice is guarded by pulmonary semilunar valve.

Heart sounds

The first *"Lub"* sound is produced due to closure of atrioventricular valves and contraction of the ventricles. It is also termed as systolic sound. Following contraction, the ventricles relax. To prevent back flow of the blood into the ventricles, the closure of aortic and pulmonary valves produce the second sound simulating *"Dup"*. This sound is synchronous to ventricular relaxing, thus it is also called as diastolic sound.

Clinical Appreciation or Examination

Clinical appreciation of haemodynamic system comprises of (a) Feeling of pulse, (b) Examination of heart and (c) the analysis of blood.

(a) Pulse: Examination of pulse is the best and easy clinical method for assessing the cardiac function in domestic animals. Still the digital perception is applicable to judge the rate, rhythm and the character of pressure in artery. These are the following types of pulse:

Rapid pulse: Increased frequency of pulse is seen in heart diseases or reflex stimulation in conditions like fear, anaemia, infections, fever and debility.

Slow pulse: There is decrease in frequency of pulse rate per minute. Decreased frequency of pulse is seen in comatose condition and heart block. Hunting horses have slow pulse at rest.

Strong pulse: Strong pulse is due to raised blood pressure. It is also called as full pulse e.g. in hypertension.

Weak pulse: When the pulse wave is imperceptible. Weakness of the heart muscle and fatigueness cause weak pulse e.g. Hydropericardium or pyopericardium.

Wiry pulse: Wiry pulse is noted when the heart beats are forceful and rapid and presence of some degree of vasoconstriction. This type of pulse is seen in acute peritonitis, pleurisy and acute traumatic pericarditis.

Thready pulse: The pulsation of artery feels weak, thin, usually rapid and scarcely perceptible. under the fingers. It indicates fatal end of a disease.

Small pulse: It is due to poor contraction of ventricles. Poor aortic and atrio-ventricular contraction also cause small pulse.

Running down pulse: Indicates progressive weakness of the heart. The tone of vessels is feeble.

Water hammer pulse: Sharp increase in blood pressure followed by sudden decrease in it emits such pulsation. Such pulse is characteristic of aortic valve incompetence.

Jugular pulse: Waves of regurgitated blood is seen in the jugular veins as in tricuspid insufficiency. Following cardiac contraction, the blood flows back and produces pulse wave in the great vein.

Venous distension: The jugular veins, auricular veins and mammary veins are generally considered to appreciate its distension. Momentary distension of superficial veins occurs following exercise. In general, whenever there is obstruction on the venous flow or when the right side of the heart is not fully emptied during systolic contraction, the condition of venous stasis develops e.g. in myocardial dystrophy, neoplasia of heart, endocarditis, pericarditis, hydropericardium, pyopericardium, pneumonia, over-distension of abdomen and chronic pulmonary emphysema. Local inflammation or tumour may compress the veins causing their engorgement.

Thrombosis (arterial/venous): The emboli may be the origin of the condition. Large emboli originated from bacterial endocarditis may occlude pulmonary artery. The smaller thrombi may lodge in brain, lungs or kidneys and the clinical symptoms speak the vessels obstructed.

(b) Examination of the Heart

Inspection of heart does not provide much information in animals, however palpation helps in assessing the cardiac cycles. Additionally, cases of valvular insufficiency or developmental defects can be detected.

Percussion of the heart can be carried out similar to that of lungs. The heart gives non-resonant sound, being air free. The area of cardiac dullness vary greatly depending on the breed, species and size of the animals.

In cattle and buffalo, percussion is carried out at the level of lower two third of the chest cavity between the 3rd and 6th ribs on the left side. It is well appreciated when the left foreleg is well drawn cranially.

In horse, the area of dullness is observable above the level of left elbow, between third and fifth intercostal spaces. Only a small area of dullness is demonstrable on the right chest. In goat and sheep, only left cardiac dullness is appreciated while on the right side, it is not demonstrable.

In dog percussion gives absolute cardiac dullness in between fourth to sixth intercostal spaces to the left. On the right side, the area of dullness lies between 4th to 5th intercostal spaces.

The area of cardiac dullness increases in conditions like pericarditis, hypertrophy of heart, hydro or pyopericardium, displacement of heart and neoplasia of heart. While in emphysema, the cardiac dullness area decreases. Pain on percussion in this region indicates acute pericarditis.

Auscultation: Auscultation provides good information on the status of the heart. The purpose of auscultation is to detect abnormal heart sound. It can be conducted either directly or indirectly (with phonendoscope or stethoscope). It must be conducted in standing position and with left foreleg fully advanced cranially. The noisy respiration in dogs can be diminished by transient closure of the mouth for better appreciation of cardiac sound.

By auscultation, the cardiac rate, rhythm, intensity and character of heart sound including abnormal sound can be assessed. The chest piece is applied between 4th and 5th left intercostal spaces. Presence of fluid close to the chest wall gives intense sound, as fluid is good sound-conductor. The systolic and the diastolic sounds are more clearer at the apex and base of the heart respectively. These are well perceived in large animals.

Normal heart sound

As stated earlier, the heart sound is composed of two distinct sounds. The first is dull, loud and of longer duration while the second is short and sharp. There is a pause between the second and first heart sounds. The first sound (systolic) is the outcome of contraction of cardiac muscle and closure of atrio-ventricular valves. The second sound (diastolic) is emitted by closure of semilunar valves. In bradycardia, these two sounds are clearly distinguished. These sounds simulate phonetically *lub-dup*. Cardiac sounds vary greatly according to the species, age and size of the animals. Thickness of the chest wall diminishes the audibility of cardiac sound. Some normal horses have a third, short and low pitched pre-diastolic heart sound while some dogs have weak sound following the second heart sound.

Abnormal heart sounds

Abnormal heart sounds, based on their rate, rhythm and character have been summarised below:

Type of heart sound	Condition	Remarks
Increased volume/loud	Cardiac hypertrophy, anaemia, strenuous work, early febrile condition, over stimulation of heart, exercise.	Increase action of heart muscles
Decreased volume/low	Cardiac displacement, hydropericardium, pericarditis, anasarca, advance cardiac insufficiency.	Myocardial weakness

Intensified first heart sound.	Ventricular hypertrophy	Strong ventricular muscle contraction
Intensified 2nd heart sound	Pneumonia, pulmonary emphysema, hypertension and renal diseases.	Increase aortic pressure
Diminshed 2nd sound	Hypotension	Low blood pressure
Reduplication of first sound	Hypotention	Low blood pressure
Reduplication of second sound	Asymmetric ventricular contraction, pulmonary hypertension	Failure of semilunar valves closure
Gallop rhythm (three sounds at regular intervals)	Myocarditis, defective transmission in bundle of His	Defective conduction
Irregular cardiac rhythm	Defective auriculo-ventricular association	Disturbed conduction

Note: Pre and post-exercise auscultation in horses and dogs gives better assessment of cardiac rhythm.

Adventitious Heart Sound (Additional Sounds)

These may be either endocardial or pericardial in origin which replace one or both heart sounds. Humming, hissing or swinging sounds are called cardiac murmurs. Murmurs are produced endocardially as in vegetative endocarditis, adhesions, valvular insufficiency or ductus arteriosus patency. Passage of blood through narrow opening produces these sounds.

Systolic murmur occurs during systole, as in atrio-ventricular insufficiency and stenosis of semilunar valves. While diastolic murmur occurs during diastole, as in semilunar valves insufficiency and stenosis of atrioventricular valves. The murmur is usually associated with valvular abnormalities but it may occur in the absence of such gross lesions or defects. Murmurs originating owing to cardiac or valvular defects, are known as organic murmur, while those occur in the absence of primary heart abnormalities are known as functional or haemic murmurs. Haemic murmurs are met in debility, anaemia, toxaemia and myocardial asthenia.

Careful auscultation and location of maximum audibility indicate affection of particular valves. The table shows the different murmurs and site of maximum audibility.

Valves (murmurs)	Site of maximum audibility
Mitral (horse)	Left side, fifth intercostal space.
Aortic (horse)	Left side, fourth intercostal space.
Mitral (cattle / buffalo)	-do-
Aortic (cattle)	Left side, just below shoulder level
Pulmonary (cattle/buffalo)	Left, third intercostal space.
Tricuspid	Right, 4th intercostal space at the level of costochondral junction.
Patent ductus arteriosus	Left, third intercostal space.

Considerable variation in the murmurs is noted when valves are affected by organic pressure like bloat and diaphragmatic hernia in cattle and buffaloes, causing loud systolic murmur. The endocardial murmurs are usually systolic and faintly audible, whereas the organic murmurs are either systolic or diastolic and are of loud intensity. Pericardial frictional sound is often heard in cattle with tuberculous pericarditis which can be differentiated from pleural friction. The former coincides with cardiac cycle, while the latter with respiratory movement. When the cardiac rate equates the respiratory rate, it becomes difficult to differentiate.

Blood pressure

Though blood pressure is not routinely recorded as diagnostic parameter in animals but it is of definite help in conditions like, shock, cardiac diseases and surgical procedures. For blood pressure measurement, two methods are usually applied.

(i) Direct method: The needle, connected directly to mercury or anaerobid manometer, is being inserted into the artery. For this brachial artery is used, both in cattle and horses.

(ii) Indirect method: Sphygmomanometer is used for this. The pneumatic cuffs are applied at the base of the tail (in horse, cattle and buffalo) and forelegs (brachial artery) or hind legs (femoral artery) in dogs. After application of the cuff through attached rubber tube to the mercury manometer, the air is filled with rubber bulb provided, until the pulse wave is blocked. A stethoscope is placed over the artery under the cuff. Slowly the air pressure is reduced by releasing the knob till a point at which blood starts flowing through the artery which is appreciated by tapping sound. Manometer reading at this point provides systolic pressure. Now release the pressure further till a point at which sound disappears completely. The manometer gives the diastolic pressure at this time. Other sophisticated technique like photoelectric cells can be used.

The blood pressure vary greatly in different species of animals and also on the artery used for its measurement. For reference, the table provides blood pressure of some animals.

Species of animal	Blood pressure (mm Hg)	
	Systolic	Diastolic
Cattle	120-190(145)	90-130 (90)
Horse (coccygeal artery)	85-135	40-70
Bracheal artery	145-195	105-150
Dog (untrained)	100-185	60-125
Trained	95-135	50-65

X-ray of the heart

Radiological picture of the heart often provides accurate diagnosis. Though it is most useful in small animals but is equally helpful in large animals (cattle/buffalo) for the confirmation of metallic objects and displacements. The radiographs are taken either vertically or laterally, depending on the requirement.

Electrocardiography

Certain organic ailment of the heart is accurately diagnosed by this technique. However, it has not been accepted as a routine diagnostic procedure. In fact it is limited to research model. The procedure is same as in human. The electrodes are applied on the upper part of the legs and recording is done with electrocardiogram. The interpretation must be carried out by an experienced clinician. For detail, standard text books on veterinary electrocardiography may be consulted.

Phonocardiography

A graphic recording of heart sounds is made with the help of phonocardiograph comprised of a microphone, sound amplifier and a galvenometer with recording attachment. With this instrument, the waves of even those sounds which are beyond the range of human audibility, are recorded.

(c) Examination of Blood

The circulating blood cells are the defence units while the soluble constituents of blood speak the nutritional/metabolic status of the body. The changes in any component (s) of the blood help in making proper diagnosis. To achieve this, blood is examined for both cellular and biochemical constituents.

Collection of blood

The preferential site(s) for the collection of blood differs species wise. The table below illustrates the sites and the requirement for blood collection.

Species of animal	Sites	Needle size (gauge x length, cm)
Cattle	Jugular vein, milk vein (Cow)	15-18x5-6
Buffalo/Camel	Jugular vein, milk vein (Female)	-do-
Horse	Jugular vein	16-18x 6
Sheep and goat	Jugular vein	18-20 x5
Dog and cat	Cephalic/tarsal vein	22x 5
Pig	Cardiac puncture, Anterior venacava, ear vein	18-20x 6-8
Rabbit	Ear vein/jugular vein/cardiac puncture	22 x 3-5

The required amount of blood for laboratory analyses also varies according to animals. Possible blood volume withdrawal in various animals is as below.

Animals	Total Volume of blood (ml/kg b.wt)	Max. safe volume to be collected (ml/kg)	Volume for routine diagnosis (ml)
Cattle/buffalo	60	7	20-30
Horse	75	7	20-30
Sheep	60	6	15-20
Goat	70	6	15-20
Pig	65	6	10
Dog	90	9	2-5

Blood is collected in two different vials. For haematology, blood biochemistry and plasma analysis, the blood is collected in vial containing a suitable anticoagulent. For harvesting serum, the blood is collected in plain vials.

List of common anticoagulents

Anticoagulents		Amount for 10 ml blood	Suitability
EDTA (Na/K salt) (Ethylenediamine tetra-acetic acid.)		10-20mg	For routine haematolgy
Oxalates mixture			
Ammonium oxalate		12mg	Not suitable for
Potassium oxalate		8mg	BUN determination
Sodium citrate (3.8%)		1.1 ml	For blood transfusion
Heparin		1 mg	For blood glucose, blood chemistry.
Sodium fluoride		100 mg	For blood glucose.
ACD solution:			
Dextrose	14.7 g		
Trisodium citrate	13.2g	2.5 ml	For blood storage and
Citric acid	4.4g		transfusion.
Distilled water	1000ml		

Blood Collection Technique

In general, the blood must be collected from the animals causing them least disturbance. Excitement while applying twitch to the horse, may raise erythrocyte count by 20 per cent. So also, the sedatives have marked effect on haematological values. In fact, it remains a challenge in veterinary practice. To some extent it depends on individual clinical acumen.

The skin must be cleaned or clipped properly. Some antiseptic (95% alcohol) is to be applied. Let the skin dry. The respective vein is to be raised either with digital pressure or with the help of suitable tourniquet. The syringe must be dry or otherwise there will be haemolysis. The bevel of the needle must face the skin to avoid clogging by cut edge of the skin. The angle between needle and skin should be 30 degree. As soon as the needle enters the blood stream, blood flows down the syringe. The piston should be drawn back gently so as to create vaccum to draw blood more efficiently. Forceful pull of the piston causes blockade owing to collapse of the vein around the point of insertion of needle. A spirit swab is placed and needle is withdrawn. Press the swab for few seconds at the point of prick.

First, the needle is detached from the syringe and blood is poured in suitable vials. The blood must be mixed with anticoagulent by rolling the vial between palmsgently.

Storage of Blood:

The whole blood can be stored for 24 hr at room temperature. Delay causes marked changes in red cell count, packed cell volume and differential pattern of white cell. At 4°C it can be stored for long time (15 days) for transfusion.

Plasma/Serum Harvest

The blood collected with anticoagulents is centrifuged at 3000-4000 rpm for 15 minutes.Centrifugations at higher speed may cause haemolysis. The plasma is transferred in a separate vial for its analysis. For serum, the blood without anticoagulents, is allowed to coagulate in slant position and incubated at 38°C. It takes 3-4 hours to ooze serum out. Lower is the temperature, more is the time required for serum separation.

Storage: The serum can be stored for 1 year at -20° C and below, at-80° C it can be kept indefinitely.

HAEMATOLOGICAL EXAMINATION

Smear preparation : Smears may be wet or dry. The wet smears are prepared by putting a small drop of blood on a cover glass and placed inversely on other cover glass. The blood spreads homogenously between the cover glasses which can be examined as per requirement. At one end of a thoroughly clean, dry glass slide, a small drop of blood is placed for dry smears. The slide is placed horizontally on the bench or table. The narrow end of a spreader slide is placed at 45° angle touching the blood droplet. The blood soon spreads along the edge of the spreader slide. Now the spreader slide is pushed forward at an angle of 30°. The blood follows the spreader slide. Lesser is the angle, thinner will be the smear. The slide is dried in air/warm air. It must be protected from flies. Dried slides may be fixed by putting few drops of either ethanol or methanol on the the smear. It prevents distortion of morphology of cells.

The slides may be stained for differential leucocytes count, protozoal and bacteriological investigation. Either Wright's, Leishman's or Giemsa stain is used in routine practice.

Wright's stain

Wright's stain powder	0.5 g
Glycerine	5 ml
Methanol	300 ml

Leishman's stain

Leishman's stain	0.5 g
Glycerine	5 ml
Methanol	300 ml

Buffer water

Potassium dihydrogen phosphate	5.47 g
Disodium hydrogen phosphate	3.80g
Distilled water	1000 ml

Wright-Leishman mixture

Wright's stain 3 parts

Leishman stain 1 part

Giemsa Stain

Commercially available.

Staining Technique

Cover the dry smear by putting 2-3 drops of either Leishman's or Wright's stain and leave for 2 minutes. Put 8-10 drops buffer water to dilute the stain and allow 10 minutes for staining. Pour off the stain, wash with buffer water and dry it for examination.

For protozoal examination Giema stain (1:10) gives the best result. The fixed blood smear is kept in coupling jar containing stain for 30-45 minutes. Higher is the dilution of stain, more is the time required but gives best result. The slide is focused, first under low power, to look for staining and distribution of erythrocytes and leucocytes. On suitable smear a drop of cedar oil is placed and examined under high power oil immersion objective. The standard battlement method is used for cellular differentiation (Fig. 12.1). The erythrocytes and blood protoza can be appreciated by same technique.

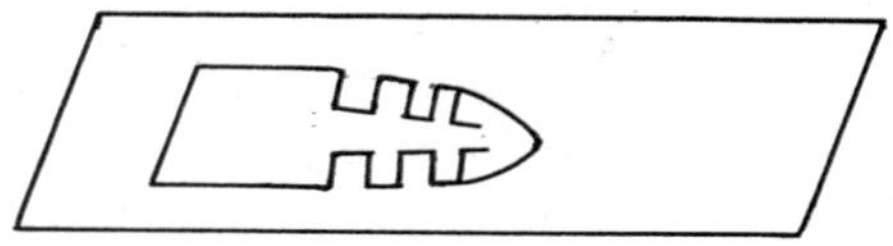

Fig. 12.1 Battlement method.

Mistakes in stained slides :

Appearance		Probable mistakes	Correction
(a)	Cell too blue	Buffer too alkaline, thick smear, prolonged staining	Decolourise in methanol
(b)	Pale cells	Understain, weak stain, excess washing	Restain
(c)	Cells with eosinophilic reaction	Buffer acidic	Check buffer pH
(d)	Invisible film	Dirty or greasy film	Clean the slide with xylene
(e)	Precipitated stain	Dry stain, insufficient wash	Proper wash

Leucocytes and its Count

Broadly the leucocytes are of two types, granulocytes (polymorphonuclear cells-neutrophils, eosinophils and basophils) and agranulocytes (mononuclear cells). From the sites of their origin, they are released in circulation. Their life span ranges from few hours (lymphocytes) to 14 days of the granulocytes. The life span and the pattern of leucocytes are greately influenced in disease conditions.

Neutrophils: The mature neutrophils are with multilobulated nucleus (upto five) joined with a thin strand (Fig. 12.2) or mononucleated. The nuclear membrane is ragged in mature neutrophils. Stained neutrophils have light pink (acidophilic) cytoplasm with fine granules and deep blue (basophilic) nucleus. The nucleus of metamyelocytes is bean or kidney shaped. The band cells are nothing but immature neutrophils.

Basophils: Have purplish granules scattered in cytoplasm as well as the nucleus.

Eosinophils: The distribution of orange-red granules in the cytoplasm of the cells makes easy recognition. The nucleus is usually non-segmented and the cytoplasm appears pale-grey. In most of the species it is usually below 10 per cent.

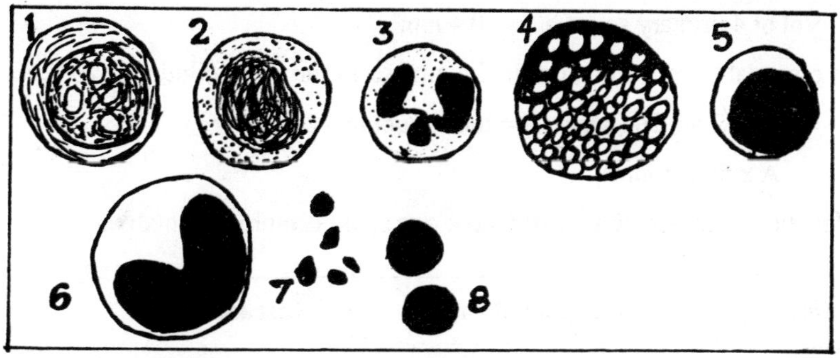

Fig. 12.2 1. Myeloblast 2. Myelocyte 3. Neutrophil 4. Eosinophil (equine) 5. Lymphocyte 6. Monocyte 8. Erythrocytes.

Total and Differential Leucocytes Patterns in Animals

	Cattle	Buffalo	Horse	Sheep	Dog	Pig
Total count						
$10^3/mm^3$	4-12	5-10	6-13	4-13	9-13	11-22
Differential %						
Neutrophils						
Segmented	15-40	25-35	50-64	15-30	60-75	40-60
Band	0-5	-	0-4	0-4	3-6	0-2
Lymphocytes	40-70	45-65	20-40	55-75	15-30	30-50
Eosinophils	3-15	2-4	4-10	0-10	2-8	1-5
Basophils	0-2	0-2	0-2	0-1	0-1	0
Monocytes	3-10	3-7	3-10	0-6	1-8	2-8

Total leucocyte count

The diluting fluids are: (1) Acetic acid 2 per cent (2 ml glacial acetic acid and distilled water upto 100 ml) and (2) hydrochloric acid 0.1 Normal (0.9 ml concentrated HCl to 100 ml with distilled water). These diluents lyse erythrocytes and leave the leucocytes intact which are counted.

Use Thoma's WBC counting pipette (Fig. 12.3). Suck properly mixed blood upto 0.5 mark. It must be very accurate. Excess sucked blood is removed by tapping on finger tips or on rubber. Never use cloth or cotton which may cause erroneous counting. Fill the pipette with any of the above fluid upto 11 mark. Roll the pipette between palms for proper mixing. Discard 1-2 drops and charge on one side of neubauer chamber covered with a glass slide. Let the cells settle for 3-4 minutes. Count in four corner primary squares. Let the count is A.

Calculation: Vol. of 1 primary square $= 1\ mm \times 1\ mm \times 0.1mm$

$= 0.1mm^3$

Vol of 4 primary squares = 0.4 mm^3

A factor of 2.5 is essential to convert counts in 0.4 mm^3 to 1 mm^3. The dilution is 20 times.

Thus total count = A x 2.5 x 20 (where A = total count in 4 corners)

= A x 50 per mm^3

Differential leucocytic count alongwith total leucocytes count is more informative.

Leucocytic reaction	Designated as	Disease (s)
Increased total leucocytes count	Leucocytosis	Bacterial infections.
Increased neutrophil count with increased total count	Absolute neutrophilia	Early suppuration.
Increased lymphocytes	Lymphocytosis	Rare, during recovery phase of the disease.
Increased eosinophils	Eosinophilia	Allergy, parasitic diseases, recovery stage.
Increased band cell	Shift to the left	Haemolytic crisis.
Increased mature neutrophils	Shift to the right	Bone marrow suppression.
Decreased leucocytes	Leucopenia	Viral diseases.
Increased monocytes	Monocytosis	TB/Brucellosis

The red blood cells (Erythrocytes):

The erythrocytes are formed in the bone marrow under the influence of renal hormone, erythropoietin. They are being discharged in the circulation regularly. About 1.25 per cent cells are destroyed daily. Their life span is also limited.

Life span of RBC in different animals

Animals	Life in days
Cattle	80-160
Horse	140-150
Sheep	52-153
Goat	125
Dog	110-120
Cat	68
Pig	62-71

The stained smear for differential leucocytic count may be used for morphological appreciation of erythrocytes.

The erythrocytes are examined in respect of abnormal size (unequal = anisocytosis), shape (distorted cells = poikilocytosis), presence of nucleus (with nucleus = erythroblasts), staining properties (deeply stained = polychromasia, less staining = hypochromic) and visualization of basophilic stippling and intraerythrocytic protozoa (anaplasma, babesia etc.).

Erythrocyte Count (Total)

Diluting fluids

A.	Normal saline:	Sodium chloride	8.5 g
		Distilled water to	1000 ml
B.	Gower's solution:	Disodium sulphate	12.5 g
		Acetic acid glacial	33.3 ml
		Distilled water to	200 ml
C.	Hayem's solution:	Mercuric chloride	0.5 g
		Sodium chloride	1 g
		Disodium sulphate	5 g
		Distilled water to	200 ml

Technique: Thoma's red cell pipette (Fig. 12.3) is filled up to 0.5 mark (up to 1 mark in severe anaemia) with well mixed blood. Any of the diluting fluid is sucked up to 101 mark. Rotate the pipette between palms. Discard 1-2 drops and charge the neubauer chamber. Avoid over or under filling. Allow the cells to settle for four minutes. Count the cells in five secondary squares (4 corner and one central), of the central primary square. Let the total count in all 5 squares is R.

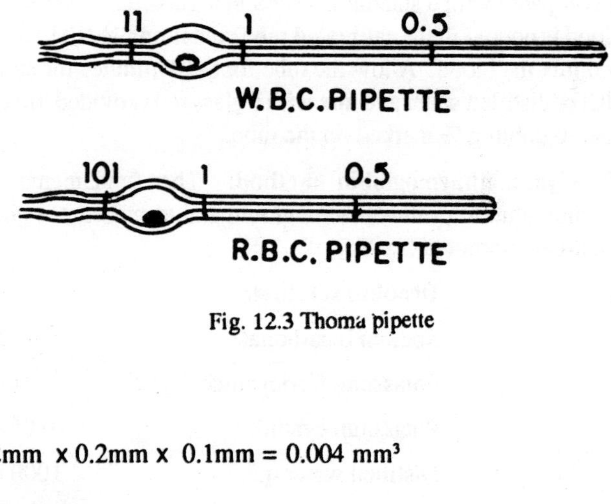

Fig. 12.3 Thoma pipette

Calculation:

Volume of one secondary square of central primary square $= 0.2\text{mm} \times 0.2\text{mm} \times 0.1\text{mm} = 0.004 \text{ mm}^3$

Volume of 5 secondary squares $= 5 \times 0.004 \text{ mm}^3$
$= 0.02 \text{ mm}^3$

To convert the count in 0.02 mm^3 in 1mm^3, a factor of 50 is necessary. The dilution is 200. Thus total erythrocyte count $= R \times 50 \times 200$ (where R is cell count in 5 squares) $= R \times 10{,}000$.

Normal erythrocyte count (millions / mm^3)

Animals	Range	Average
Cattle	5-10	7.5
Buffalo	5-7.30	6.65
Camel	4.2-5.5	4.85
Horse	5.5-13.5	8.5
Sheep	8.5-13.5	10.8
Goat	8-18	15
Dog	5-7	6.2
Pig	5.0-8.5	6.8
Cat	6-9.5	7.5

Haemoglobin Estimation

In routine clinical practice the methods used for determination of haemoglobin are:

(1) **Sahli's method (acid haematin method):** The method is based on formation of acid haematin, which is compared with a standard, sealed in a glass tube. With the help of haemoglobinometer pipette, 20 mm^3 blood is poured in the calibrated tube containing N /10 hydrochloric acid to 2 mark. Rinse the pipette twice and mix the blood. Allow the tube for 8-10 minutes for acid haematin formation. Add drop by drop N/10 HCl or distilled water and mix with a glass rod provided, till the colour matches with the standard tube. Read haemoglobin g % marked on the tube.

(2) **Cyanmethaemoglobin method:** The fundamental behind this method is the conversion of haemoglobin to cyanmethaemoglobin and to measure it photometrically at 640 nm or with Erma (Japan) haemoglobinometer.

Drabkin solution:

Sodium bicarbonate	1 g
Potassium ferricyanide	0.2 g
Potassium cyanide	0.052 g
Distilled water q.s.	1000 ml

Five ml drabkin solution is pipetted in a test tube and 20 mm^3 blood is mixed. Allow to stand for 10-15 minutes. Set the instrument at zero scale with Drabkin solution and fix the scale to 15.8 with the knob provided, while the push button is pressed. Put the sample tube and note the reading. The value obtained by this technique is very accurate.

Packed cell volume (Haematocrit): It is the measurement of red cells volume per cent in the blood. Either Wintrobe method or microhaematocrit method is in routine use.

Wintrobe method: The tube is filled with heparinized blood with a long needle and syringe avoiding gas bubbles in the tube. The tubes are calibrated in 100 mm scale. The tubes are placed in a centrifuge machine, and spun at 3000 rpm for a standard time of one hour. Take out the tubes and read PCV % on the calibrated tube. The buffy coat is to be ignored. The method is cumbersome and time consuming and also the packing of cells is not so complete.

Microhaematocrit method: Capillary tubes are used in this method. The packing of RBC is rather better than Wintrobe tube. The capillary tubes are filled 2/3 its length with well mixed blood. One end of the tube is closed with sealing clay. The tubes are placed in the microhaemocrit centrifuge with sealed end towards periphery. Close the lid and centrifuge only for 2 minutes. It rotates at 12000 rpm or above. Remove the tubes and read with the help of microhaematocrit reader provided with the machine. The bottom of RBC column lies on zero line while top level of plasma at 100 line. The line coinciding the top level of RBC provides PCV per cent.

Erythrocytic indices: Based on erythrocytes count, haemoglobin g per cent and haematocrit (PCV), the average volume of a red blood cell and its haemoglobin content. can be deduced indirectly. The values help in classification and type of anaemia and in rationalisation of treatment.

Mean corpuscular volume (MCV) : It is the average volume of one red cell.

$$MCV = \frac{\text{Haematocrit (PCV)} \times 10}{\text{Erythrocytes count}} = \text{fl. or } \mu^3$$

Example: PCV = 35, erythrocyte 5 million/mm^3

MCV = 35/5 x 10 = 70 fl. or μ^3

MCV allows to classify red cell to be normocytic, macrocytic or microcytic.

Mean Corpuscular Haemoglobin (MCH): It is the amount of haemoglobin in average erythrocyte

$$MCH = \frac{\text{Haemoglobin g\%} \times 10}{\text{Erythrocytes count (million/mm}^3\text{)}} = \text{pg.}$$

Example: Haemoglobin = 12 g %, erythrocytes- 5 million / mm^3

MCH = 12/5 x 10 = 24 pg

Mean Corpuscular Haemoglobin Concentration (MCHC): It is per cent haemoglobin concentration in average erythrocyte

$$MCH\ C = \frac{\text{Haemoglobin g\%}}{\text{PCV}} \times 100 = \%$$

Example: Haemoglobin 14g%, PVC=35%

$$MCHC = \frac{14}{35} \times 100 = 40\%$$

Normal MCV, MCH and MCHC in Animals

	Cattle	Buffalo	Horse	Pig	Dog
MCV(fl^3)	62.0	56.0	51.0	61.6	64.0
MCH (pg)	21.3	19.2	13.0	15.0	15.3
MCHC (%)	31.0	34.1	25.0	26.0	23.7

Interpretations:

	1	2	3	4
MCV	Increased	Normal	Decreased	Decreased
MCH	Increased	Normal	Decreased	Decreased
MCHC	Normal	Normal	Normal	Decreased
Type of anaemia	Macrocytic	Normocytic	Simple microcytic	Microcytic hypochromic
Conditions	Folic acid, vit B12 deficiency	Haemorrhage, Iron deficiency	Iron deficiency	Iron deficiency Infections

Complete haematology including total leucocytes, erythrocytes, haemoglobin, packed cell volume, MCV, MCH and MCHC can be calculated most accurately with automated blood cell counter (Erma, Japan, Colour Plate-B).

Haemoglobin and PCV (%) of Animals

	Haemoglobin (g %)	PCV (%)
Cattle	8.5-13.5(11)	28-42(35)
Buffalo	9-12.9(10.8)	30-36(33)
Sheep	9.3-14.8(11.5)	27-43(35)
Goat	8.8-13.8(11.3)	25-40(34)
Horse	8.5-13(11)	28-45(36)
Dog	11.8-16.9(14.3)	36-51(43.5)
Pig	8.3-12.7(10.4)	32-46(40)
Camel	8.7-10.5(9.6)	26.25-32.70(29.50)

Erythrocyte sedimentation rate (ESR): Provides the rate of settling of RBC in the calibrated column. It varies markedly in different diseases. The Wintrobe method and Westergren method are in routine use.

Wintrobe technique: The Wintrobe tubes are filled with fresh heparinised blood as for the determination of PCV. The tubes are placed vertically in Wintrobe stand and left. At the end of one hour, the upper level of RBC is recorded. The calibration starts from upper level. It gives mm fall of erythrocytes per hour.

Westergren method: The Westergren tubes are graduated from 0 to 140 mm. The blood samples are sucked up to 0 mark and the tubes are fitted vertically in the stand. After one hour the upper miniscus of erythrocytes is noted as mm fall per hour. There is a great variation in erythrocyte sedimentation rate in different species of animals. In sheep and goat, for a period of 8 and 24 hrs respectively, has been recommended for recording the ESR values. Formation of rouleau in horse, dog and cat causes rapid settling of RBCs. This property lacks in cattle, sheep and goats. ESR is more in anaemia, filariasis, neoplasia, tuberculosis, pregnancy and acute general infections.

Normal ESR in Animals

Animal	ESR mm/hr
Cattle	0-3
Buffalo	30-60
Horse	15-38
Sheep	0-3
Goat	2-2.5
Dog	5-8
Pig	1-14

Bleeding and Clotting Time (BT and CT) :

The bleeding time is determined by making a prick in the mucosa of lower lip with a hypodermic needle. The blood is soaked on filter paper at every 30 seconds till the oozing of blood ceases. Normally bleeding stops by 3 minutes. Thrombocytopenia and deficiency of Vit. K cause prolonged bleeding time in animals.

Determination of clotting time is a bit cumbersome and provides the similar inference to that of clotting time. For estimation, four clean saline rinsed test tubes are used. About 5 ml blood is collected from a jugular vein with 10 ml plastic syringe rinsed with normal saline. Remove the needle and put 1 ml in each 3 tubes and 2 ml in the 4th tube. Incubate the tubes at 38°C. After 4 minutes, tilt the 1st tube to see formation of clot. Repeat this procedure with tubes 1st and 2nd at every 1/2 minute till blood does not spill. Note the time when the blood enters the syringe and when the blood of 3rd tube does not spill. Generally clotting time ranges from 2-11 minutes. The fourth tube can be used for determination of clot retraction.

Platelet count: Whenever there is clotting defect, the platelets count is essential

Diluting fluid:

Saponin	0.25 g
Sodium citrate	3.5 G
Formalin	1 ml
Distilled water to	100 ml

Freshly drawn blood in a siliconised vial with anticoagulent is diluted in the above fluid to 1:20 dilution. The WBC pipette is used in the same way as for total white cell count. The neubauer chamber is charged and allowed to settle for 30 minutes in a petridish containing wet filter paper. Observe under microscope. The platelets appear round or oval refractile bodies. In the five squares, used for erythrocyte count, the number of platelets is counted. The count is multiplied by 1000, providing the number of platelets per mm^3.

Bone Marrow Evaluation:

The erythrocytes, granulocytes and thrombocytes are produced in bone marrow. Evaluation of bone marrow smear speaks the functional status of the marrow.

Technique: Bone marrow aspiration needle is used for collection. The preferable sites are iliac crest, sternal crest and rib in cattle, buffaloes and horses, while the trochanter fossa of the femur in case of dogs. Local anaesthetic is injected at the site and the skin is incised with pointed blade. The needle is pierced through the bone cortex by rotation. As soon as the resistance is decreased, the needle crossed the cortex. Withdraw the stylet and attach 10-20 ml heparinized syringe. Aspirate about 0.25 ml or more of bone marrow and transfer in a vial. Prepare the smear immediately and stain as the blood films. The nucleated cells are counted with haemocytometer. A count of $10^5/mm^3$or more is normal. While high and low counts indicate hyperplasia and hypoplasia of bone marrow respectively.

Reticulocytes count: Reticulocytes are immature erythrocytes which stain deeply with methylene blue (supravital stain).

Technique:

Staining solution:		
	New methylene bule (N)	0.5 g
	Potassium oxalate	1.4 g
	Sodium chloride	0.8 g
	Distilled water up to	100 ml.

- Take 4 drops each of venous blood and stain in a small test tube, mix and allow to stand for 10 minutes.
- Place one drop of the above mixture on clean slides and smears are prepared.
- Dry the smears rapidly by warming in air and examine under oil and count 1000 erythrocytes. Separate out the cells with deeply stained reticulum i.e. reticulocytes.

Calculation :

$$\text{Reticulocyte \%} = \frac{\text{Number of reticulocytes}}{\text{Number of erythrocyte}} \times 100$$

Reticulocytes are more in haemorrhage, haemolysis and less in aplastic anaemia.

Blood Compatibility and Blood Transfusion:

In emergency (haemoglobin > 6 g %), first transfusion can be done as there is less chance of reaction particularly in cattle and horses. However, blood compatibility or cross-matching is the rational approach for safe blood transfusion

Compatibility technique: In field, this test can be performed easily. One drop of donor's blood is diluted in 3 ml normal saline. A drop of this suspension is mixed with 1 drop of recipient serum on a clean glass slide and agitated for 3-5 minutes. The mixture is seen for the agglutination of red cells. Uniformly distributed cells indicate compatible blood.

Cross matching: For this, heparinised blood and serum are collected from both the donor and the recipient. The erythrocytes are separated from plasma by centrifuging at 3000 rpm for 5 minutes. Two drops of erythrocytes mass is suspended in 3 ml normal saline and is centrifuged at 3000 rpm for 2 minutes. The supernatant is discarded and by repeating the procedure, the erythrocytes are washed thrice and finally resuspended in 3 ml normal saline.

Procedure: In four clean test tubes, labelled as 1,2,3 and 4, the test is being carried out. Tubes 1 and 2 represent major and minor system while tubes 3 and 4 are respective controls for donor and recipient.

Tubes	1	2	3	4
Donor's RBC	2 drops	—	2 drops	—
Recipient's serum	2 drops	—	—	2rops
Donor's serum	—	2 drops	2 drops	—
Recipient's RBC	—	2 drops	—	2 drops

Mix the content of the tubes and keep it for 30 minutes at 38°C and centrifuge at 1000 rpm for 1 min. Examine the tubes for haemolysis or agglutination. Absence of colour in the supernatant and settling of erythrocytes in the bottom suggest no haemolysis. Absence of both haemolysis and RBC's clumps, indicates compatible blood.

Blood Transfusion Technique:

In a bottle containing ACD solution @ 25 ml per 100 ml blood and autoclaved at 15 pound pressure for 5 minutes, the blood is collected. A 13 gauge needle is suitable for blood collection in large animals. The collected blood can be kept for 10-15 days at 4-6°C. The transfusion is performed aseptically by gravitational method. The rate of blood inflow should be 70-100 drops per minute. The blood can be infused upto 10-20 ml/kg body weight of the recipient. In transfusion reacion, adrenaline or dexamethasone my prove life saving.

Blood chemistry: The whole blood, serum and plasma are analysed in respect of important biochemicals like bilirubin, ketone, creatinine, macroelements (calcium, phosphorus, magnesium), microelements (iron, copper, cobalt, zinc) and certain enzymes like AST (GOT), ALT (GPT), LDH and creatine phosphokinase in routine clinical practice. Their significant variations have relations with diseases, which have been summarised in the table below:

Blood constituents	Variation	Associated diseases
Blood glucose	Decrease	Hypoglycaemia, ketosis, starvation
	Increase	Diabetes mellitus, hyperglycaemia, hypoinsulinaemia.
Urea nitrogen	Increase	Nephritis, urinary calculi.
Creatinine	Increase	Severe renal damage, wasting disease, increased protein breakdown.
Bilirubin	Increase	Intra/extra biliary obstruction, severe hepatopathy or haemolysis.
Calcium	Decrease	Milk-fever, hypocalcaemia, osteoporosis.
	Increase	hyperthyroidism, hypervitaminosis D_3
Phosphorus	Decrease	Hypophosphataemia, osteomalasia.
	Increase	Bone fracture healing, advance chronic renal insufficiency.
Magnesium	Decrease	Hypomagnesaemia, grass tetany, whole milk tetany in calves.
Ketone	Increase	Ketosis, starvation, advance diabetes mellitus.
Alkaline phosphatase	Increase	Bone repair, fracture healing.
Aspartate amino transferase (AST or GOT)	Increase	Myocardial necrosis, muscle dystophy, hepatitis, azoturia.
Alanine amino transferase (ALT or GPT)	Increase	Liver damage, carbon tetrachloride toxicosis.
LDH & CPK	Increase	Muscular dystrophy and muscle damage.
Sodium	Decrease	Hyponatraemia, excess sweating, low sodium intake, diarrhoea.
Potassium	Decrease	Vomition, diarrhoea, low intake.
	Increase	Hyperkalaemia, acidosis
Chloride	Decrease	Vomition, diarrhoea, low intake of salt.
Bicarbonate	Decrease	Acidosis, grain engorgement.
	Increase	Alkalosis, urea toxicity, ammonia toxicosis.

Normal Blood Biochemicals in Animals

Blood constituents	Cattle	Buffalo	Horse	Sheep	Goat	Dog	Pig
Whole blood							
Glucose (mg/100 ml)	40-70	50-70	60-100	40-60	45-50	60-100	65-95
Urea nitrogen (mg/100 ml)	6-27	5.6-7.8	10-20	8-20	13-28	10-20	8-24
Serum:							
Creatinine (mg/100 ml)	1-2	1-2	1.2-1.9	1.2-1.9	0.9-1.8	1-1.7	1-2.7
Calcium (mg/100 ml)	10.5-12.25	10.80	10-14	9-12.25	9.25-11.5	8.5-11.5	9-13.25
Phosphorus (mg/100 ml)	3.2-8.4	6.0	2.4-4.5	2.9-7.4	4-9.7	2.4-4.2	4.6-10.2
Magnesium (mg/100 ml)	1.8-3	3.4	2.2-4.5	2.6-3.5	2.7-3.5	1.8-2.5	2.4-3.6
Bilirubin (mg/100 ml)	0.2-0.5	0.3-0.4	0.8-3	0-0.4	0-0.1	0-0.3	0-0.4
AST (Units/ml)	38-50	20-30	130-200	150	90-275	17-50	15-45
ALT (Units/ml)	7-32	13-15	7-15	24	15-50	15-40	20-35
CPK (unit/ml)	4.8-12.1	2.65-2.90	2.4-23.4	8.1-12.9	0.8-8.9	1.15-28.4	2.4-22.5
Sodium (m Eq/L)	147	145-150	149	153	137	147	140-160
Potassium (m Eq/L)	4.8	5-6.2	3.3	4.8	3.6	4.4	4.9-7.1
Total Protein (g%)	7.6	6.8	6.7	5.2	6.2	5.4-7	7.4
Bicarbonate (m Eq/L)	29.5	26.4	28.6	25	24.8	18.6	
Iron (mg/100 ml)	57-162	300	73-140	166-222	150.0	94-122	91-199

Reference

Boddie, G.F. (1969) *Diagnostic Methods in Veterinary Medicine, 6th ed.* Oliver and Boyd, Edinburgh.

Frankel, S., Reitman, S. and Sonnenwirth, A.C. (1977) Gradwohl's Clinical Laboratory Methods and Diagnosis. 7th ed. C.V. Mosby Company, Saint Louis.

Sastry, A. Ganti (1983) *Veterinary Clinical Pathology. 3rd ed.* CBS Publishers and Distributors, Delhi, India.

Schalm, O.W; Jain, N.C. and Carrol, E.J. (1975) *Veterinary Haematology, 3rd ed.* Lea and Febiger, Philadelphia.

13

LYMPHATIC SYSTEM

Appreciation of lymph nodes and lymph vessels is important to assess their direct involvement and specific characteristics in diseases like equine lymphangitis, tuberculosis, bovine leucosis, actinobacillosis and theileriasis. Swelling, tenderness and hardening of regional lymph nodes speak about the abnormalities in the area and sometimes it may physically block the function of certain normal organ e.g. swelling of mediastinal lymph node causes vagus indigestion in ruminants.

Clinically, the superficial lymph nodes (Fig. 6.2) are inspected and palpated for abnormalities. The course of lymphatics as well as its biopsy are helpful in the diagnosis. Following lymph nodes are palpable in cattle and buffaloes.

Prefemoral lymph nodes: Are elongated body, situated about 6 inch above the flank fold and cranial to the mid thigh.

Mammary lymph nodes: Situated between bony floor of the pelvis and the posterior margin of udder on both the sides.

Scrotal lymph nodes: They are palpable on each side above the scrotal neck, behind the spermatic cord and under the abdominal wall. They are of the size of small arecanut.

Mandibular lymph nodes: They lie in the intermandibular space. Normal nodes are embedded in adipose tissue, hence not easily felt.

Parotid lymph nodes: Are situated just below the mandibular joint. Their size approximates a walnut.

Retropharyngeal lymph nodes: They lie caudally and dorsal to the roof of the pharynx. For palpation , the fingers are placed behind the ramous of mandible.

Prescapular cervical lymph nodes: Are located cranial to the shoulder edge. They are easily palpable by sliding the extended fingers. Normally,they are elongated mass.

Internal lymph nodes: In large animals, iliofemoral lymph nodes are palpable. They lie on each side of pelvic inlet at the upper part of the body of ileum. Other lymph nodes like renal lymph nodes and mesentric lymph nodes are only palpable when they are abnormally enlarged.

Lymph vessels: These are only appreciable when they are distended. They run through the regional lymph nodes, showing nodules or abscesses.

Examination of lymph: Major lymph vessels like thoracic duct or intestinal duct is punctured for lymph collection in cattle and buffalo. The lymph is examined for leucocytes and biochemicals. The lymph of cattle is alkaline and its protein content B 2--5.2g per cent.

Lymph nodes biopsy: Lymph nodes fluid smear is prepared by aspirating it with the help of needle and syringe. The smear may be examined for leucocytes or bacteria after staining. For histological examination, the lymph nodes are exposed surgically. A piece of 0.5-1 cm is preserved in 5 per cent formaldehyde solution for the analysis.

14

REPRODUCTIVE SYSTEM

The system of reproduction comprises the male and female genital organs and the mammary glands. The purposes of clinical examination of reproductive system are to locate the presence of disease, assessing reproductive ability and to identify the genital defects.

The male Reproductive Organs:

Visual as well as palpation techniques are used to examine the external genitalia e.g. the prepucial skin, the scrotum, the glans penis and some distal portion of penis. The penis of bull and male buffalo can be examined by allowing them to mount on a teaser female and diverting the organ on side. Epidural anaesthesia may help in loosening the sigmoid flexure manually. In stallion, the penis can be drawn by grasping it through prepucial cavity or by noosing a bandage behind the glans penis and pulling it out. The penis of dog can be exposed for examination, when the dog is in lateral recumbency. The prepuce is held and slided back by one hand while the penis is pushed forward by the other hand. In ram, buck and boar, the technique for bull can be applied.

The abnormalities like protrusion of penis in pudic nerve paralysis, narrow prepucial opening (paraphimosis), unexposable penis (phimosis), and inflammations are detected. During urination, exposure of penis is usual but absence of urination and frequent exposure of penis must be suspected for obstruction of urethra.

The concentration of smegma (prepucial secretion of peculiar smell) causes retention of urine in bullocks by blocking the prepucial orifice. Similarly smegmatic prepucial calculi is seen in gelding. The prepuce may show papules, vesicles or ulcers in specific diseases like glanders and dourine in horses. Purulent discharge from the prepucial orifice of dog is very common indicating suppurative balanitis. Increased libido has been seen in dog when glans penis get inflammed.

Both the inguinal region and scrotum must be examined cautiously for the presence of hernia, particularly in colt foals and stallion. Hot, painful and unilateral swelling of scrotum indicate inguinal hernia. Congential scrotal hernia is very common in horse, but of not much worry.

The testicles are examined for its shape, size, consistency and sensitivity by moving the skin of scrotum. Cryptorchidism (absence of desending of testes), marked asymmetrical testes (testicular hypoplasia), unilateral orchitis, neoplasia of testes and testicular atrophy are recorded. Inflammation will cause swelling of scrotum and animal feels pain on palpation. Neoplasia of testes is very common in dogs of over 5 years. The mispositioned testes are more prone to become neoplastic. The bulls and dogs suffer more commonly from interstital cell tumours. The sertoli-cell tumour affected dogs become faminized which include alopecia of ventral abdomen, decreased libido, gynaecomastia and sexual attraction for male dogs, owing to more estrogen production by the tumour.

Manual examinations of internal genital part of bull, male buffalo and male horses are feasible per-rectum. In small animals, this procedure is seldom applicable. The seminal vesicles and prostate glands can be palpated in bullocks and the stallion. The seminal vesicles of bullock are in pair about 4-5 inch in dimension which extend cranially from anterior portion of pelvic urethra where the prostate gland remains surrounding. The two lobes of the prostate in stallion are directed outward and forward from the neck of the bladder. The paired seminal vesicles of horses are of 6-8 x 2 inch in dimension.

In dog only digital exploration of caudal part of internal sex organ is possible. Appreciation of bilobed prostate surrounding the urethro-cystic junction is of importance in dogs. However, in large dogs it may not be feasible to feel it. Hyperplasia, prostitis and neoplasia are common problems in dogs. Dogs above 5 years suffering from hyperplasia of the prostate develop constipation, ribbon like faeces with straining and dysurea. Prostitis in dog is characterized by acute pain, arched back and insertion of finger or lifting the tail leads moaning or crying. Neoplasia of prostate is least common, however, when present it causes discomfort, severe pain and straining while defaecation.

Libido test: Frequent priapism (erection of penis) is common in young males reaching sexual maturity. Reduced libido is characterised by unwillingness to mount the female. Conditions like ankylosis, spondylitis, spastic syndrome, peritonitis, pain in the hind limbs and certain genital defects are responsible for poor libido.

Examination of prepucial secretion: Organisms like *Trichomonas foetus, Vibrio foetus* and *M. tuberculosis* can be demonstrated in prepucial secretion microscopically or culturally. The secretion can be obtained by inserting plastic tube fitted in a glass syringe or a pipette with rubber bulb, deep into the prepucial cavity. The washing of prepucial cavity with normal saline can be achieved in the same way.

Semen collection and evaluation: The performance of pedigree males is dependant on the quality of semen. For determination of quality, the semen is collected by using artificial vagina and its examination under microscope. For collection of semen, the male is persuaded to mount on a female dummy. As soon as the penis is protruded out while mounting, it is grasped and diverted in suitable artificial vagina (Plate 3) maintained at 98°F inner temperature.

Properties of Semen of Domestic Animals

Animal	Volume per ejaculation (ml)	Count of sperms million/ml	pH
Bull	5-8	1000-1800	6.4-6.8
Buffalo bull	2-3	600-1200	6.2-6.6
Stallion	25-250	100-150	7.3-7.9
Ram	0.8-1	2000-3000	5.9-6.8
Boar	200-250	200-300	7.3-7.9
Dog	1-25	20-540	6.0-6.8

Examination: Grossly, semen is evaluated in respect of its volume, colour and consistency. Microscopic examination is done by putting a drop of fresh semen on a clean slide and motility is assessed at 37°C. Stained semen smear is used for the determination of good spermatozoa, abnormal spermatozoa and leucocytes or the bacteria. Satisfactory evaluation can be made in the field by examining fresh unstained semen smear. At least 3-4 ejaculations at regular interval are to be evaluated for final decision. While transporting the semen for other places it must be protected from rough handling and environmental temperature. Diluted semen should be used for artificial insemination.

Semen dilutors

Bull	Buffalo bull	Ram	Buck
Buffer			
Sodium citrate	Tris (hydroxy methyl	Sodium citrate	Skimmed or homo
dihydrate 2.94 g	amino methane)	2.37g	genised cow milk
	3.786 g		heated at 95°C for 10
Sulphanilamide 0.3 g	Citric acid 2.115 g	Glucose 0.8 g	minutes and cooled.
Distilled water 100 ml	Distilled water 100 ml	Distilled water 80 ml	Dihydrostreptomycin
Buffer 4 parts	Buffer 4 parts	Egg Yolk 20 ml	750 μg
Egg Yolk 1 part	Egg yolk 1 part	Penicillin G	
Penicillin G Sodium	Penicillin G	Sodium 1000 IU/ml	
1000 IU/ml	Sodium 1000 IU/ml	Dihydrostreptomycin	
Dihydrostreptomycin	Dihydrostreptomycin	sulpate 1 mg/ml	
Sulphate 1 mg/ml	Sulphate 1 mg/ml		
Dilution ratio	Dilution ratio	Dilution ratio	Dilution ratio
(semen:dilutor)			
1:10-20	1:10	1:5 or 10	1:5 or 10
Store at 4-5°C	Store at 4-5°C	Store at 5°C	Store at 5°C
Use within 48-72 hrs.	Use within 48 hrs.	Use within 24 hrs.	Use within 24 hrs.

The diluted semen can be stored for longer period, even up to 10 years in liquid nitrogen (—196°C) after addition of glycerol, DMXO or other cryoprotectives in the dilutors, while processing.

The female Reproductive Organs:

Clinical examination of external genitalia, the vulva and vagina of females starts with inspection. The inner vulval mucous membrane is visualised by aparting the vulvar lips, however for deeper inspection upto cervix, vaginal speculum is necessary. Inner vulva can be palpated by introducing either the fingers or the hands, depending on the size of the animal. In large animals, the internal reproductive organ can be appreciated by rectal manouvring.

Careful examination may reveal presence of persistent hymen. It must not be confused with freemartinism, which should be ascertained by the history of twin-born heifer. Insertion of blunt end of a test tube (15 X 1.5 cm) will help in measuring the vagina. In freemartin, only 6-7 cm length of the tube goes in.

Prolapse of vagina occurs commonly in advance pregnant cows, she buffaloes, mares, ewes and goats, particularly in sitting posture. Hyperplasia of vagina is frequently observed in bitches usually after oestrus. Mares suffering from vesicular exanthema, show multiple small vesicles, which develop into pustules and ulcers subsequently. Swollen vulva, switching or elevation of tail and arched back are seen in such condition. Pneumovagina is seen in multiparous mare. Cows with pustular vulvo-vaginitis have similar symptoms to that of mare. Vaginitis in cows is a sequela of pyelonephritis. The bitches suffer more commonly with vulvitis and vaginitis and show straining following urination, restlessness, lick vulva frequently and have a desire to accept males

Rectal palpation: The technique is useful in assessing the cervix, uterus, the fallopian tubes and the ovaries in large animals.

Cervix: The cervix of cattle and buffalo lies on the pelvic floor close to public bridge, usually on the right median line. Roughly it measures 5-10 cm long and 2-7 cm thick. Adult cows and buffaloes have firm cervix while in the heifers it is shorter and softer. The cervix may be absent in freemartinism and white heifer disease.

Palpation of uterus: The uterus of large animals is palpated to ascertain pregnancy, obstetrical manipulation and to assess its normal status during oestrus cycle. Direct internal palpation is possible in recently parturited cows or otherwise rectal palpation is applied mostly. The examiner must put on gum boot, rubber coat and full sleeved gloves before manipulation of uterus. The gloves must be well lubricated with sterile jelly or other suitable antiseptic ointment.

For better appreciation, the uterus is scooped by passing the hand down in the abdominal cavity (per rectal), slightly to the right midline. Giving half clench, the hand is withdrawn near the pubic bridge (Fig. 14.1 & 14.2). Attention is to be paid in respect of symmetry, size, consistency, contractibility and motility of the uterus. The size is gauged by comparing with the thickness of fingers. The symmetry is judged by putting middle finger into the false bifurcation and the index and the right fingers help in assessing the symmetry. Pregnant uterus show asymmetry.

Contractibility and consistency: Speak the state of uterine muscle. Longitudinal folds are appreciated in recently calved animals. The inflammed uterus appears firm in consistency. The presence of blood, mucous, mummified foetus and pus alter its consistency.

Motility: The non-pregnant uterus is motile. It ceases when there is adhesion with adjascent organs.

Oviducts: They are fairly firm structures between the tip of the horns and the ovaries. Salpingitis and hydrosalpinx cause swelling and fluctuation respectively.

The ovaries: To find ovaries, locate the iliopubic junction and explore forwards and downwards. The other way, scoop the organ near pubic bridge and try to grasp the ovary little downward and side way. The ovaries should be examined for graffian follicle, corpus luteum, cyst, depression or any abnormality in the size.

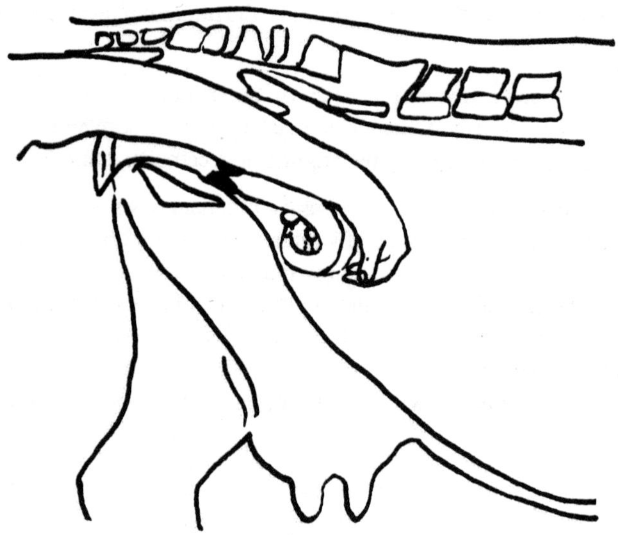

Fig. 14.1 Palpation of uterus in cow and buffalo (non-pregnant)

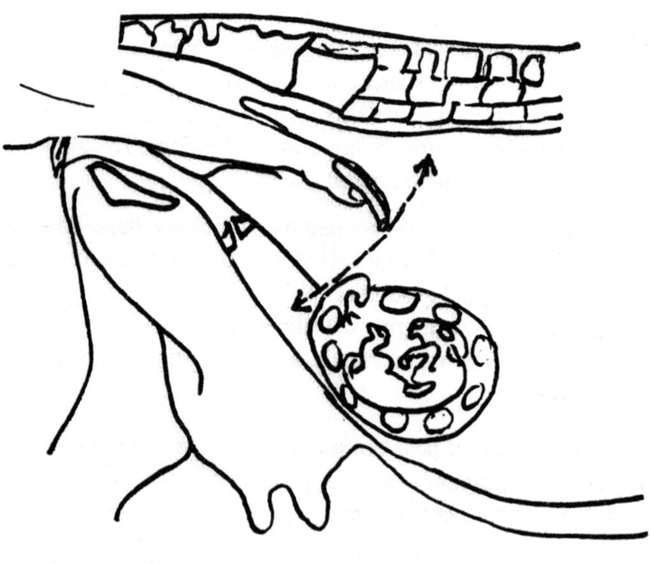

Fig. 14.2 Pregnancy diagnosis (5th months)

Examination of cervical mucous: The mucous coming out of vulva or adhering the speculum or the inseminating catheter can be examined grossly. A portion of mucous is tensed between two fingers and is seen. Normal mucous is transparent. Presence of blood indicates ovulation. Fern pattern crystallization on glass slide is indicative of oestrus mucous. In doubtful case, the mucous can be examined bacteriologically.

Collection of cervicovaginal and uterine contents: For culture and sensitivity test, cervico-vaginal secretion is scooped by uterine swab catheter or a spoon with long handle. The uterine content can be collected by introducing plastic catheter attached to a syringe. Where mucous is less, a sterile swab attached to 50-60cm long wire, is passed.

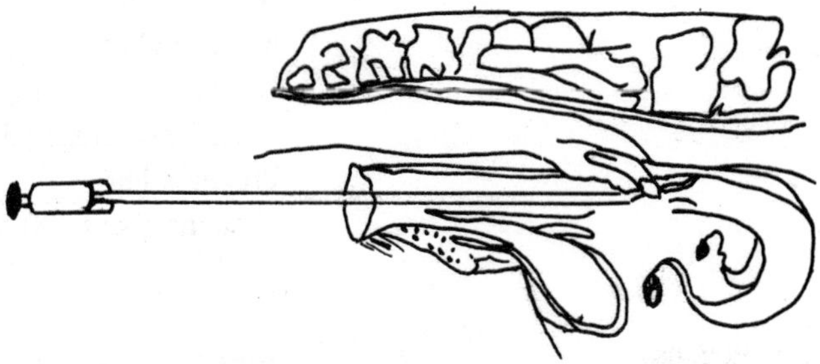

Fig. 14.3 Artificial insemination

Oestrus detection: Examination of external genitalia of female helps in detection of oestrus. The external manifestation like bellowing, polyurea, inappetence, reduced milk yield, anxious look, mounting on the mates and acceptance for the males are characteristics of oestrus. Tolerance of mounting by other animal is the surest sign of oestrus. Help of teaser bull can be taken in organised herd.

Artificial insemination: Semen is deposited either in vagina, cervix or uterus manually. However, cervical insemination is preferred.

Technique: Rectovaginal technique is most practical and effective. The semen is deposited in the cervix which is located through rectal wall by introducing gloved hand (Fig. 14.3). Lubrication with soap or jelly makes easy introduction. The inseminating pipette is inserted into the vagina at 20-30° angle to avoid blind pouch or uretheral opening. As soon as the tip of the tube is felt near the cervix, it is directed into the cervical opening with the help of thumb of gloved hand. The cervix feels firm incomparision to vaginal wall. The pipette is advanced 4-6cm in to cervix and the semen (1-1.5 ml) is deposited with the help of attached syringe.

Pregnancy diagnosis: Rectal exploration is still the routine method for pregnancy diagnosis in cows, buffaloes and mares. Abdominal ballottement is used in small animals, where the above technique can not be applied.

Summary of rectal palpation for pregnancy diagnosis in cattle buffalo and mare

Days post conception	Cattle/buffaloes	Mares
Ist 30 days	Absence of oestrus Large C.L. on one or both ovaries Slight enlargement of pregnant horn No other change Cervix closed.	Slight enlargement of uterus Increased uterine tone

31st-60th days	Absence of oestrus Asymmetry of uterine horns (right horn 60%) Double wall feeling Foetal membrane slips finger tips Pregnant horn contains about 300-500 ml fluid.	Oval enlargement of body of the uterus The buldging measures football size 12-15 x 8-10 cm
61st-90th day	Absence of oestrus Very apparent asymmetry of uterine horns. Rebound of foetus is appreciable (foetal bump) Uterus sinks towards abdominal cavity. About 500 ml-1500 ml fluid present.	Uterus begins to descend in the abdominal cavity. Ballottement reveals presence of foetus.
91st-120th days	Large ballooned uterus with 2-5 litres content. Placentomes detectable Uterine arterial tremor (frimitus) C.L. of pregnancy present Pregnant horn hangs on pelvic brim	Uterus descends Ballottement reveals presence of foetus.
121st-180th days	Uterus descends into abdomen. Foetus is beyond the reach of palpation.	Foetus goes deep in the abdomen Cannot be palpated unless abdominal floor is raised.
7th-10th months	Foetal movement can be appreciated externally	Externally careful examination will show foetal movement.
(210-300 days)	Deep palpation of abdomen with fist will help recognise foetal movement (Foetal ballottement)	Fist may be utilised externally to feel the foetus.

Laboratory Tests for Pregnancy Diagnosis:

1. **Biological test (Mare):** The serum of pregnant mare (40-120 days) contains gonadotropins (PMSG). Half ml serum is injected s/c into 3 1/2 weeks old mice daily for 2-4 days. The positive test is characterised by production of ripe follicle on the ovaries and oedema of uterus, examined 96-120 hours later.

2. **Chemical test (Mare) :** The urine of pregnant mare (150-300 days), contains oestrogens (oestrone and oestradiol 17B). To 15 ml of urine, 3 ml hydrochloric acid (conc) is mixed and heated for 10 minutes at 100°C in a water bath. After cooling to room temperature, 18 ml benzene is added. The test tube is shaken vigorously. After decanting the benzene layer in other tube, 10 ml sulfuric acid (conc.) is added slowly. The tube is stoppered, shaken and heated for 5 minutes at 80°C. Development of dark green fluorescene indicates postive pregnancy.

3. **Copper sulphate test :** Mix 1 ml milk from pregnant cow and 2-3 ml pure copper sulphate solution (3%). Formation of coagulum indicates positive pregnancy, while homogenicity non-pregnancy. The accuracy vary between 90-92 per cent if tested at 30-40 day post-service/insemination.

4. **Barium chloride test:** Add 4-5 drops of barium chloride (1%) to 4-5 ml urine of pregnant and non-pregnant animals separately. Absence of precipitate formation confirms pregnancy. The test is 95-100% accurate, provided it is done between 15-210 days post-service.

5. **Radioimmunoassay or Enzyme linked immuno-serum assay (hormone assay):** This method is very sensitive for early and rapid pregnancy diagnosis. Less than 1 ng/ml plasma progesterone or 3 ng/ml of milk is classed as non-pregnant while about 2 ng/ml plasma or 7 ng/ml milk is classed as pregnant (21-24 days) in cows.

6. **Ultrasonic method:** When high frequency sound waves strike a moving object, they are reflected at slightly altered frequency (Dopler's phenomenon). Ultrasonic instrument can detect early pregnancy, when uterus contains more fluid in comprision to foetal size. The probe of the instrument is placed directly on the ventral side of abdominal wall, cranial to the pelvic brim. A postive sound is heard if animal is pregnant. It is 92-100 per cent accurate.

Assessment of Infertility

Reproductive disorders lead to infertility in female which are characterised by repeat breeding, irregular or absence of oestrus cycle and premature delivery. The following conditions are responsible for infertility.

1. **Congenital defects:** Include free-martinism, hypoplasia of genital organs and persistence of median walls of the Mullerian ducts. Other conditions like persistent hymen and double cervix are rare.

2. **Anoestrus:** The factors like managemental failure to detect the silent oestrus, malnutrition, deficiency of Co, Cu, P and other elements and persistent corpus luteum play major role for anoestrus.

3. **Cystic ovary:** Formation of cysts on the ovaries owing to cystic degeneration of follicle. Some times several cysts, deep in the ovaries, are present. Such animals show continuous heat known as nymphomanic.

4. **Vaginitis/cervicitis:** Visual examination shows inflammation. On palpation, the cervix feels firm. Sometimes pus may be present.

5. **Endometritis:** Usually occurs as a postparturient infection associated usually with retained placenta. Presence of greyish-white exudate near cervix or anterior vagina indicates endometritis. Rectal exploration reveals bilateral enlargement of uterine horns.

6. **Chronic metritis:** It may be purulent or non-purulent. Purulent diacharge from vagina is noted. Uterus feels large and firm on palpation.

7. **Pyometra:** Pus is accumulated in the uterus. It is usually associated with post-partum infection. It may be open or close type. Rectal examination reveals enlargement of both horns of uterus and atonic. The trichomonad and post-partum pyometra differ in the following ways:

Trichomonad pyometra	Post-partum pyometra
- Occurs post-service	- Post-parturition
- Pus is potato-soup like	- Thick in consistency
- Creamy in appearance	- Yellowish
- No smell	- Foul smell
- Volume 6-8 litres	- 150-300 ml

8. **Mummification:** Detachment of foetal membrane from the uterus leads to mummification, usually at 3-4 months pregnancy. The fluid is absorbed and dessicated foetus may be palpated near the brim of the pelvis. There is absence of oestrus owing to persistent corpus luteum.

9. **Foetal maceration:** Usually associated with uterine infection. The uterus contains purulent material with foetal bones, which is palpable. Anoestrus is due to corpus luteum.

10. **Salpingitis:** Inflammation of oviduct leads to failure of conception.

11. **Miscellaneous factors:** Deficiency of progesterone and habitual abortions. More or less the above factors are resposible for infertility in most of the females.

Pseudopregnancy in Bitches:

Excess level of luteinizing hormone conditions delayed regression of corpus luteum. It often gives symptoms simulating pregnancy. The bitches show preparatory symptoms of whelping. X-ray examination of abdominal cavity will confirm the diagnosis.

Obstetrical Techniques

Before making an effort to correct the cases of difficult parturition or distocia, careful history like date of insemination/service, time of showing signs of calving, personal or mechanical help to induce delivery are to be recorded.

In general, causes of distocia are narrow birth canal, uterine torsion, uterine inertia, abnormal presentation of foetus, abnormal size of the foetus and weakness of the dam.

To ascertain the nature of obstruction in parturition, manual examination of external as well as internal organs in cows, buffaloes and mares is possible. The abnormal presentation (Fig. 14.4) of the foetus is being corrected with the different tools (Plate 3) as and when necessary. In small animals, where manipulation by hand is not feasible, forcep delivery should be preferred or otherwise caesarian should be attempted.

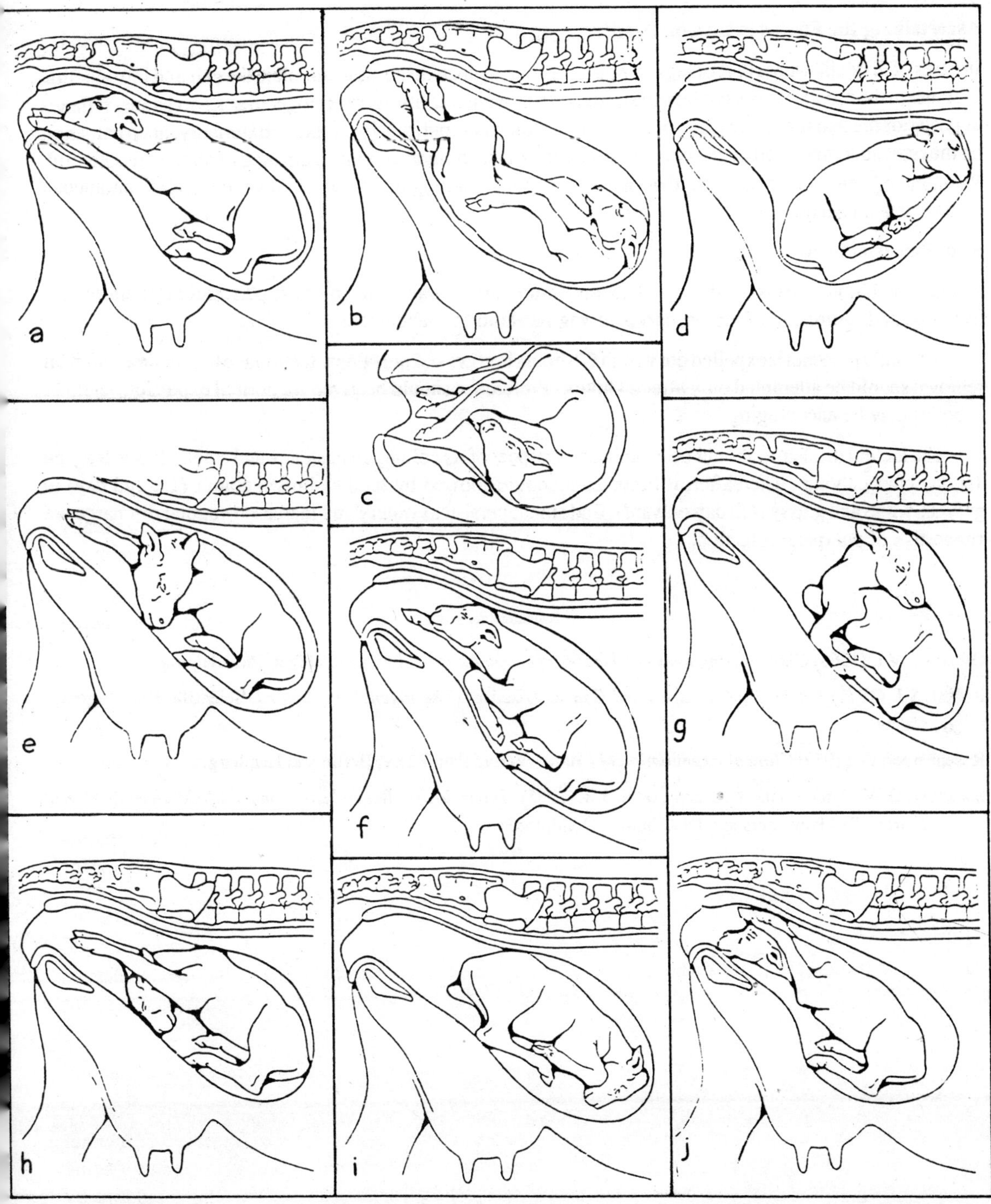

a. Anterior presentation
b. Posterior presentation
c. Breech presentation
d. Spinal presentation
e. Head turned to the left
f. Left carpal flection
g. Head turned to one side
h. Downward head deviation
i. Hip (left) and hock (right) deviation
j. Fore limbs over the neck

Ascertaining the Foetus is Live or Dead

In cases of distocia, where part of legs is protruding out, a pinch in the cleft stimulate the calf and introduction of finger in the mouth causes swallowing or sucking movement. Insertion of finger in anus gives anal reflexes in posterior presentation. Presence of uterine pulsation also confirms live foetus. Externally, deep palpation on the right abdomen appreciates the movement of foetus. In small animals, palpation of abdomen is helpful. Shedding of hair, detached claw, abnormal odour, foul smelling discharge from vagina and subcutaneous emphysema are suggestive of dead foetus.

Post-Parturient Care

Rupture of blood-vessels, undelivered foetus (multiparus), traumatic injuries, perforation of uterus (in dystocia) and protrusion of uterus, cervix or vagina should be taken care.

Normally placenta is expelled out within 6-8 hours in cows and buffaloes. It may take longer time. Manual removal should be attempted only after 24 hours. Preference should be given for normal expulsion. Help of ecbolics may be encouraging.

The lochial discharge should be examined in respect of its colour, consistency and smell. It is watery on 1st day after calving. Thereafter, it becomes mucoid followed by reddish-brown colour (1st-2nd day) to greyish-white and glassy (4th day onward). Bad smell, persistent watery and increased vaginal discharge are suggestive of puerperal infection.

References

Gibbons, W.J. (1966) *Clinical Diagnosis of Diseases of Large Animals.* Lea and Febiger, Philadelphia.

Robert, S.J. (1971) *Veterinary Obstetrics and Genital Diseases (Theriogenology) 2nd ed.* Scientific Book Agency, Calcutta.

Rosenberger, G. (1979) *Clinical Examination of Cattle.* Verlag Paul Parey, Berlin and Hamberg.

Salisbury, G.W. Van Demark, N.L. and Lodge, J.R. (1985). *Physiology of Reproduction and Artificial Insemination of Cattle.* CBS Publishers and Distributors, Delhi, India.

15

THE UDDER AND TEATS

The udder and teats (mammary gland) are the organs of production in dairy animals while the organ of nourishment for youngs in other animals. The location and size of mammary gland and the number of teats vary in different species of animals.

Animals	Location of udder	Number of teats	Number of milk ducts per teat
Cow	Inguinal region	Four	1
She buffalo	— do —	Four	1
Mare	— do —	Two	2-4
Goat	— do —	Two	1
Ewe	— do —	Two	1
Bitch	Abdomino-pectoral	8-12	8-20
Sow	Abdomino-pectoral	10-12	2-3
She elephant	Pectoral	Two	—
Camel	Inguinal	Two	—
Cat	Abdomino-pectoral	8	4-7

The location, size of udder and teats and system of milking, condition the high milch animals to suffer from diseases of the mammary gland. It has great economic significance. Early detection of mastitis and its prevention help curb the economic loss.

General examination: Comprises inspection in general, palpation and examination of mammary secretion physically, chemically and microbiologically.

Inspection of udder and teats: The size, location and the shape of udder and teats should be viewed from the front, the behind and from each sides. Pendulous udder is seen in aged cows and buffaloes. This is due to the weakness of connective tissues or may be the outcome of repeated attacks of inflammation. Atrophy of either quarter gives asymmetric appearance of the udder.

The teats should be examined for size, shape and presence of supernumerary teats. Presence of supernumerary teat causes concern with milking and may act as the route of entery of infection. It may have its own parenchyma or arising from the main teat.

The skin of udder and teats: The skin is inspected for the presence of crusts, vesicles, pustules, ulcers or injuries. Violet discolouration of skin indicates gangrenous mastitis while hyperaemia in acute mastitis. Swelling of underlying skin of the udder is seen in oedema, haematoma, abscess and tumours growth. Perforating wound in teat cistern and loose teat sphincters cause spontaneous flow of milk.

Palpation : The teat canal, teat cistern, teat wall, udder cistern, udder skin and the glandular tissue of all quarters are palpated to appreciate any deformity.

The tip of the teat is being rolled between fingers. Change in consistency, swelling and blockade are recorded. The patency of teat canal is judged by stripping the milk in a cup or by probing sterile milk tube or cannula. Proliferation of epithelium of teat canal or congenital abnormalities cause difficult milking.

To assess the mucous membrane of teat cistern, the teat is rolled between fingers. Normally it should be uniform. Presence of cords, lumps, blood clots or any other objects should be recorded. These objects hinder the milk flow and they need necessary correction. Interconnection of congenital teat fistula with the main teat or its independancy is judged by probing the main teat and fistula separately. The other way is to inject bromocresol dye in to the main teat, using syringe. If the dye comes out of the fistula, indicates communication with the main teat. The fistula may have its own glandular mass.

Udder skin: Palpation of udder skin reveals its warmth, thickness, tenderness and its elasticity. Normally, the skin fold of empty udder is pulled out easily. Acute mastitis gives warm feeling while in gangrenous mastitis, it feels cold. The mammary skin becomes oedematous in inflammatory swelling and also in physiological udder oedema, just before calving, particularly in heifers.

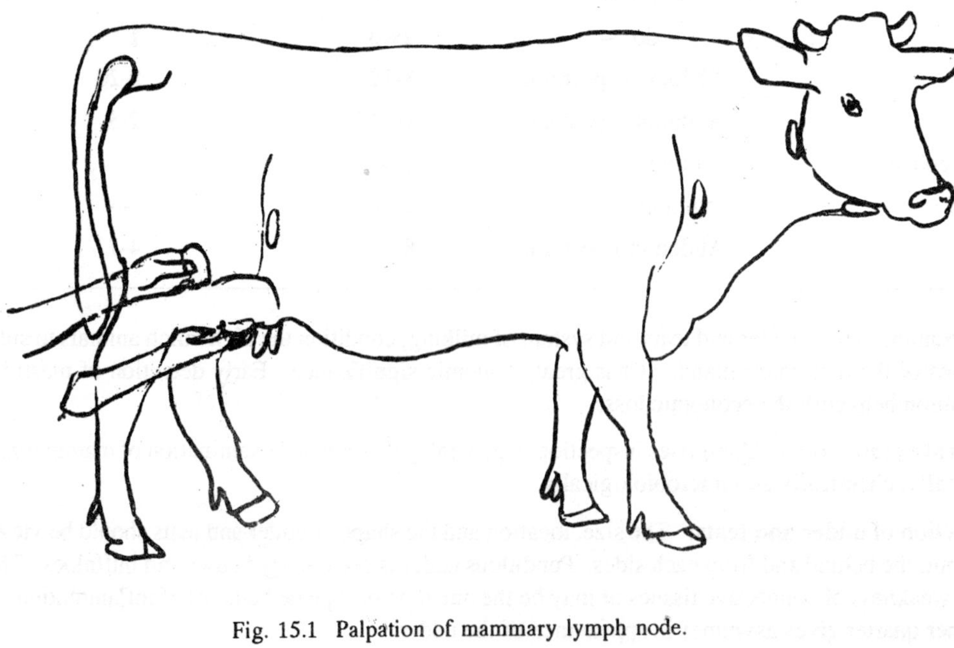

Fig. 15.1 Palpation of mammary lymph node.

Udder Glandular Tissues:

Normal consistency of udder is softer or grained. Acute swelling, localised or diffuse hardening, feeling of hardness and tumour or nodules are appreciated. Diffuse hardening of mammary tissues occurs in tuberculosis mastitis. Localised hardening is seen in chronic mastitis.

Mammary Lymph Nodes:

Appreciation of mammary lymph nodes indicates whether mastitis is of infective origin, in particular the tuberculous mastitis. In cows and buffaloes they lie posteriorly on each side of the udder lateral to mid line at a level half way between the lower commisure of vulva and the hock (Fig. 15.1).

Examination of Milk:

Milk is examined grossly for flakes, colour, consistency and smell, followed by chemical and microbial evaluation which help diagnosis of mastitis.

Flakes: Streaks of milk are drawn on black painted cup(Fig. 15.1) and the presence of flaks is detected.

Colour: Normal colour of milk is white. Colostral milk and milk of cows and buffaloes fed on carotene rich diet appears yellowish. Discolouration of milk is also seen in horse tail (plant) poisoning. Haemorrhages give redish colouration, while generalised infection (FMD) causes yellowish colouration. Dosing the animal with tetracyclines or acridine dyes turns the milk yellow, while phenothiazine causes pink coluration.

Odour: Normally vary from species to species e.g. goat milk has peculiar goaty odour. Ketotic milk has fruity smell. Mastitis caused by *Corynebacterium pyogens* gives offensive odour of milk. The odour of milk changes when the animal is fed on rape, kale, turnip, silage or applied externally with disinfectants.

Consistency: It changes during the course of inflammatory changes in the mammary glands. It may be honey like, serosanguinous, watery, with flakes or pusy.

Chemical tests: Are applied when mere appearance of milk fails to detect disorders in the udder.

Milk pH: Normal pH of cow milk ranges between 6.4 to 6.8. Colostral milk has slight lower pH (6.0-6.4). In mastitis milk turns alkaline. Only in gangrenous mastitis the milk pH is around 6.0. The following field tests have been evolved based on the change in milk pH. The test can be applied on indiviual or bulk milk samples.

Bromthymol blue test: The test can be applied on filter paper or in a test tube. A 2 per cent solution of the dye in alcohol is prepared. One drop of the dye is placed on four corners of a square filter paper and dried in shade and labelled as RH, RF, LH and LF. 1-2 drops of milk are put on each spot and the change in colour noted. Change of colour from yellow to yellow-green or green indicates mastitis. The degree of change in colour is dependant on the alkalinity of milk. Otherwise in a test tube containing 3 ml milk, 4 drops of the dye is added and mixed and change in colour is observed. Dye bromcresol purple is also used in place of bromthymol blue.

White side test: On a clean glass slides 5 drops of milk are mixed with 2 drops of sodium hydroxide (4%). Formation of flakes or stringy solution indicates high leucocytes count in the milk. Negative test is indicated by opacity of milk and free from precipitate while trace is characterised by fine coagulated particles.

California Mastitis Test (CMT): The test is based on leucocytes content of milk. A white plastic paddle with four cups is used. About 3ml of milk to each cup is mixed with equal volume of the reagent *alkylaryl* sulphate and bromcresol purple by swirling. The change in colour and its consistency are noted.

A positive reaction is characterised by a change from blue to purple and formation of gel. The reaction is with four cups is used. About 3 ml of milk to each cup is mixed with equal volume of the reagent *alkylaryl* sulphate and bromcresol purple, by swirling. The change in colour and its consistency are noted. A positive reaction is characterised by a change from blue to purple colour and formation of jelly. The reaction is directly proportional to the leucocytes present in the milk.

Immunodiffusion test: The method is helpful in detecting sub-clinical mastitis. Due to change in blood-udder-barrier, the increased whey albumin content is detected.

Microbial test: Milk must be collected before infusion of antibiotics. Contamination of milk can be avoided by washing and drying the udder. Few streaks of milk of affected quarter are collected in strip and discarded. The quarter is swabed with 70 per cent alcohol or methylated spirit and allowed to dry. The milk is collected in sterile vial or test tube holding horizontally. Avoiding contamination, the collection is done from the nearest quarter first, then from the others. Last stripping of milk is collected from suspected tuberculous mastitis.

A smear is prepared and stained for differential leucocytes count. For the diagnosis of tuberculous mastitis, the milk is centrifuged and smear is prepared from sediment and stained with acid-fast stain and examined under microscope for *M. tuberculosis.*

The milk sample is used further for microbial culture and sensitivity test, which help the treatment of mastitis.

Other Mammary Abnormalities

Tumours: Most frequently seen in bitches above 5 years of age.

Leucosis: Enlargement of supramammary lymph nodes of cows in leucosis may be confused with tumour in the udder.

Teat spider: Formation of mass in teat cistern blocks the passage of milk. It can be removed safely with the teat tumour extractor. A teat bistoury may be needed for intrusion of the former.

Constriction of teat canal: Milking becomes difficult. Fine streak of milk comes out. Most often, plugging the canal with teat dilator between each milking is helpful.

Leaking of milk: Continuous dripping of milk is seen when there is increased milk pressure or when the teat sphincter is loose. Temporary prevention can be achieved with teat clamps.

Agalactia: A real problem is mares and sows but less in cows and buffaloes. Congestion and painful condition in udder or teat hinder virtually let down of milk in heifers. True agalactia in sows is usually of hormone origin where there is absence of general disturbance. Agalactia is also seen in post-parturient toxaemia of infectious or metabolic origin. Temporary agalactia is noted in all milch animals suffering from severe systemic diseases.

Clinical Classification of Mastitis

Inflammation of glandular tissue is known as mastitis. In the litis, all layers of the teat are affected and in cisternitis only mucuos membrane of cistern is involved.

Types of mastitis	Udder and teat palpation	Systemic reactions
Acute mastitis	Hot, oedematous, hard and painful, scanty and watery milk.	Anorexia, rise in body temperature, depression, increased heart rate and pulse.
Acute gangrenous mastitis	Initially hot, followed by cold, oedematous, hard, sero-sanguinous milk, subsequently the mammary tissue sloughs out.	Toxaemia, depression, anorexia, increased heart and pulse rate and temperature. In fatal cases, temperature becomes sub-normal.
Chronic mastitis	Feels hard due to fibrosis of quarter, milk is water or may contain flakes or pus.	Clinically the animals appear otherwise normal.

16

LOCOMOTORY SYSTEM

The supports provided jointly by the bones, muscles, tendons, joints and nerves help the animals in getting up and down and the movement. Abnormalities in any of the above support structures lead to difficult or absence of locomotion. The systems may be affected directly (trauma, congenital defects etc) or associated with nutritional deficiency (osteomalacia, muscular dystrophy, downer syndrome), infectious polyarthritis and selenium or flourine toxicity. Locomotory disturbances must be carefully examined in order to reach a concrete diagnosis.

Herd history is important. Occurrence of good number of cases of lameness gives idea of some managemental problems (i.e. housing or feeding). The type of housing, spacing and flooring affect the system of locomotion. Short chain, narrow calves boxes, feeding stall and too narrow bays, insufficient standing area, very low feeding trough, uneven and hard lying area cause abnormalities in the system of locomotion.

Nutritional deficiency may lead to laminitis. Vitamin E or selenium deficiency causes enzootic muscular dystrophy, while phosphorus deficiency produces osteomalacia. Laminitis is seen due to excess intake of fermentable carbohydrate (lactic acidosis) in ruminants.

General examination: Starts with behavioural inspection. Subsequently the locomotory organs should be examined for weakness, stiffness, lameness, swelling, posture, sensation, sores or any other lesions on the skin of the legs. Further, the methods of palpation, percussion, passive movement of legs, probing, puncture, diagnostic desensitization, radiography and electro-myography, neurography are to be used. Apart from these tests, analysis of blood (cells, enzymes, electrolytes), urine (ketone), synovial fluid and cerebrospinal fluid (turbidity, cells) help in rationalising the diagnosis.

Natural posture of animal: The animals suffering from defects in support organs show abnormal posture e.g. lying down in paralysis, dog-sitting posture in cattle with hip—dislocation etc. Careful look should be given for abnormal position of head, neck, back, the joints, limbs, toes and claws for deviation from the normal.

The process of standing differs in different species of animals. Cattle and buffalo raise their hind legs first followed by forelegs. Horses put weight first on the forelegs in the process of getting up. Any deviation from normal warrants to suspect the locomotor system. Kneeling in cattle is suggestive of carpal joint problem. Goose stepping is characteristic of pantothenic acid deficiency in pigs. Wooden horse appearance is suggestive of tetanus in animals.

Sudden lameness is the result of accidental trauma, nail pricking, overstreching of tendon, ligament or muscle, dislocation of joint, fracture of bones or nerve paralysis. Whereas, slow degenerative changes and neoplasia are responsible for the development of gradual increase of lameness in animals.

Physical examination of foot: The foot should be examined for overgrowth, change in shape, crack, swelling or pain in hoofed and soliped animals while the claws and the nails in dogs and cats. Deformed hoof or foot may be congenital, acquired and due to diseases like foot and mouth disease in ruminants. Deformity in hooves and bleeding around coronary band are seen in buffalo suffering from **degnala** disease. Movement on rough road may tear the hoof of animals. Overgrown nails cause restricted gait or lameness in dogs.

Palpation: Manual palpation of hoof by lifting the leg is rewarding. The wall, heel and sole and coronary band should be examined by applying pressure. The pain on pressure is characterised by withdrawal of leg or pain expression by the animals. If manual pressure fails, the use of hoof-testing-plier or forceps is useful. The foot must be moved or twisted in all possible ways to assess pain. The interdigital space should be viewed carefully for the presence of any lesion.

Percussion with hammer to the wall and sole of large animals helps in the diagnosis of localised lesions while probing with the help of metallic probe helps determining the extent and structure involved.

Wooden block test: This technique is applied to acertain the affected claw of ruminant. The wooden block is placed under each claw turn by turn. The lameness increases when the block is under affected claw.

Similar diagnosis can be made by nerve block. Infiltration of local anaesthetic (10-15 ml) is done around dorsal and volar branches of digital nerve, about 3-4 fingers width above the fetlock joint, just lateral and medial to extensor and flexor tendon respectively. Lastly radiographic examination of the foot is advised.

The Joints and its Structures

Inspection of joint, its capsule, tendon, sheath and bursa helps in detecting abnormal swelling, which occurs due to accumulation of excess synovial fluid. The joint is palpated for consistency and for cellulitis, haematoma, abscess and sensitivity to pressure. Crepitation at hip, stiffle or shoulder joint points for dislocation. This can be achieved by bending, streching and rotating the limbs.

Articular puncture: To ascertain, whether the joint swelling is hemorrhagic or purulent, the synovial fluid is examined. Care must be taken during puncture to avoid introduction of infection. The site must be thoroughly cleaned and disinfected with tincture of iodine. Fine needle fails to collect viscous fluid. The punctured site should be covered with adhesive plaster. The colour, consistency, transparency, odour, coagulation, protein content, total and differential cell count and bacterial culture and sensitivity of synovial fluid are to be recorded. Protein is estimated by colorimetric method and the leucocytes are counted similar to blood. The dilution depends on the number of cells expected.

Properties of Normal Synovial Fluid (Cattle)

Colour	Colourless or slightly straw colour
Consistency	Viscous/stringy
Odour	Odourless
Transparency	Clear
Protein	2 g %
White cell count	$300/mm^3$
Neutrophil	10%
RBC	Very few

Deviation from normal must be considered pathological.

Haematogical analysis is also helpful. An increase in neutrophils (left shift) indicates purulent arthritis. Elevated serum alkaline phosphatase and altered calcium and phosphorus are characteristic of abnormal bone growth, osteomalacia and rickets. Radiological examination of joint is useful to judge the presence of exostosis. Air may be injected as contrast media.

Ankylosis of joints may be either congenital or acquired. Inheritence or faulty diets during pregnancy may be responsible for the congenital ankylosis, while in chronic inflammation also, the joints get ankylosed.

The Bones

Clinical examination of bones comprises inspection, palpation and radiography. The major defects in bone are of developmental origin in most of the species of animals followed by metabolic and other origin.

Multifactoral developmental defects are ankylosed vertebral bones, vertebral disc protrusion (enzootic ataxia/wobbler), dwarfism, abnormal mandible joint, chondrodystrophy, rickets, beding of radius, osteomalacia and metastatic calcification.

Ricket is a disease of young animals. The bone near epiphyseal cartilage is swollen. Curving of limbs, marked swelling at costo-chondral joint (ricket rosary) and varying degree of lameness are characteristic of rickets. Inadequate dietary calcium and Vit.D_3 and excess phosphorus are responsible for it. Enlargement of bone near joint in foals has been recorded in copper deficient areas. However, direct involvement of copper is not well illucidated.

Osteomalacia is a condition of adult animals, in which the long bones get demineralised and become fragile. Phosphorus deficiency is responsible for this. Depraved appetite, painful or stiff gait and crackling sound from the joints while movement, are the clinical signs. Blood analysis of such animals show low phosphorus and increased alkaline phosphatase activity. Osteoporotic bones are visible on radiography.

Osteodystrophia fibrosa is horses is nutritional in origin. There is deposition of soft celluar fibrous tissue on bones. In the beginning there is shifting lameness without appreciable defects. Occurrence of secondary hypocalcaemia and excess dietary phosphorus through exclusive or excess bran feeding have been attributed for this.

Ostitis/osteomyelitis is not so common in animals. The factors responsible are traumatic injury, associated infection, joint ill, actinomycosis, brucellosis, atrophic rhinitis (swine) and tuberculosis. Swelling, pain and lameness are characteristic if limb bones are involved. In horse, tuberculosis causes cervical ostitis leading to stiffness of neck. Kneeling while feeding in buffalo with occipititis has been seen. Osteosarcoma is commonly seen in most species of animals affecting different bones.

Fracture of bones: Fracture of long bones is appreciated by palpation and feeling for haematoma or tenderness, grating sounds and passive movement of limb. For pelvic bones fracture, rectal exploration is necessary. Animals with pelvic fracture are unable to get up. For the fracture of small or well concealed bones, radiological appreciation is advisable. It also helps in assessing the nature of fractures.

Biopsy evaluation: For bone biopsy appraisal, the material must be collected aseptically. In large animals, the sample is harvested, either from the tubercoxae, the ribs or xyphoid cartilage. A special punch, needle is introduced following local anaesthesia. A bone sample size of 5 mm x 10 mm is suitable. For histological examination, the sample is preserved in 10 per cent formalin. The findings necessitate comparison with the same species, age and sex of animals.

The Muscles, Tendons and Nerves:

Injury, inflammation, displacement and overstreching of muscle or tendon cause lameness in animals. Malformation and atrophy of muscle also cripple the livestock. Topographicl knowledge of muscles and their innervation is important to assess their normal functions. Palpation of torn or ruptured muscles reveals

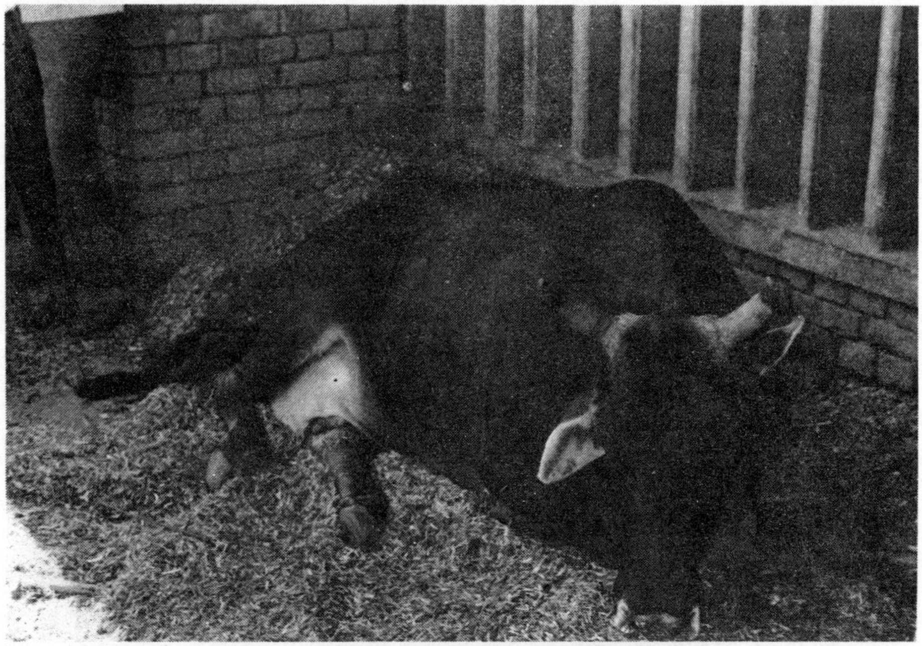

Fig. 16.1 A downer cow

swelling, warmth and increased tension of the part. Tonic-clonic contractions of muscles occur in tetanus and grass sickness. Muscular dystrophy causes hardening of muscles, however, localised hardening is seen in early abscess, tumour or calcified lesions. Muscle degeneration gives tympanic crepitating sound as in black leg and emphysematous myositis. Normal tendon feels under tension. Denervation leads to paralysis of muscles. Sensation is tested by pin prick

Muscle degeneration can be diagnosed by demonstration of myoglobin in urine. The clinical signs including lameness and swelling of muscle, indicate myoglobinuria. It must be differentiated from haemoglobinuria in which anaemia is present. Myoglobinuric urine is acidic and positive for protein. Elevated level of creatine phosphokinase and AST in blood serum is very senstitive indicator of muscular damage.

Electromyography and electroneurography measure the motor action potential and velocity of conduction of motor nerve fibers respectively. However, these techniques have not been applied fully in animal disease diagnosis.

Histological and Histochemical studies: Changes in muscle are appreciated histologically. Muscles, nerves and tendon samples are analysed histochemically for enzymes ATP ase, LDH and others.

Examination of Downer Animals

Inability in getting up by the animals due to paresis of hindquarters is most common. It originates from malfunctioning of mucles, nerves, bones or joints associated with number of disorders. Classical downer cow syndrome (Fig. 16.1 & 16.2) may be the outcome of unresponsive parturient paresis cases. Elucidation of such problem becomes most difficult task for the practising veterinarians.

Fig. 16.2 A downer she buffalo (abnormal posture)

Case history is often helpful in determination of etiological factors. Date of calving, handling during parturition, difficult calving, feeding schedules, previous history of milk fever, treatment adopted by the farmer, duration of recumbency and type of housing should be reviewed.

Table showing possible causes of downer syndrome

Metabolic	Toxaemic	Calving injury	Post-parturient injury	Managemental/ other
Hypocalcaemia	Septic metritis (acute)	Obturator paralysis	Pelvic fracture, femur fracture,	Slippery floor Parasitism Malnutrition
Hypophosphataemia Post-parturient haemoglo-binurea				
Hypomagnesaemia	Per-acute mastitis	Internal bleeding	Round ligament rupture,	Prolonged anaesthesia
Hypokalemia	Acute diffuse peritonitis,	Pelvic fracture	Hip dislocation,	Delayed calcium therapy,
Ketosis	Reticulum, abomasum, & uterus rupture	Sciatic nerve paralysis, Fatigueness	Damaged peripheral nerves, Ruptured gastrocnemius muscle,	Hypothermia Hyperthermia Heat stroke
Fatty cow syndrome	acidosis, drenching			
Bloat	pneumonia, traumatic pericarditis		Pressure atrophy	

General Clinical Examination: Includes recording of position of legs, temperature, respiration, rumination, cardiac rhythm and feed intake. The posture of the animal, tail movement and general appearance (alert or non-alert), colour of mucous membrane and pupillary reflexes should be noted.

Palpation will reveal any abnormal swelling, pain or tenderness in the area. Passive movements of the limbs are to be ascertained by flexion, extension, adduction and abduction of limb. Hammer or deep finger percussion often reveals deep seated pain. Vertebral column should be percussed in the same ways.

The sensory test is carried out with the help of a pin or needle prick. It must start from the lower portion of the limb and subsequently upward. The paralysed skin area may determine the involvement of particular nerve.

Testing of urine samples for the presence of myoglobin, ketone bodies and bile pigment often helps to elucidate the type of associated condition. Blood chemistry in respect of glucose, protein, urea, calcium, phosphorus, magnesium, potassium, sodium, transaminases and creatine kinase helps in rationalising the therapeutic approaches.

Reference

Andrews, Tony (1986). *The Downer Cow. In Practice*, September issue.

17

THE NERVOUS SYSTEM

The central nervous system is almost inaccessable for direct clinical examination in large animals as the brain and spinal cord are situated in the bony frames. However, the same can be better appreciated in dogs and cats. For better understanding and diagnosis of nerves involvement, the students are advised to refer the text describing anatomical and physiological function of different nerves.

As basic reference, the nervous system has been classified into (a) central nervous system (CNS), (b) peripheral nervous system and (c) autonomic nervous system.

(a) Central nervous system: It is comprised of brain, cerebrum, cerebellum and brain stem which are located in the skull and the spinal cord, enclosed in the vertebral column.

(b) Peripheral nervous system: It is comprised of cranial and spinal nerves.

(c) Autonomic nervous system: It originates from cranio-sacral region and supplies the internal organs which work involuntarily.

The cerebrum is the seat of psychic functions for feeling, thought and wish or will. The pyramidal and extrapyramidal motor systems are concerned with cutaneous sensation, joints, muscles tone and reflexes. Cerebral disorders are characterised by loss of conciousness, motor irritations, (spasms or convulsions), paralysis, loss of vision, hearing and cutaneous perception. The cerebellar damage is characterised by disturbance in voluntary movement. Inco-ordination in movement and abnormal rotation of eye ball (nystagmus) are noted when cerebellum is damaged. Spinal and peripheral nerves dysfunctions lead to paresis or paralysis of both the hind legs.

In general, the following features, if noted clinically, speak the involvement of nervous system.

- Abnormal behaviour.
- Disturbance in conciousness.
- Involuntary movement.
- Abnormal motor functions
- Abnormal sensory functions
- Disturbed co-ordination.

Abnormal behaviour: Behavioural changes in respect of deglutation (partial or intermittent intake), waste excretion (uncontrolled and/or urination), locomotion (staggering gait, crossing of legs, inco-ordination), voice (changed voice or repeated unprovoked) and reaction to a person (attacks to butt or runs away or any other aggressive reaction) indicate involvement of nervous system.

Disturbance in consciousness: The affected animals are oblivious to the environment. The manifestations may be either depressive or aggressive. Dullness, somnolence, apathy and comma represent depressive manifestations which are seen in cerebral congestion, haemorrhage, contusion, tumours, hydrocephalus and degeneration of brain. The aggressive disturbances are characterised by bellowing, excitement, mania and delirium, which are the outcome of meningitis, brain abscess, intoxication, lead poisoning, encephalitis, rabies and sunstroke.

Involuntary movement: Disturbances of the motor centers of the brain lead to twiching, tremors, clonic/ tonic spasms and tetanic contraction of forced movements. These occur in meningitis, meningo-encephalitis, brain abscess, lead, copper and nitrite toxicosis. Tremors and twichings are seen in acetonaemia, convulsions are seen in cerebrocortical necrosis (thiamine deficiency), toxic encephalitis, increased intracranial pressure, brain tuberculosis and acute fatty degeneration of liver. Tetanic spasms of muscles occur in grass tetany, hypomagnesaemic tetany and tetanus.

Circling to the left or right and dashing movement are seen in space occupying lesions, coenurosis, lead poisoning, cirrhosis of liver, listeriosis and sinusitis. Backward falling points cerebellar aplasia or degeneration.

Abnormal motor functions: These can be assessed from active and passive movement of limbs, tail, neck and head. Complete paralysis of muscles leads to swallowing, drinking, respiration, switching and locomotion difficult. Limbs may develop mono, hemi, para, or quadriplegia, usually associated with nerve injuries. Paresis is seen in milk fever and ketosis in cattle and buffaloes.

Increased motor activity causes tonic or clonic contractions of muscles in which either localised or generalised spasm may take place. While difficulty in standing (inco-ordination), the animal may put limbs wide apart, crossing over, disproportionate movement, stumble or fall repeatedly.

Abnormal sensory functions: The impulse perceptions are either increased (hyperaesthesia) or decreased (anaesthesia=complete loss or hypoesthesia = partial loss of sensation). Hyperaesthesia is characterised by abnormal action when the animal is handled and/or touched as in case of cerebromeningitis. Paraesthesia (itching sensation) is manifested by rubbing, licking or biting the skin, seen in Aujeszky's disease, nervous form of ketosis and rabies. Skin reflexes are tested by touch, pin pricks, skin pinch or by use of electric goads. Other reflexes like corneal, eyelids, ear flap, anal and interdigital, are tested by touch or prick. Acute brain diseases, brain tumours and hydrocephalus cause loss of sight and hearing reflexes. Spinal compression leads to loss of skin sensation.

Disturbance of co-ordination: Inco-ordination is seen in early milk fever and ketotic cases. In horses, inco-ordination (wobbling) occurs usually by rear limbs. Affected animals fail to lift the fore legs when forced for backward movement. Cirrhosis leads to inco-ordination. In swine, pantothenic acid deficiency leads to peculiar mongoose stepping.

Degeneration of cerebellum, middle ear infection and compression of intervertebral disc at lumbosacral junction lead to inco-ordination of gait in animals.

Examination of the skull and vertebral column: The whole bony cover of the CNS must be checked for swelling, depression and abnormal mobility. Keen observation, palpation and percussion techniques are to be applied. Abnormal curvature of the spine and kinking (kyphosis, opisthotonos, torticolis etc) are recorded. The tenderness as well as the consistency of the lesions are determined with blunt end of percussion hammer. Softness in bony consistency is appreciable in hydatidosis. Sometimes trephining of skull becomes necessary to confirm the diagnosis.

Clinical syndromes in relation to the location of CNS disorders

Affected area	Syndromes
Brain:	
Increased intracranial pressure	Somnolence, vacant look, head pressing, semiclosed eyes, lethargy, dragging of legs, prostration, opisthotonos, blindness, paresis, inco-ordination and circling.
Cerebellum	Ataxia, asymetric and compulsive gait, legs wide apart, paresis, tremor, nystagmus and fall on one side.
Cerebrum	Oblivious to the surroundings, impaired vision, little automatic feeding and drinking, abnormal noding (up and down or side ways), recumbency.
Base of the brain	Restriction of jaw movement, mandibular paralysis, tongue immobile, unable to ingest, chew or drink.
Cerebral nerves:	
Olfactory nerve (I)	No response even with compulsive fume.
Ophthalmic N (II)	Impaired or no vision, the animal is apparently blind.
Oculomotor N (III)	Mydriasis (dilatation of pupil) and ptosis (dropped upper eye-lid), and squint.
Trochlear N (IV)	Downwards and side ways squint.
Trigeminal N (V)	Absence of sensation in forehead, eyelids, cornea, nose, cheecks, lips and tongue. Uni or bilateral chewing restriction, cuds drop from affected side.

Abducent N(VI)	Exophthalmus
Facial N (VII)	Paralysis of facial muscles, upper eye-lid and lower lip.
Acoustic N (VIII)	Loss of hearing, head rotation and nystagmus.
Glossopharyngeal N (IX)	Cud dropping syndrome due to pharyngeal paralysis, regurgitation of drinking water through nostril, unable to swallow feed or water.
Vagus N (X)	Difficult swallowing, roaring, bloat and coughing.
Spinal accessory N	Paralysis and atrophy of neck and shoulder.
Hypoglossal N	Protrusion or turning of tongue.
Spinal cord	Partial or complete loss of sensory and motor function of area innervated, injury to cervical region leads to respiration failure or whole caudal parts get paralysed.

Special examination of CNS: The failure to reach a conclusive diagnosis based on the syndromes observed necessitates to go for special examination like evaluation of cerebrospinal fluid (CSF), roentgenological views and electroencephalography. The latter method is limited to research laboratory, while X-ray examination is limited to small animals and the calves.

Cerebrospinal Fluid (CSF)

Collection: The CSF is collected generally from two sites (i) lumbosacral junction (Cattle, buffalo,sheep, goat) and (ii) atlanto-occipital (horse, cattle, dog, cat) junction. In horse epidural (sacro-coccygeal) puncture is rewarding inplace of sacral puncture. The size and length of needle vary from species and age of the animals. For adult large animals, 15-16 gauge x 3.5-4.5", for calves, foal, sheep and goat 16-18 g x 2.5" and for dog and cat 22-24 g x 1.5-2.5", needles are required. The collection is made either in standing or in recumbent position. The needle is punctured, taking all the aseptic precautions (shaving, sterilization) in the midline at right angle.

Infiltration of local anaesthesia is good. Introduction of air or suction with sterile glass syringe is necessary.

For post-occipital puncture, the animal should be casted and the head is flexed as far as possible and the rest procedure is as lumber puncture. As soon on the needle reaches the site, the CSF flows out easily. Some times blood contaminations make the sample useless for evaluation.

Physical and chemical properties of normal cerebrospinal fluid of animals

Properties	Cattle	Buffalo	Sheep	Horse	Dog
Colour	Watery	Watery	Watery	Watery	Watery
Transparency	Clear	Clear	Clear	Clear	Clear
Sp. gravity	1.005-1.01	-	1.007	1.006	1.005
Pressure (mm H_2O)	200	-	60-270	272-490	135-150
Leucocytes (per mm^3)	0-25	5-7	0-5	1-7	5-8
Differential cells	95% lymphocytes				
Protein (mg%)	24-30	17	8-70	28-71	11-55
Pandy's Test	- ve	- ve	- ve	- ve	- ve
Glucose (mg %)	30-80	65-70	48-109	40-80	61-116
pH	7-7.4	7.5	7.35	7.25	7.4-7.6
Chloride (mg %)	620-750	458.50	650-860	690-792	761-883
Calcium (mg %)	5.1-6.3	5.0	5.8	6.30	6.50
Phosphorus (mg %)	0.9-4	2.8	-	1.5	3.1
Magnesium (mg %)	2.1	2.5	2.85	1.98	3.0
Urea (mg %)	6-12	—	5.6	2-3	6-10
Sodium (m Eq/L)	119	337	-	620-760	157
Potassium (m Eq/L)	11-13	.11	-	10-14	10-12

CSF examination: Physical and biochemical properties of normal CSF are given in the table. Normal CSF is watery, transparent and does not clot. In CNS affections, the physical, cytological and biochemical composition change. CSF pressure, which can be measured with manometer, increases in cranial bone compression and in vitamin A deficiency.

CSF leucocytes count:

Diluting fluid:

Glacial acetic acid	10 ml
Distilled water	90 ml
Crystal violet	100 mg
Phenol (5%)	3 drops

The diluting fluid is taken up to mark 1 of the WBC diluting pipette and filled up to 11 mark with CSF. Mix, discard few drops and charge the neubauer chamber on both the ruled sides. Focus and count all the cells in 18 primary squares (9 on each side). Multiply the count with factor 0.6, which gives leucocytes/mm³. Total area = (3 x 3 x 0.1 mm+3 x 3 x 0.1 mm) =1.8 mm³and the dilution is 10/9.

Calculation:

1•8mm³ contains A number of cells

1 mm³ contians 1 x A/1•8 x 10/9 = 0•6 x A

A leucocyte count more than 30 per mm³ suggests non-purulent encephalomyelitis. The differential patterns of leucocytes are performed after making a smear and staining with suitable stain a similar to blood. Normally lymphocytes are numerous but in suppuration the neutrophils dominate.

Pandy test: The test detects globulin in CSF qualitatively.

Reagent: Phenol pure 10 g

Distilled water 150 ml.

Discard the solution when discoloured.

A drop of CSF is mixed with 5 ml of reagent. Development of turbidity is proportional to the amount of globulin present suggesting inflammatory changes in CNS.

Radiological examination: The technique is not helpful in adult large animals. However, it is best used in small animals and the calves because of their small sizes. The animals are immobilized with sedatives or anaesthetics. Myelography is used for the detection of CNS compression due to vertebral disc dislocation, haemorrhage and meningeal tumour. Following withdrawal of CSF, contrast medium is injected either through lumber or cisternal puncture. The dog's table is tilted slightly to promote posterior migration of the contrast medium.

Contrast radiography of the brain includes cerebral angiography, pneumoencephalography and ventriculography. For cerebral angiography, the carotid artery is canulated and contrast medium is injected and the radiographs are taken in sequence. Pneumoencephalography is done by introducing air as contrast media through cisternal or lumber route. The technique is useful for locating space occupying lesions or blockades. The ventricular fluid is removed by air or a suitable contrast medium for ventriculography. The needle is passed through a trephined hole on the skull between lateral canthus of the eye and external occipital protuberance. Correct insertion of needle leads to emergence of cerebrospinal fluid. About 5-15 ml air or 2- 3 ml contrast medium is injected carefully. The head is shaken for proper dispersal of medium and the rediograph is being taken.

Collection of nervous tissues: Whenever an animal is dead or euthanised showing nervous symptoms, the brain and the spinal cord must be exposed very carefully. The gross changes must be noted before sending the sample. The piece must be removed with durameter. For histopathological examination, the tissue is fixed in 10 per cent formaldehyde solution. For bacterial, viral or fungal investigation, unfixed tissue is packed in sterile cool container and is sent soonest possible to the nearest laboratory. For histochemistry, the tissue must be frozen. Alongwith the specimen, the clinical symptoms and changes observed must be sent.

REFERENCES

Benjamin, M.M (1978). Outline of Veterinary Clinical Pathology. 3rd edn. The Iowa State University Press, Ames, Iowa, U.S.A.

Joshi, H.C, Kumar, Amresh and Prasad, B. (1982). A note on the composition of cerebrospinal fluid in buffalo, cow and dog. Indian vet med. j. 6:50-51.

18

EXAMINATION OF EYE

Bright and shining eyes are indicators of good health. There are number of conditions in which the eyes or its accessories are affected. A careful general examination, preferably in day light followed by instrumental examination with aided light should be carried out.

Inspection: The eye ball, eye-lids, sclera and cornea are examined in day light. A battery light is needed for the anterior chamber of eye, iris and the lenses.

Symmetry: Normal eyes are symmetric. Asymmetry in the size of eyes may be due to inflammations, swelling, abscess or tumours. The discharge of the eyes, whether watery, mucoid or purulent should be noted.

The eyelids: Are examined for swelling, inward turning (entropian), outward turning (ectropian) papillomas or adhesions (ankyloblephron) or paralysis (ptosis).

Third eyelid: It is appreciable when the head is turned to one side. Prolapse of third eye-lid, which crosses the inner canthus, is very characteristic of tetanus in animals. Bilateral eversion of third eyelid occurs in dog due to oedema of harderian glands.

The eye ball: The movement, size and position of eye ball should be noted. Macrophthalamus (large eye ball) or microphthalmus may be congenital. Sunken eye ball is seen in dehydration, extreme malnutrition and weakness. Exophthalmia may be due to inflammation or iodine deficiency and in acute theileriosis in calves. (Colour Plate). Deviation of visual axis (squint) may be unilateral or bilateral, usually congenital in origin. Nystagmus (abnormal rotation) is seen in comatosed animals.

Cornea: Corneal opacity develops in malignant bovine catarrh, equine influenza, distemper, swine influenze and trauma.

A torch light is sufficient for viewing the cornea. Its smoothness, deposits and transparency are to be noted. With the help of keratoscope, the corneal surface is studied best in human. The keratoscopic image is blurred in interrupted cornea. The corneal defects are easily assessed by instilling few drops of fluorescein or 0•5 per cent methylene blue into the conjunctiva. The debraded corneal surface retains dye, which can be seen easily. Excess dye is washed off with normal saline.

The iris: The shape, colour and pattern of iris are to be noted. The iris pattern of cattle and buffalo is such that the shape of pupil is oval. Adhesion of iris with lens or posterior part of cornea alters the shape of pupil, which are known as posterior and anterior synechia respectively.

Pupillary reflex: On exposure to bright light, normal pupil constricts instantly. Failure of pupillary constriction is termed as mydriasis which is seen in encephalitis, atropine and strychnine toxicity, vitamin A deficiency and optic nerve or brain damage. Permanent constriction (miosis) occurs in OPI poisoning, pupillary muscle paralysis and acute keratitis.

The lens: Lens is affected in number of diseases. Opacity of lens develops in diabetes mellitus, chronic nephritis and aged dogs.

The lens can be visualised in day light. Preference should be given to use ophthalmoscope for the lens, ciliary body, vitreous body and the fundus. Students are advised to consult text book on examination of eye. About 10-30 minutes before ophthalmoscopy, homatropine (2%) is instilled for better visualization. Lenses of + 12 to +20 for anterior eye, +8 to +12 for lens, 0 to 18 for vitreous humour and -3 or less for optic disc and retina are used.

Corneal reflex: A sterile cotton swab is touched to the corneal surface. Normal reflex causes closure of eyelids. This reflex is absent in trigeminal nerve paralysis, anaesthesia, comatose condition, brain damage and increased intraocular pressure.

Tonometry: Increased intraocular pressure (glaucoma), which may be the outcome of malabsorption of aqueous humour necessitates to note its pressure. Normally, intraocular pressure in cattle ranges 15-30 mm; in dog 16-30 mm and in man 15-20 mm mercury.

Eye function test: Mild loss of sight may necessitate to use specific test. For general purpose, finger ring is opened just near the eye of the animal without touching the eye. Normal eye gets closed as finger opens. The test can be repeated on both sides. Failure of closure of eyelids shows absence of sight.

19

ROUTINE OPERATIVE TECHNIQUES

Common operative procedures necessitate the use of sterilised equipments. The following techniques are to be used for this:

Techniques of Sterilization

Methods	Temperature (°C)	Duration (min)	Suitability
Autoclave	120 at 15 lb pressure	20-30	Surgical packs, cotton pads and threads, gauze etc.
Dry heat	160	60	Glasswares
Boiling	100	20-30	Metallic instruments, needle, catheter, glass syringes, teat instrument etc.

Castration: To make the male docile and to enhance the performance of draft animals, castration is done. The preferable age of castration is below two years. Either close or open method is used.

Close method: For this Burdizzo emasculator (Plate - 20) is used. The animal is being secured in lateral recumbency. The spermatic cord of one side is grasped with skin. The cord is crushed at two places one inch apart, on both the sides. The crushing is made first dorsal and then at ventral sites. Care must be taken to avoid crushing of testicles. Apply betadine for 3-5 days locally.

Open method: Spermatic nerve block or epidural anaesthesia is necessary in this method. The scrotum is made aseptic. The testicles are grasped making the scrotal skin tense. Ventral incision is made. The testicles are exposed out by traction. Following ligature of the blood vessels, vasdeferences and tunica vaginalis are severed with scissors as high as possible. A gauze soaked in tincture iodine or betadine is packed. The incision in not sutured. The site is dressed with iodine preparation for 5-7 days along with streptopenicillin injection. Injection of tetanus toxoid (3000 IU) a week prior to castration is essential in horse.

Urethrotomy: Generally urethral calculi in male bullocks and buffaloes necessitate this operation.

The animal is secured in lateral recumbency. The urethral tract is washed externally and the site of obstruction is located by palpation. Infiltration of lignocaine (2%) 10-15 ml is done locally. After 10 minutes a 5" long incision is made along the midline. The sigmoid flexure is pulled out and is made straight. The calculi are felt by palpation. The most common sites are sigmoid flexure, tip of the penis, ischeal arch and the neck of the bladder. By making a small incision, the stone is removed. Sandy deposit needs passage of catheter and washing with aseptic water. A polythene tube is passed down from the site of incision protruding 2"-3" out of the prepuce. It is kept as such for a month or so. Catheterization prevents subcutaneous infiltration of urine. Urethral incision is not sutured to avoid constriction of urethra. Suture the skin with silk thread No. 3. Dressing the site aseptically and a course of streptomycin-penicillin injection are advised.

Amputation of Limb:

Gangrenous and irreparable fractures justify limb amputation. Either fore or hind limb may require this operation.

The operation is done under general anaesthesia. The common sites are radial and tibial region in fore and hind leg respectively. A tourniquet is applied below elbow or stiffle joint. An incision shaping V is made on lateral and medial sides of the skin. The bone is sawn following dissection of muscles. The blood vessels are ligated. The flaps of skin are made in apposition and sutured with silk thread No. 3 covering the bone and bandaged. The tourniquet is removed. Daily antiseptic dressing and injection of streptomycin-penicillin are indicated for a week.

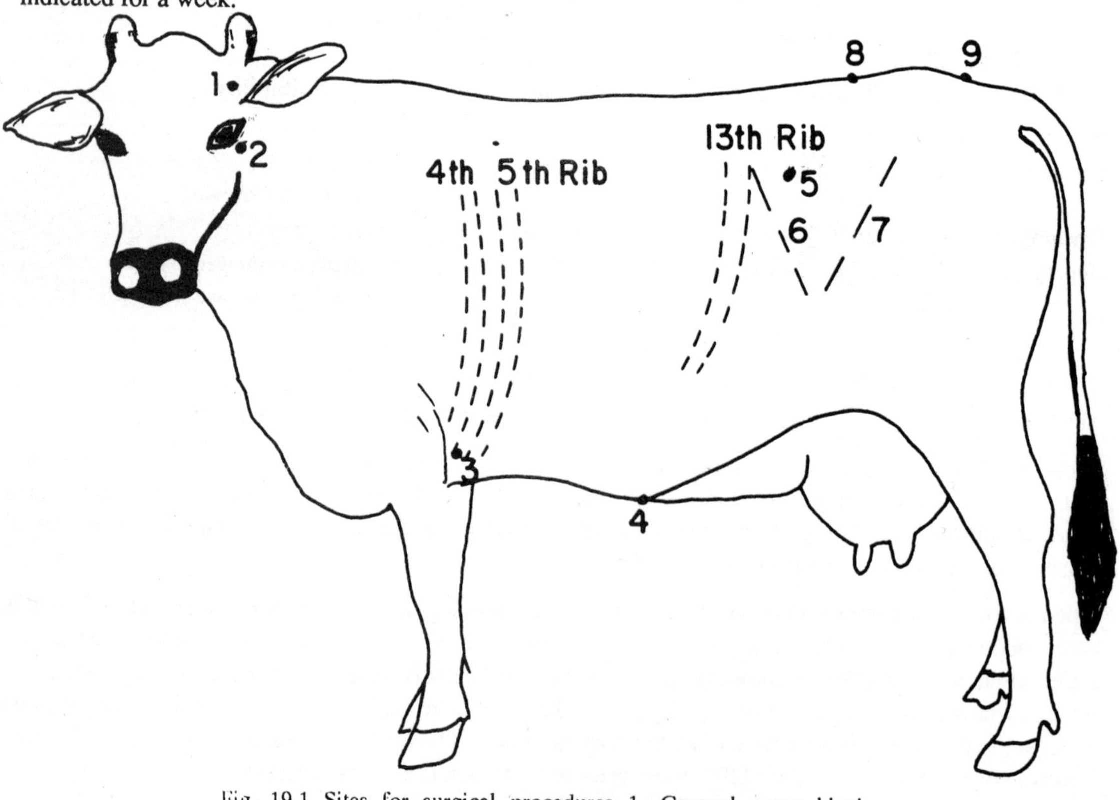

Fig. 19.1 Sites for surgical procedures 1. Cornual nerve block 2. Retrobulbar nerve block, 3. Thoracocentesis, 4. Abomasal puncture, 5. Rumen puncture, 6. Line for rumenotomy, 7. Line for cystectomy, 8. Cerebrospinal fluid collection, 9. Epidural anaesthesia.

Medial Patellar Desmotomy:

Medial patellar ligament originates from medial aspect of patella and inserts at the tibial tuberosity medially. Shortening of this ligament leads to upper fixation of patella hindering the flexion of affected limb.

Technique:

Animal is casted on the affected side. The leg is restrained on a wooden log to prevent movement. The area of medial stiffle joint is prepared aseptically and lignocaine (2%), about 10-15 ml is infiltrated locally. The anterior tibial tuberosity is located. About 1.5-2" above the tuberosity, a depresion (between middle and medial ligaments) is felt, Give 1-1.5"' long incision vertically on the skin. Insert bistury (No.12) and cut the medical ligament. An appreciable gap is formed between the cut edges. Put tincture iodine plug. The wound heals within a week.

Rumenotomy:

For removal of foreign bodies, abomasal impaction, correction of diaphragmatic hernia, acute rumen overload and acute urea toxicosis warrant rumenotomy.

Technique: The animal is restrained in standing position. Left paralumber fossa is shaved and prepared aseptic. Lignocaine (2%), 30-40 ml is infiltrated either in T or inverted L fashion. About 2" caudal and parallel to the last rib a 9-10" long incision is made (Fig. 19.1). Remove the fascia and cut through the abdominal muscles and expose the rumen. The rumen wall is secured with forceps and the wall is incised.. Now fix the wall of rumen in Weingart's frame perfectly.

Remove about 1/3rd of the rumen content for better manipulation. Following correction, the rumen wall is sutured in double rows Lembert suture with catgut No.2. The muscles and peritoneum are sutured with apposition type of suture in continuous lock stitch pattern with catgut No. 2. Eversion pattern is used for skin with interrupted horizontal mattress pattern. Silk thread is used for it. The lesion is dressed daily along with a course of antibiotics for 7-10 days. The suture is removed after 15 days. The animal should be kept half fed post-operation for a week.

Amputation of Tail

Cattle and buffaloes: Drying of tail, irreparable damage and development of gangrene necessitate its amputation.

Technique: The animal may be restrained either in standing or lateral recumbency. Epidural anaesthesia is given. Few inch above the site of damage or gangrene or if possible the length covering anus and vulva, the hair are shaved and dressed with antiseptic. A tourniquet is applied to check the bleeding. On the dorsal and ventral skin surfaces of the tail, V shaped incisions are made.Both dorsal and ventral triangular flaps are separated basing exactly at inter-coccygeal joint. A sharp cut is made with a docker through this junction. Arterial bleeding is ligated. The flaps are brought in apposition and sutured in simple interrupted or mattress suture pattern.

Dogs: For breeds of dog like Spaniels (2/3), Poodles, Terriers (1/3), Boxer and Doberman, docking of tail is advised. From 1/3 to leaving only two coccygeal vertebrae, the tail is removed. Preferably the docking is to be done before 15 days old. Regional anaesthesia is not required at this age. Pulling the skin upward, a cut with scalpel is made through the intercoccygeal joint. The skin is loosened which covers the stump and stitches are made on the skin in apposition.

Dishorning and Disbudding

Dishorning (dehorning): It is indicated in horn fracture, horn cancer or to make the animal controlable.

Technique: The adult is restrained in either standing or recumbent position. Cornual nerve block is done For horn-cancer, flap method is used. At the base of the horn, anterior and posterior flaps of skin are made by giving long elliptical incision around the horn, which extends from the nuchal crest to the frontal ridge. The bleeding is checked with artery forceps or ligature. The horn is sawn and skin is sutured after proper trimming. The sawing may be done at any level of the horn in which thermocautery technique is used for the control of bleeding. The other method of dehorning is wiring the horn till it separates.

Disbudding: It is done in calf below one month of age. There are two methods (i) chemical and (ii) physical.

Chemical method: Shave the area around horn buds. Apply vaseline at the peripheri of the buds. Apply potassium hydroxide sticks. This suppresses the growth of the horn buds.

Physical method: Either red hot iron or electric debudder/dishorner is used (Plate 21). The buds are cauterised till a depression is left. Tincture of iodine is applied.

Ear Haematoma

Accumulation of blood between the skin and the ear cartilage is commonly seen in dogs. It may occur on both sides of the cartilage. The dog feels discomfort and has continuous itching tendency, which further aggravates the condition.

Technique: In early case, where there is absence of fibrin formation, the blood may be sucked out with sterile needle and syringe but it often necessitates incision. The site is infiltrated with local anaesthetic, Lignocaine 2%, 3 ml. The ear canal is plugged with cotton. A vertical incision throughout the haematoma is given. The blood clots are removed. A little elliptical portion of the skin of either side is removed. Mattress sutures are applied passing through the concha. The ear flap is bandaged with head. A course of streptomycin and penicillin is required for rapid healing.

Nail Trimming (Dogs)

Overgrown nails produce lameness or careful gait in dogs. Lack of exercise and or absence of trimming periodically lead to this condition.

Technique: The dog is restrained on the table or in lap. The avascular portion of the nail is cut using dog nail cutter. Overcutting causes pain and bleeding. Application of tincture of iodine or betadine (aqueous iodine) is helpful.

Trephining:

For the removal of cysts, fragments of bone and pus from the cavities of skull, trephining is needed. Usually the frontal sinus, superior sinus and inferior maxillary sinuses are trephined in equine. Sites for trephining the various sinuses are as below.

Sinus(es)	Location
(i) Frontal Sinus:	
(a) Upper site	At inferior angle of intersecting, imaginary lines drawn between supra-orbital processes and along the mesial suture.
(b) Lower site	One inch medially and about 2•5" below the inner eye canthus, at a point where the lines joining the inner canthuses and nasomaxillary notch meet.
(c) Middle site	At superior angle of the point of intersection of line between two inner canthuses of the eyes and along the mesial suture.
(ii) Superior maxillary sinus	About 1" inward from the centre of facial crest.
(iii) Inferior maxillary sinus	About 1" inward from the lower level of facial crest

Technique: The animal is restrained in standing position and the skin is infiltrated with local anaesthetic. An area coinciding the head of the trephine is estimated. Giving cruciated incisions, four flaps of skin are made. The trephine is put on the site and rotated till it cuts the bone. The cut piece of bone is removed and sinus is approached for the purpose. After removal of cyst or pus, the piece of bone is placed and skin is sutured. A course of antibiotic is advised.

Reference

O'connor, J.J. (1985) Dollar's Veterinary Surgery. Indian ed. C.B.S. Publishers and Distributors, 485, Jain Bhawan, Bhola Nath Nagar, Shahdra, Delhi-110032.

20

IMMUNOLOGICAL TESTS

The immunological tests are dependant on the reaction between the antigen and the antibody. The important diseases of domestic animals including tuberculosis, paratuberculosis, glanders and brucellosis can be diagnosed in routine practice. The implications of immunological tests are vast and too accurate for the diagnosis of diseases of livestock and poultry for which consultation of text book on immunology is advised.

Tuberculin Test

Single Intradermal Test (SID): The test is very easily applicable in cattle and buffalo. The skin of middle neck is preferred. A 2" x 2" area is shaved. The thickness of the skin fold is measured (mm) with a dial or ordinary calliper and 0.1 ml (0.2 ml in positive herd) tuberculin or its PPD is injected intradermally with special syringe and needle. The pressure is applied on the needle at 30° angle with the skin. A small pea sized elevation indicates proper placing of the antigen. The skin fold thickness of the site is noted 72-96 hours later. If the thickness increases by 4 mm or more, with or without painful swelling, indicates the test positive. In doubtful case, the test is converted into stormont test or repeated after a month.

Stormont test (ST): The SID test may be converted into stormont test in less sensitized animals. The first test is conducted as mentioned above. After 7 days, again 0.1 ml tuberculin or its PPD is injected intradermally at the same site. The reaction and thickness of skin is recorded 24 hours later and is interpreted as above. The tested animal gets desensitized for 6 months.

Horse: SID test may be used for tuberculin test but the specificity remains questionable.

Sheep and goat: In the caudal fold 0.1 ml tuberculin is injected intradermally and read 72 hours later.

Pigs: The outer skin of base of the ear provides acceptable site for conducting SID test. Tuberculin is injected intradermally. Inflammatory reaction occurs by 24 hours in positive case.

The tuberculin tests employing subcutaneous and intravenous routes are not in routine use as anaphylactic rections are often observed.

Limitations: Animals get sensitized with other infections like paratuberculosis, liver fluke infestations, skin tuberculosis, saprophytic acid fast bacilli and avian tuberculosis, which can be ruled out by conducting comparative test similar to SID test at two places about 5" down on the same side of the neck of cattle and buffaloes. The injection showing more reaction is considered positive.

The test may give either false positive or negative cases in following conditions.

False positive	False negative
• Sensitized with paratuberculosis, liver fluke.	• Early stage of disease.
• Skin tuberculosis	• Advance stage of disease
• Attended by tuberculous attendant	• Old age
• Calves fed with TB positive dam's colostrum	• Recent tuberculin test
	• Recent parturition
• Drinking of water infected with acid fast bacteria	• Advance pregnancy

Johnin Test: It is applicable for the diagnosis of Johne's disease in cattle, buffaloes, sheep and goats. Single intradermal test is used. Johnin 0.1ml is injected in the skin of neck similar to tuberculin test. Skin fold thickness is measured pre and 48-72 hours post-inoculation. A positive test is characterised by oedematous swelling.

For the diagnosis of subclinical Johne's disease, short thermal test has been advised. One ml Johnin, diluted with 9 ml normal saline, is injected intravenously. A rise in body temperature by 2° F around 5-8 hours. post-inoculation indicates the test positive.

Limitation: Early and very advance cases fail to give positive test.

Mallein test: Used for glander test in horses and mules.

Intradermopalpebral test: This test is used widely. The eye is cleaned properly. The lower eyelid is restrained with fingers and 0. 1 ml mallein is injected intradermally about 1/2" down the palpebral margin. Development of severe conjunctivitis or oedema of whole orbit by 24-48 hours, indicates the test positive.

Subcutaneous test: One ml diluted mallein (1:9 in normal saline) is injected subcutaneously in the middle third of the neck. The body temperature is recorded at 0, 9, 12, 15, 18, 21, and 24 hours post-inoculation. The start of rising in body temperature 18 hours onward and reaching to 103-104°F or more with or without local inflammation, indicates the test positive.

Ophthalmic test: The test is infrequently applied. Few drops of mallein are instilled in the normal conjunctival sac with a suitable dropper or syringe. A positive test is characterised by purulent conjunctivitis, photophobia and swollen eyelids within 24 hours of instillation, which persists for 48-72 hours.

Brucellosis: Milk, milk - whey or serum agglutination test is applied for the diagnosis of brucellosis in almost all species of animal. To a small test tube containing 2 ml milk, 2 drops brucella antigen (coloured) are added and mixed. The tube is incubated at 37°C for one hour. In positive case, the antigen gets agglutinated and forms deep blue layer on the surface of milk.

21

BACTERIOLOGICAL TECHNIQUES

For better appreciation, consultation of text book of bacteriology is essential. The techniques for the determination of type of the bacteria (gram positive, gram negative or acid fast) and their sensitivity to antimicrobials are essential in routine verterinary practice.

Gram's Stain

(a) Methyl violet : To 100 ml distilled water, 0.5 g methyl violet is dissolved and filtered.

(b) Iodine Solution : To 100 ml distilled water, add 1 g iodine and 2 g potassium iodide crystals.

(c) Carbol fuchsin : Mix 1 ml of Ziehl Neelsen's carbol fuchsin and 9 ml distilled water.

Staining Technique

Prepare blood, sputum or aspiration fluid smear and fix in methanol for 2 minutes and dry. Cover the smear with methyl violet solution and leave for 3 minutes. Keep the slide in slant for removing stain and pour iodine solution and allow one minute. Wash the iodine with absolute alcohol completely till no colour comes out further. Wash the smear for 15 seconds. Counter stain with carbol fuchsin for one minute. Wash with water, dry and examine under microscope.

Result: Gram positive bacteria appear deep violet while the gram negative bacteria, pus cells and tissue appear pink.

Acid Fast Stain: The method is applied to demonstrate the acid fast organisms *(M. tuberculosis* and *M. paratuberculosis).*

(a) Ziehl-Neelsen's carbol Fuchsin: Contains 1 g basic fuchsin powder, dissolved in 10 ml absolute alcohol and 100 ml carbolic acid (5 % aqueous).

(b) Decolourising solution: Alcoholic solution of sulphuric acid (1%) or hydrochloric acid (3%) can be used.

(c) Counter stain (Loeffler's methylene blue): Mix 30 ml alcoholic solution of methylene blue (1%) and 100 ml of $1/10^4$ aqueous solution of potassium hydroxide.

Staining Technique

— Flood the dry smear (blood, sputum, milk, peritoneal fluid, rectal pinch) with filtered carbol fuchsin solution.

— Heat the slide gently to begin evaporation and leave for five minutes. Repeat heating during this period. Care must be taken to avoid drying the stain.

— Wash the smear with water and dip it for one minute in decolourising acid solution and wash it. These steps are repeated till the smear appears faint pink colour. Wash with water.

— Counter stain by pouring Loeffler's stain for 2-3 minutes.

— Wash with water and dry the smear for examination. The acid-fast organisms appear red and non-acid-fast blue.

Note: For demonstration of tubercle bacilli, the thick vicid portion of sputum is spread with blade and fixed under heat. The centrifuged sediment of peritoneal-fluid, milk and urine should be used for preparation of smear. For paratuberculosis, the faeces should be spread in 2 x 2 cm area and 0.25 mm thick.

Bacterial Sensitivity Test

In clinical practice, determination of sensitivity/resistance of micro-organism is of real value for rational and satisfactory therapy. The availability of drug impregnated discs made this task practicable. Basically two media are required for this:

1. **Muller Hinton agar Media**

Lab lemco	6g
Starch	1.5g
Bactocasmino acid	17.5g
Distilled water to	1000ml

Adjust pH 7.4, distribute in 100 or 200 ml flask and autoclave it at 15 lbs for 15 minutes. Melt it before use. The above agar media is commercially available (Hi-media Bombay), which can be used.

2. **Tryptose phosphate broth/Nutrient broth.**

Tryptose	20g
Dextrose	2g
Sodium chloride	5g
Disodium hydrogen phosphate	2.2g
Distilled water to	1000 ml

Dissolve by heat, distribute 5 ml in tubes and autoclave at 15 lbs for 5 minutes.

Technique: Pour 15 ml of Muller Hinton agar in 4" diameter petridishes and allow it to solidify.

Inoculate the suspected material (blood, urine, sputum, milk etc.) in test tube contaning tryptose phosphate broth and incubate at 37°C for 4-5 hours. Growth of bacteria is proportional to the development of turbidity. With sterile cotton swab or platinum loop, smear the growth evenly on culture plate and press gently the standard antibiotic discs (Pasteur Biological Laboratories, Umbergaon Road, Bulsar, Gujrat) on the plate and incubate at 37°C for 18-24 hours. Note the zone of inhibition around each disc. No zone of inhibition is considered as resistant.

Common Antibiotic Discs Available

Antibiotics	Amount per disc
Ampicillin	10/μg
Bacitracin	10/μg
Cephaloridine	30/μg
Chloramphenicol	30/μg
Erythromycin	15/μg
Gentamycin	10/μg
Kanamycin	30/μg
Neomycin	30/μg
Nitrofurantoin	300/μg
Penicillin G	10 units
Streptomycin	10/μg
Sulphonamides	300/μg
Tetracyclines	30/μg

22

TOXICOLOGICAL TECHNIQUES

Toxicoses remain a real challange for the practising veterinarians. The unselective eating habits of animals, particularly cattle and buffaloes, pose them at great risk for the entry of toxicants. Indiscriminate use of insecticides, weedicides and pesticides leaves toxic levels of these chemicals in the plants. These chemicals causes poisoning not only directly but also alter the metabolism of plants conditioning them to store poisonous metabolites in them. For example application of 2-4-D, (2,4-Dichloro phenoxy acetic acid) conditions the plants to accumulate toxic level of nitrate in them. Improper concentration of acaricides often cause poisoning in animals through cutaneous absorption.

The problem of toxicosis is more complicated unlike human, where the veterinarian has to determine first the surce of poison as well as to confirm the actual poison. Considering these facts, it appears necessary to indicate the ways toxins act, the routes of entry, the sources and the laboratory diagnostic techniques for some common poisons.

Ways the toxins act: The toxins act in the following ways.

1. **Surface injury:** e.g. strong acids or alkalies.
2. **Necrosis of the tissue:** e.g. Thallium.
3. **Gastro-intestinal irritation:** e.g. Lead, urea, lactic acid and heavy metals.
4. **Central nervous system stimulation:** e.g. Strychine.
5. **Central Nervous system depressant:** e.g. Barbiturates, anaesthetics etc.
6. **Blood vascular abnormalities:** e.g. Bracken fern.
    a. Haemolysis of RBC: e.g. Copper, Lead, Saponin, Kaleect.
    b. Bone marrow suppression: e.g. Bracken fern, X-radiation, tetrachlorethylene.
    c. Endothelial damage: e.g. Thallium and ergot poisoning.
    d. Alters haemoglobin: e.g. Methaemoglobin (Nitrite, aniline dyes, excess methylene blue), cyanmethaemoglobin (cyanide), carboxyhaemoglobin (CO or CO_2)
    e. Alters blood coagulation:e.g. warfarin, rodenticides, dicoumarol, snake venom etc.

Routes of Entry:

Ingestion: It is the most common route in animals. The toxicants get entry either through feed and fodder or the drinking water.

Inhalation: Only accidental, when the animals are forced to inhale gases like CO_2, CO or the volatile anaesthetics.

Cutaneous: Application of strong or neat solution or spray thereof to control the ticks, lice, fleas and mites, often lead to toxicoses e.g. Malathion, BHC etc.

Parentral: By mistake or in ignorance, certain chemical is used in lieu of other e.g. i/v administration of potassium iodide inplace of sodium iodide or administration of sodium nitrite in excess.

Bite: Snake bite.

Source of Poisoning:

Plants: They constitute the major source of poisoning in animal. Cereal plants, wild plants, weeds & grasses (wild or cultivated) are attributed to cause toxicity e.g. Oat hay, bajra (Nitrate/nitrite), Jwar, sorghum, linseed meal (cyanide) and bracken fern *(Pteris aquilina)* causes haematuria in cattle, thiamine deficiency in horses and bright blindness in sheep.

Toxic Spray:

Either on the plants or animals, spray of insecticides or pesticides, like chlorinated hydrocarbons, (aldrin, dieldrin), organo-phosphate compounds (Malathion/parathion etc) and arsernic and mercurial compounds.

Weedicides: Arsenic preparations and 2-4 D are commonly used for this purpose.

Rodenticides: Zinc phosphides, dicoumarol compounds and strychnine are used as rodenticides. The poisoned bait is often taken in by the dogs and cats leading to toxicosis.

Dips: Arsenical preparations are commonly used as dips for the control of ectoparasites. Chlorinated hydrocarbons and organo-phosphates are also used.

Other sources: Paints contain lead. Poisoning occurs in animals after licking or accidental intake through fodders. The other sources of lead are car batteries, plumber paints for leak proof and insulating tapes.

Laboratory Diagnostic Techniques:

Arsenic : Faeces, minced liver or urine may be analysed for arsenic detection.

In a clean beaker, put about 20g of faeces or minced material.

Add 100 ml dilute hydrochloric acid (1:4) and mix.

Place a bright copper coin or wire in it.

Boil gently under cover for 10-30 minutes.

Take out copper piece, wash and let it dry.

A dark or blackish deposit on the copper coin indicates presence of arsenic, mercury, silver or antimony. In the absence of these, copper remains bright. Further differentiation is made symptomatologically.

Lead: Either kidney cortex or liver is suitable for lead.

Put a small piece of kidney cortex (10x 5 m.m) in a small flask and add few drops of nitric acid.

Heat gently till dry.

Add few drops of water and only two drops of potassium iodide (10%).

Development of dark yellow colouration indicates positive for lead.

Cyanide: Rumen content, plant and feed materials or blood may be tested.

Prepare reagent solution containg sodium bicarbonate 5 g, picric acid 0.5g and distilled water to 100 ml (stable for 6 months in refrigerator).

Dip strips of filter paper (2" x 6") and dry in cool place. Prepare the picrate paper every week.

In a test tube, put the material to be tested and add few drops of water and chloroform.

Cork the test tube hanging the dried picrate paper. The paper should not touch the fluid in the tube.

Heat the tube gently till evaporation.

Wait for few minutes. If the colour of paper changes from yellow to brown or red, indicates positive for cyanide.

Simply the presence of free cyanide in rumen may be tested by putting few drops of rumen fluid on the picrate paper. Change of colour of paper from yellow to brown suggests positive for cyanide.

Nitrate/Nitrite: Rumen content, plant materials, blood, serum, urine and CSF are analysed.

Dissolve diphenylamine 1 g in 100 ml. concentrated sulfuric acid.

Place gently 8 drops, each of the above mixture and fluid material to be tested on clean glass slide. Allow to mix the two by slight tilting or blowing. Development of blue colour indicates positive for nitrate and/or nitrite.

Nitrite: Rumen content, plant extract/slices, blood, urine and CSF are used. The reagents are:

Solution A:

Dissove sulfanilic acid 1 g in 100 ml distilled water or 1g sulfanilamide in 100 ml 1.5 N hydrochloric acid (13.5 ml conc. HCl to 100 ml with distilled water).

Solution B:

Mix 20 mg of N-ethylene diamine dihydrochloride in 100 ml absolute alcohol.

On a clean glass slide place few drops of mixture (1:1) of solutions A&B.

Put suspected fluid material to be tested equally side by (8 drops each).

Allow to mix these two fluids and observe the colour.

Development of pink colouration speaks positive for nitrite.

carbon monoxide Poisoning: This qualitative test is applicable only when blood contains above 20% carbon monoxide. A negative blank and a positive control are to be run simultaneously.

Pyrotannic Acid Test:

Reagents: Dissolve 1 g pyrogallol and 1 g. tannic acid in 100 ml distilled water.

Procedure: In a test tube, dilute blood (1:10) with distilled water.

Add 10 ml pyrotannic acid solution to it, mix and allow 15 minutes.

Blood containing above 20% carbon monoxide, develops pink colouration. The degree depends on the amount present. Normal blood develops grey-brown colour.

Organophosphate Insecticides(OPI):

There is no suitable field test for the qualitative detection of OPI. However, colorimetric method for the determination of cholinestrase is avilable. The activity/level of cholinestrase decreases in poisoned animals. Normal buffalo plasma cholinestrase activity ranges from 180-254 nm/min per ml. For determination, text book on analytical chemistry should be consulted.

Phenothiazine: Toxicosis due to phenothiazine has been observed in horses, when used as dewormer. Though the available test is not very specific but can be applied on urine and compared with control test.

Reagents:

1. Ferric chloride (5%) w/v
2. Perchloric acid (20%) v/v
3. Nitric acid (50%) v/v
4. FPN reagent-contains 5 ml Ferric chloride solution, 45 ml. per chloric acid solution and 50 ml nitric acid solution.

Method:

Mix equal amount of urine and FPN (1 ml each) in a test tube, mix and allow for 10 seconds. Different shades of pink colour are observed depending on the amount of phenothiazine in urine.

23
NECROPSY (POST-MORTEM) TECHNIQUES

As set of equipments is required for routine post-mortem examination including rubber gloves, apron and gum boots. Wherever, zoonotic diseases are suspected (e.g. tuberculosis, glander, rabies etc), use of rubber gloves is essential. In addition to the metallic tools (Plate), formalin (5%), glass jars, thermos flask, spirit lamps, slides, platinum loops, thread, soap and antiseptics must be ready.

For case of litigation, the recording must be complete from all possible angles, which includes:

1. Owner's name and complete address.
2. Place, date and time of post-mortem conduction.
3. Description of animal: Species, sex, age and identification number.
4. Date and time of death.
5. External appearance of the carcass e.g. rigors, putrefaction, tympany, skin lesions etc.
6. Post-mortem finding (abnormality)
7. Material sent for laboratory finding.
8. Probable cause of death.

Technique

Before opening the carcass, it must be thoroughly inspected. Inspection of surrounding, electric wires, insecticides, paint materials and feeds often helps to solve the problem. In cattle, buffaloes, sheep and pigs, the presence of anthrax must be ruled out before *taking knife in hand.*

The carcass is held on its back. The ruminants may be held on left recumbency. A longitudinal incision on the skin beginning from intermandibular space to the pelvic brim is made. The skin is reflected on both the sides. Both upper legs are removed preferably and in females, the mammary gland should be seen for its consistency.

The abdominal cavity is opened by putting incision from xiphoid cartilage to pelvis. Transverse incision is made on both the flank extending to lumber region. The abdominal cavity is inspected and nature of fluid is recorded. Xiphoid cartilage is cut through the cotochondral junction and the ribs are cut through vertebral coloumn exposing the thoracic cavity. Examine for the presence of fluid etc.

Now remove the abdominal organs and record systematically. Ligate rectum duodenum and oesophagus. For examination, incise the organ between ligatures. The peritoneal cavity should be viewed for inflammation. The rumen, reticulum, omasum and the abomasum in ruminants are incised sequentially and its content, change (s) and presence of parasites are to be noted. The intestinal loops are looked for intussusception, strangulation or volvulus and whole length is examined for its content and changes by incising. The lymph nodes and the diaphragm are examined. The liver is incised into pieces. Its appearance, consistency, and biliary system are recorded. Similarly, the kidney, adrenal gland and spleen are examined. All organs or reproductive and urinary systems of both the sexes are examined thoroughly.

Remove tongue, trachea, lungs and heart, and inspect these alongwith associated lymph nodes. Presence of cysts or nodules should be recorded. If needed, impression smears are prepared from cut surface of lungs and other organs.

For examination of the brain, the skull is opened while for spinal cord, the transverse laminae and spinus processes are cut, better starting from lumber region. If external examination fails to provide any clue about the disease, submission of materials for further analysis and histological/histochemical examination, is essential.

Despatch of Material for Investigation:

Leak proof and sterilized containers are required for the despatch of materials. For microbial investigation and chemical analysis, the preservatives are not used. The pieces of organ must be fixed in formalin (5-10%) for histomorphological examination. Submission of materials depends on the purposes for which they are to be examined.

Purposes	Organ of choice
Toxicosis	Rumen content, piece of intestine (tied), liver, kidney, hair.
Microbial	Long bone (metacarpal, metatarsal, humerus or radius and ulna).
Histopathological	Any organ e.g. liver, brain, spleen, etc.
Histochemisty	Any organ e.g. muscle, brain, liver, kidney, nerve etc. (Frozen)

During summer, unpreserved specimen must be sent in container packed in ice crystals. The container with specimen be packed in comfortable wooden case packed with saw dust, which absorbs fluid if there is leakage. The outer face of the pack is labelled with full address of the sender and the laboratory, the nature of specimen and the analysis required. A covering letter is must, elaborating the above matters. The container should be sent either by train or in person.

APPENDIX —A

Miscellaneous Clinical and Surgical Tools:

A number of clinical as well as surgical tools did not appear in the text. Here monographic appearances of some of the tools have been provided for the acquaintence of the readers. At present a good number of automated analytical equipments are in use in most of the diagnostic and clinical laboratories. These equipments take not only the least time and samples (blood, serum, C.S.F. etc) for the analysis but also the accuracy is unequivocal. These automated equipments are nationally or internationally manufactured. Foreign make analysers are readily marketed by various authorised dealers of the country. Below are the addresses of some of the suppliers of standard clinical and surgical equipments, chemicals, glasswares, wooden equipments and laboratory analytical equipments equipping the clinical diagnostic laboratory in the best and latest possible manners.

Items	Supliers
1. **Clinical and Surgical Equipments**	(i) Rajdhani Surgical Co, 1701, Bhagirath Palace, Opp. Bhagirath Hotel, Chandni Chowk-N. Delhi-110006.
	(ii) IDPL Surgical Instruments) N.13 South Extension Part-I, New Delhi-110049.
	(iii) RMT International, Post Box-52, Main Road Ranchi-834001 (India), Tel 21525, 24123.
	(iv) Stridewel International, GL-9, Ansal Bhawan Kasturba Gandhi Marg, New Delhi-110001. Tel. 3318378, 3313578.
2. **Diagnostic Laboratory Equipments** (Atomic absorption spectrophotometer, gas analysers, spectro-photometer, PH meter etc).	(i) Rachho Scientifiques, 59, Sant Nagar, East of Kailash, New Delhi-110065. Tel: 6415543
All sorts of laboratory equipments	(ii) Systronics, Grover Mansion, 3/17 A Asaf Ali Road, New Delhi-2. Tel: 277219.

Plate I

Bull Leader. with remote control release operated by a cord,

Restraining and **Dressing Clip** for **Cattle**

Bull Nose Rings stainless

Bull Holder with thumb

Cattle nose Twitch

Bull Nose Rings

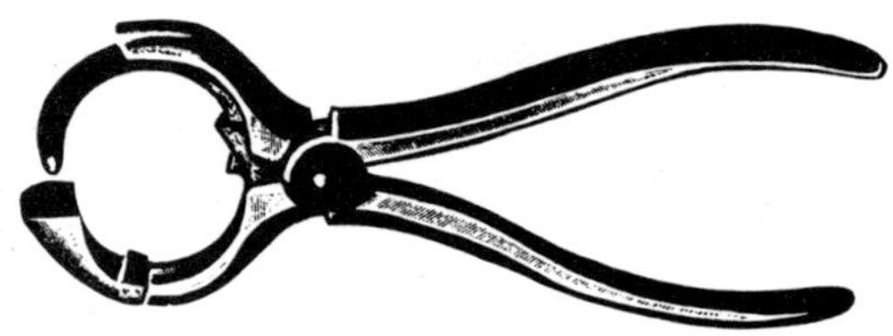

Forceps for applying **Bull Rings**

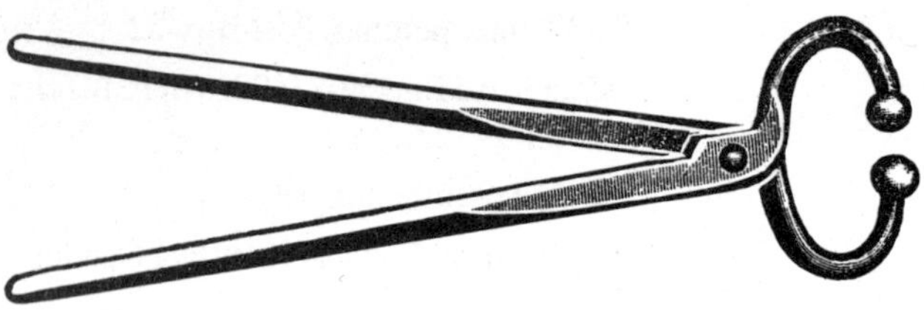

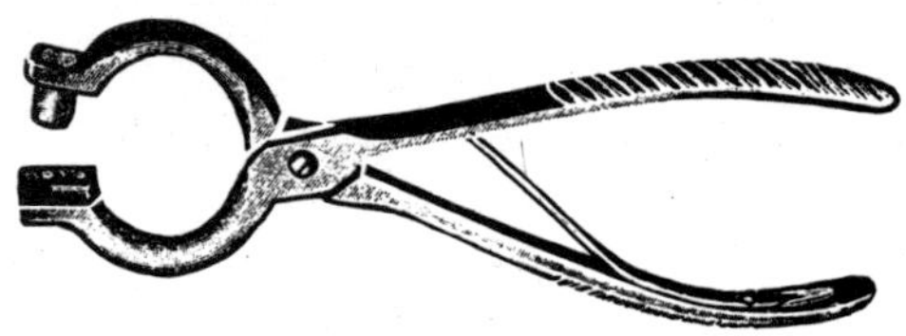

Bull Nose Punch. with spring

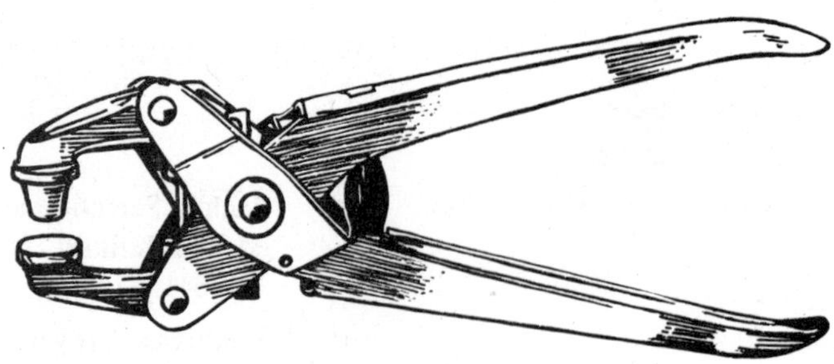

Bullnose Punch,

Plate II

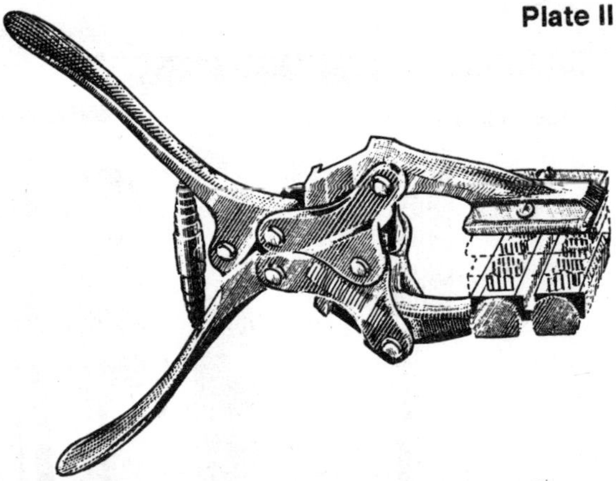

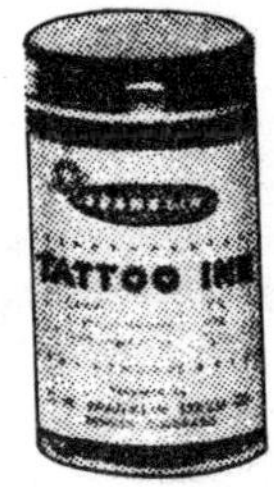

Parralled Action Tattooing Forceps, A built of highgrade steel. Joints firmly rivetted Return spring is of stout well-tempered steel ribbon. Made with 3,4,5 or 6 spaces in one row, or with 6,8,10 or 12 spaces in two rows of 3,4,5 or 6.

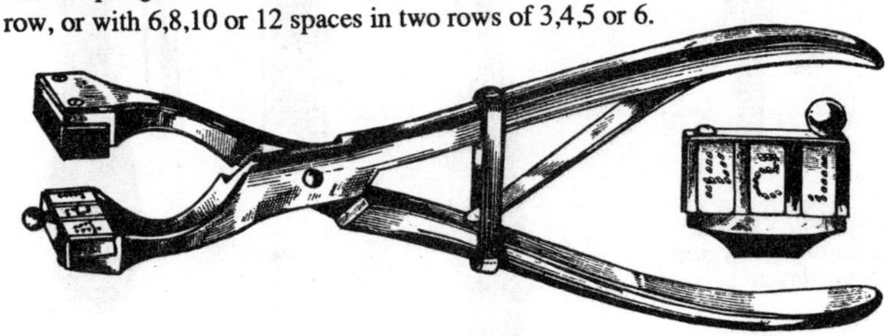

Tattooing Forceps,

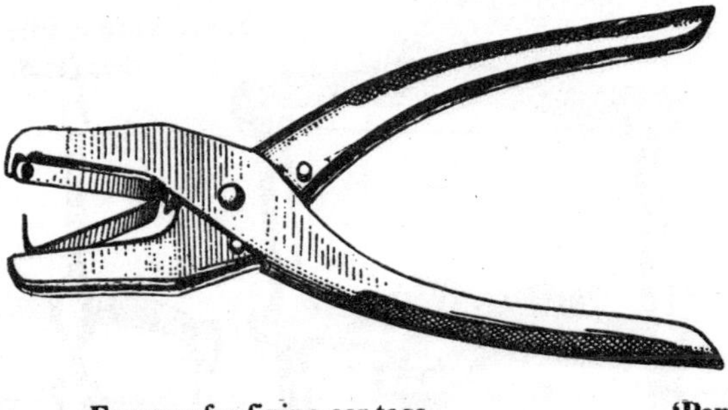

Forceps for fixing ear tags.

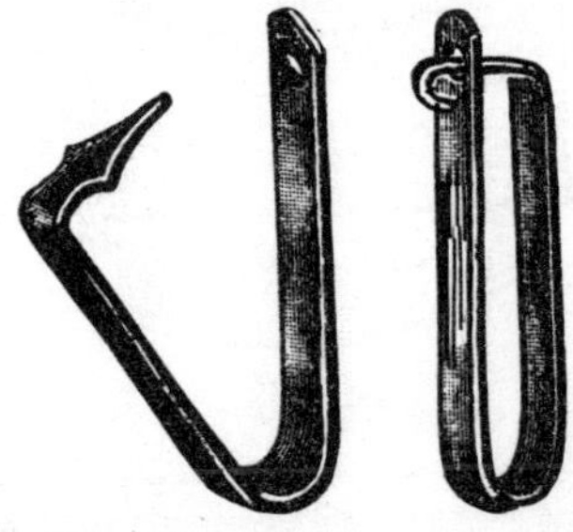

'Perfect' Aluminium Ear Tags, for cattle, Hogs and sheep. The tag is applied in one operation and stays put.

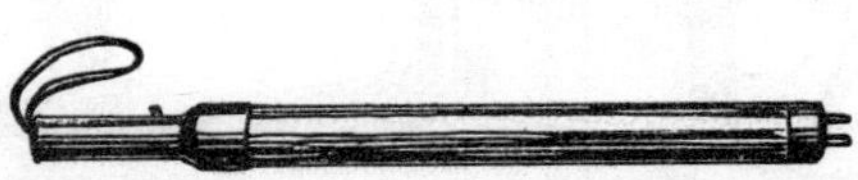

Cattle, Pig and **Sheep** Goad, with 4 ordinary battery cells. Complete **with safety** switch and wrist loop.

Plate III

Tooth Chisel with guard.

Dental Wedge, assorted
Dental Probe.

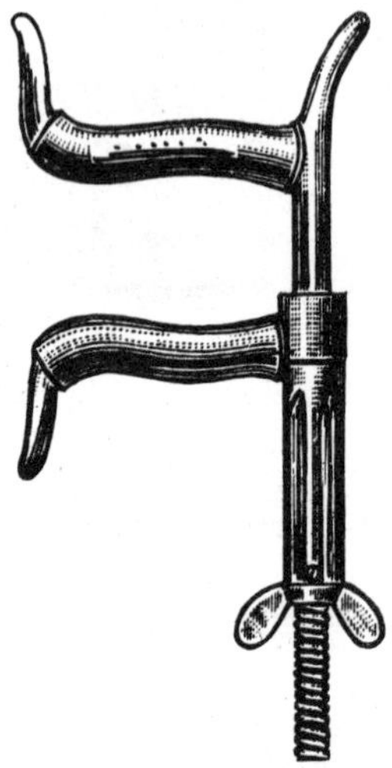

Mouth Gag, Varnell's with regulating screw and rubber cover jaws.

Tooth Rasp
Danish pattern long shaft and hinged movable plate.

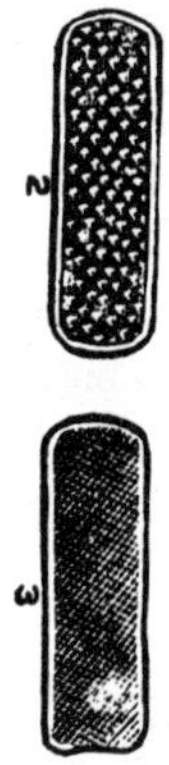

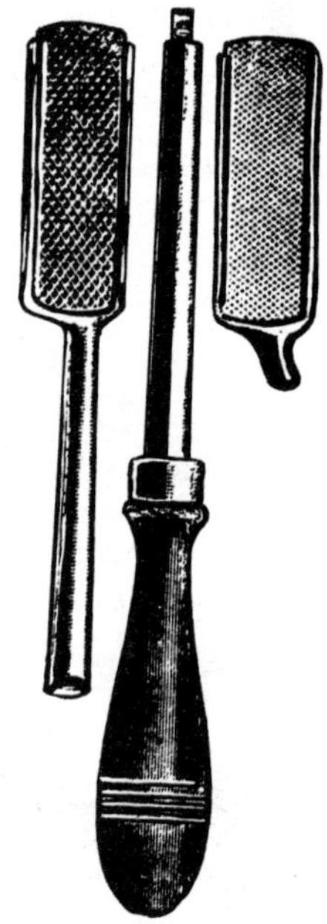

Tooth Rasp with guard-one handle and 2 heads (one straight and the other angular) fitted with rasp and file plates.
Spare Rasp & File Plates.

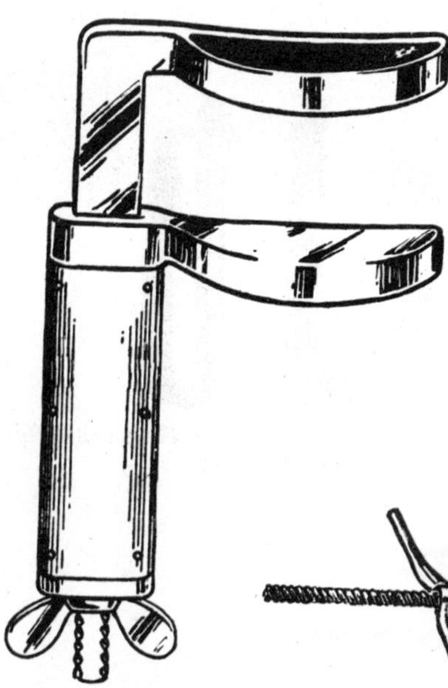

Hitching's Horse Gag.

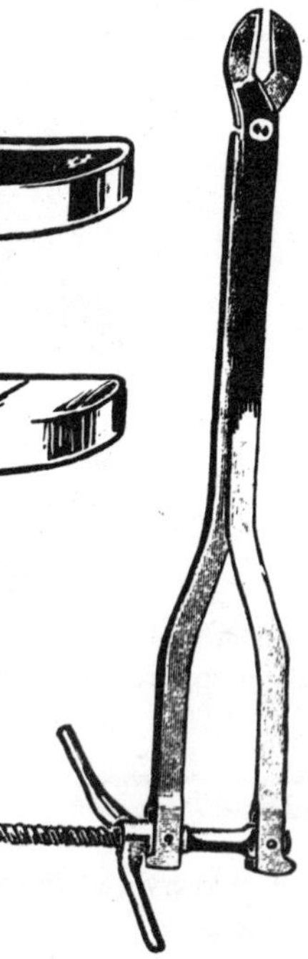

Molar Tooth Cutter

Butter's Mouth Gag.

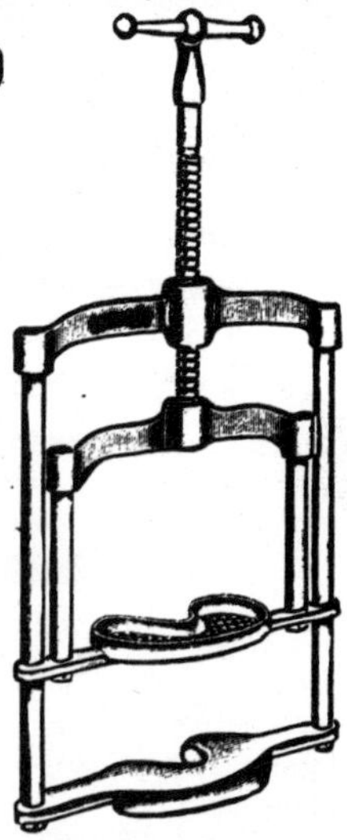

Gunther's Mouth Gag.

Plate IV

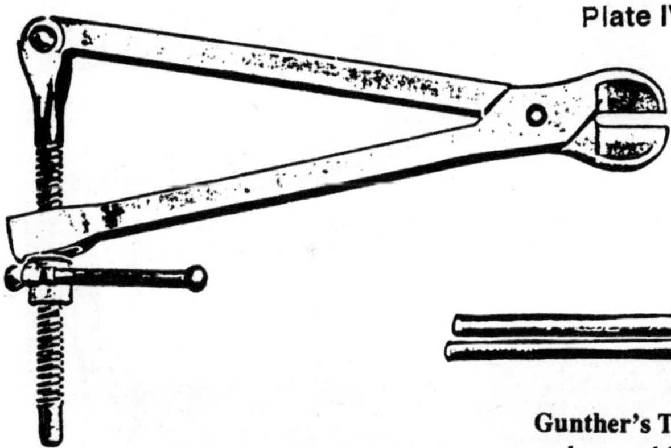

Gunther's Tooth Forceps, $17^{1}/_{2}$ in. long for lower molars and $20^{1}/_{2}$ in long for upper molars.

Thompson's Heavy Tooth Shears with Duplex screw clamp.

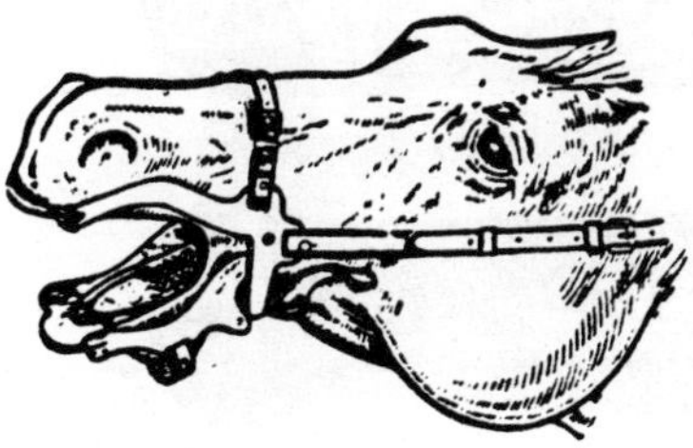

Mouth Gag McPherson's Allow for a large opening without any obstruction, for examination and dental work, and is fitted with 2 sets of dental plates. One set, covered with rubber cushions is used when working on the incisors. The semi-lunar cup shaped plates fit on the incisor teeth and are used when working on the molars. Fitted with leather straps.

Probang
Horse, Whalebone

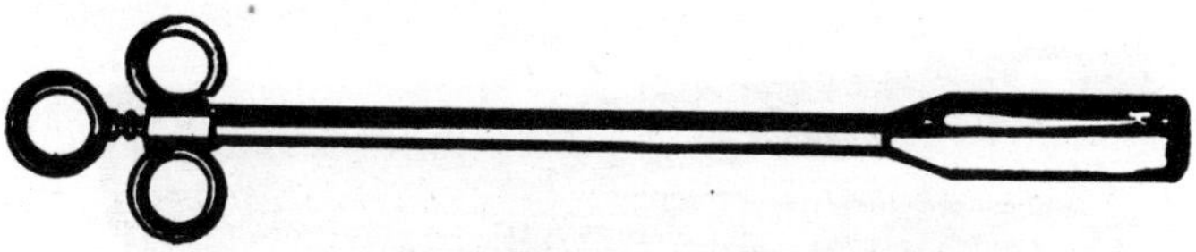

Bailing Gun for horses, with spring.

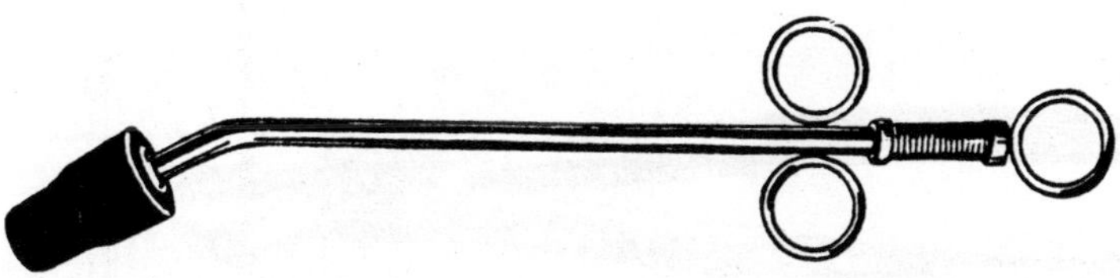

Fook's Balling Gun with rubber covered mouth piece.

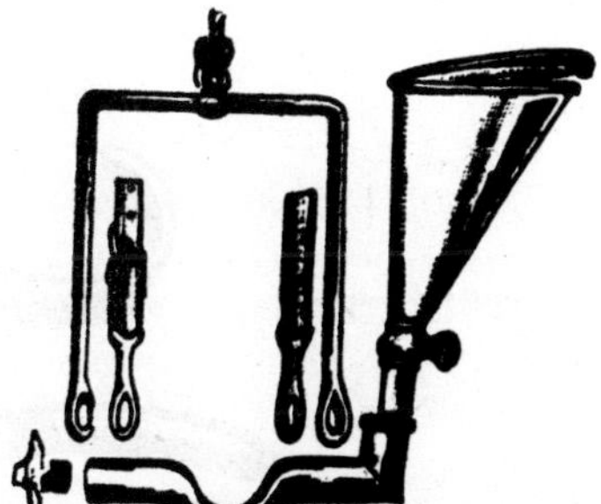

Drenching Bit for Horses, leather straps.

Drenching Bottle, all-metal, Pattern.

Drenching Bottle, leather.

Balling Gun Flexible made of spiral steel wire.

Plate V

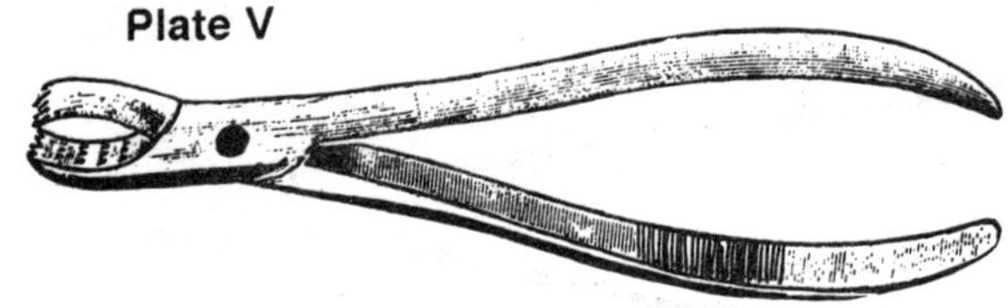

Pritchard's Tooth Forceps for Incisors.

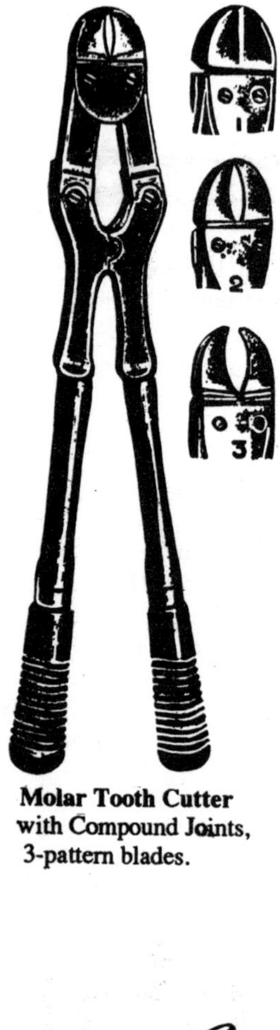

Molar Tooth Cutter
with Compound Joints,
3-pattern blades.

Molar Tooth Extractor with handles.

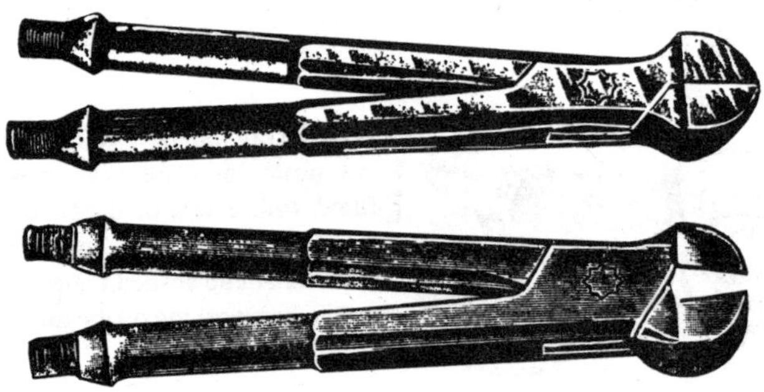

Molar Tooth Cutters, 3 pattern blades.

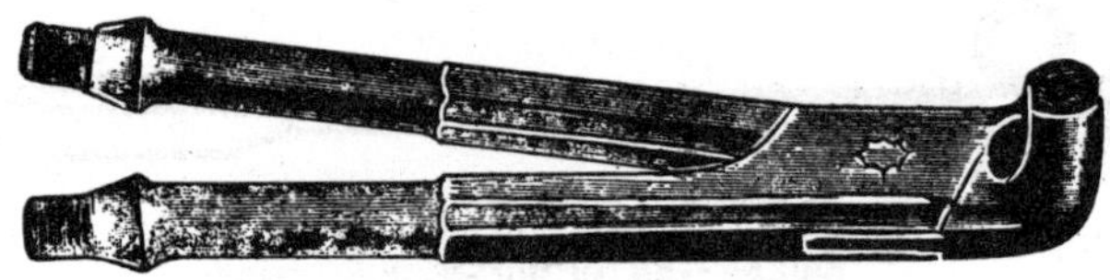

Root extractor with handles.

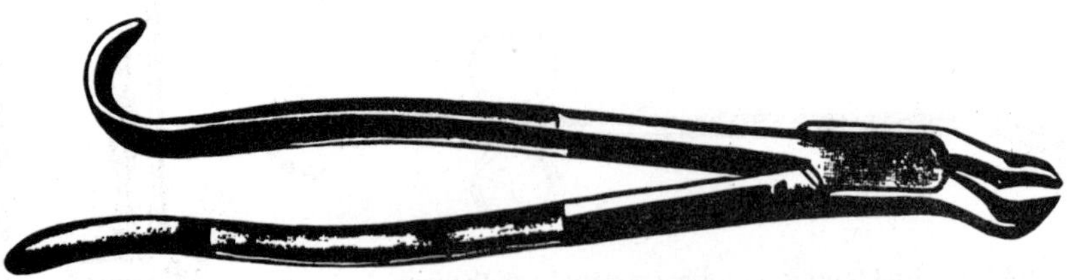

Horse Tooth Forceps for wolf teeth.

Tooth Chisel,
English pattern.

Plate VI

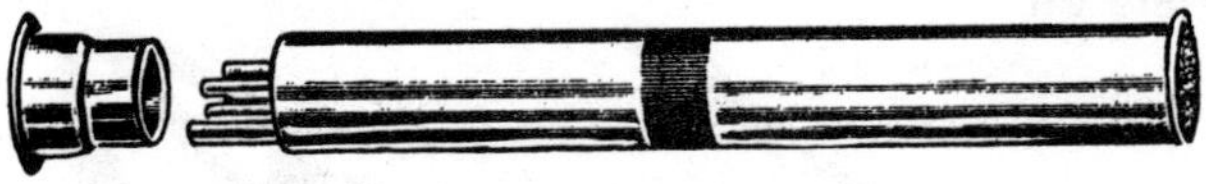

Metal Container for carrying inseminating (catheter)

Vaginascope, Perex with light attachment for large and small animals

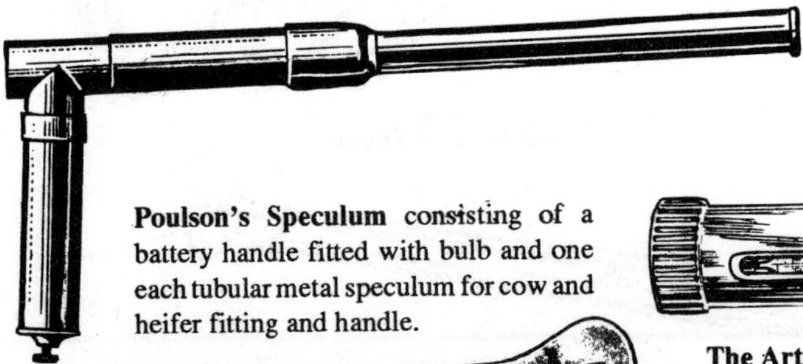

Poulson's Speculum consisting of a battery handle fitted with bulb and one each tubular metal speculum for cow and heifer fitting and handle.

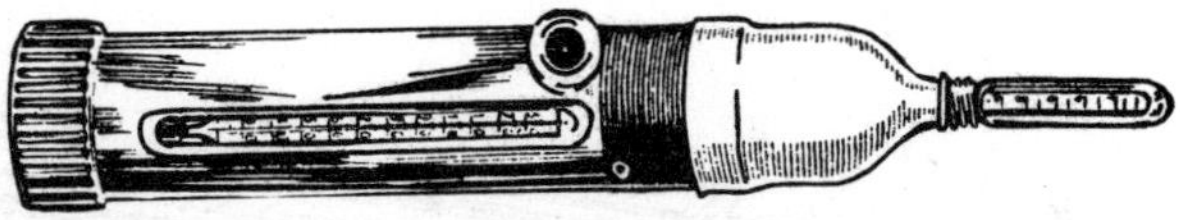

The Artificial Vagina, **Model "Kieler Scheide"**

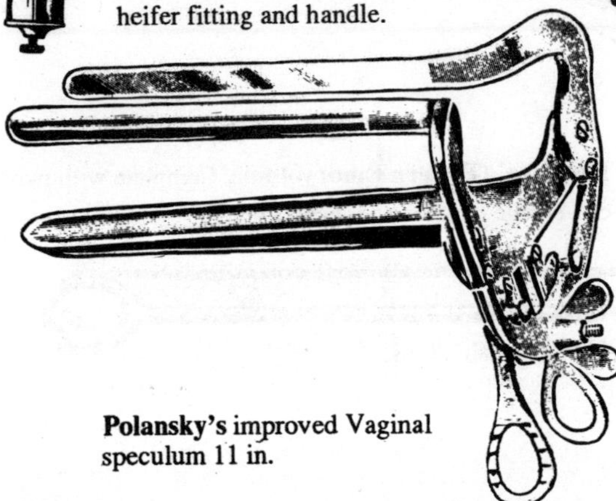

Polansky's improved Vaginal speculum 11 in.

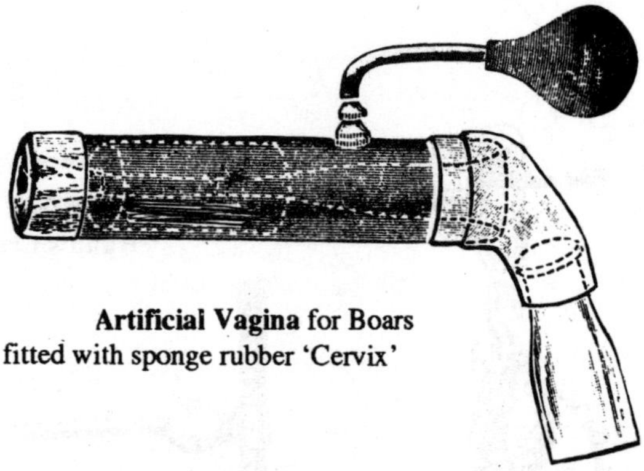

Artificial Vagina for Boars fitted with sponge rubber 'Cervix'

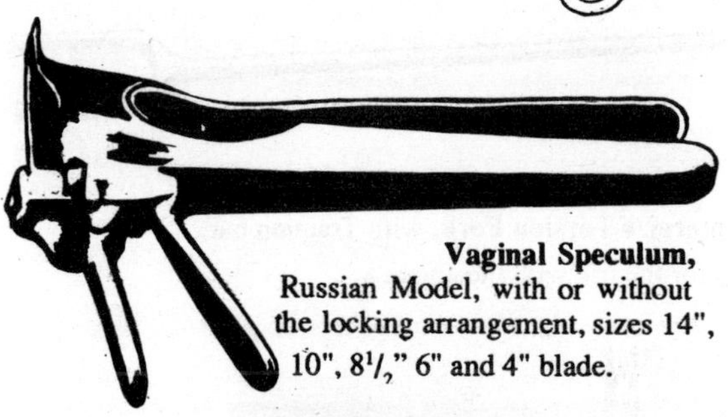

Vaginal Speculum, Russian Model, with or without the locking arrangement, sizes 14", 10", 8½," 6" and 4" blade.

Rubber Junction, to take inseminating Pipette and syringe.

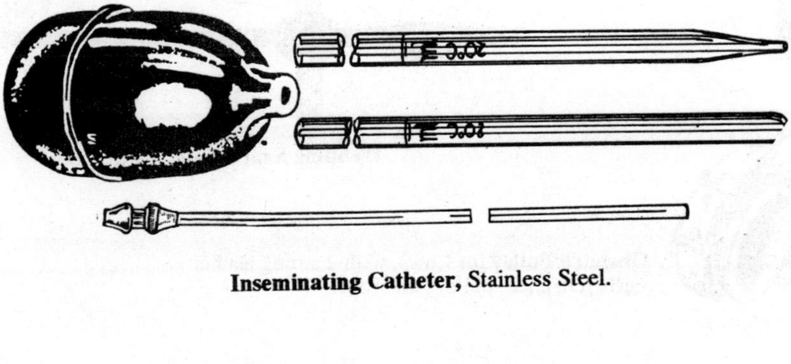

Inseminating Catheter, Stainless Steel.

Plate VII

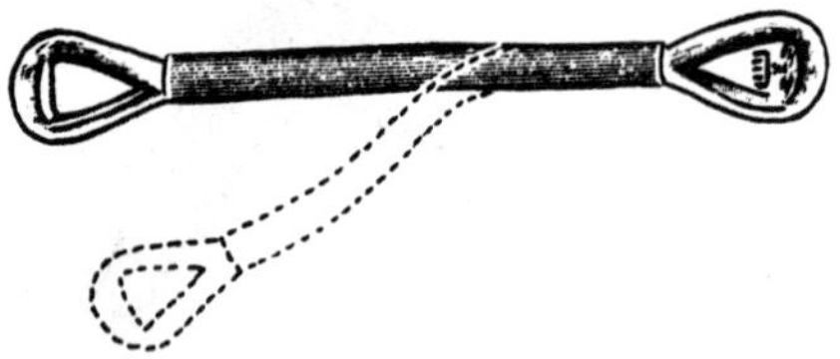

Calving Rope Carrier,

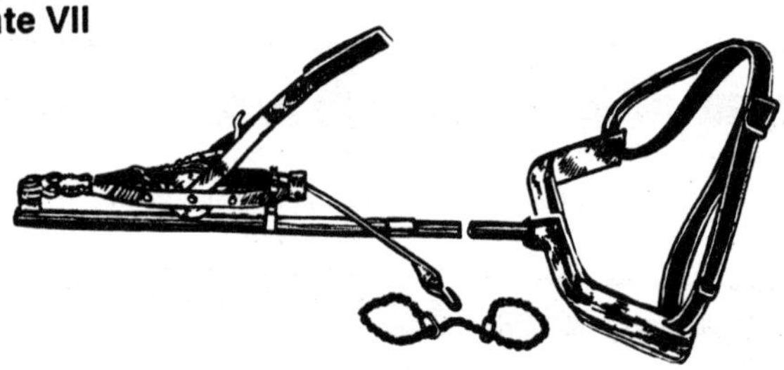

'Franklin' Calf Puller

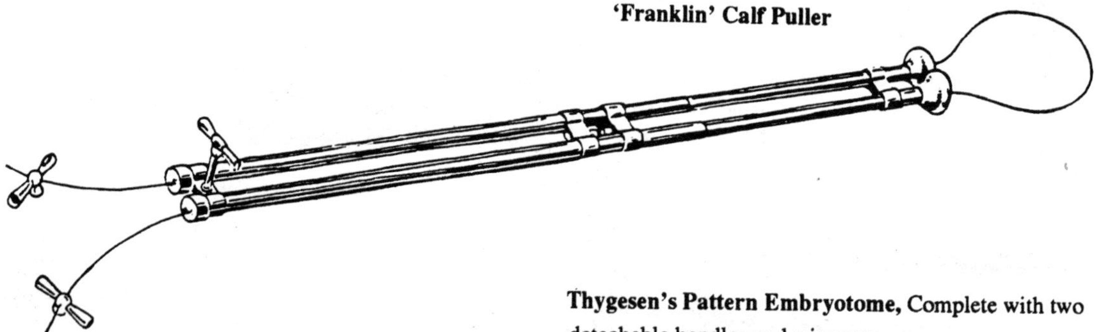

Thygesen's Pattern Embryotome, Complete with two detachable handles and wire saw.

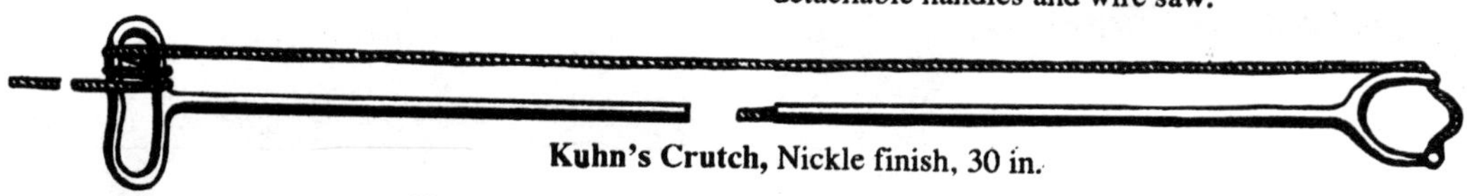

Kuhn's Crutch, Nickle finish, 30 in.

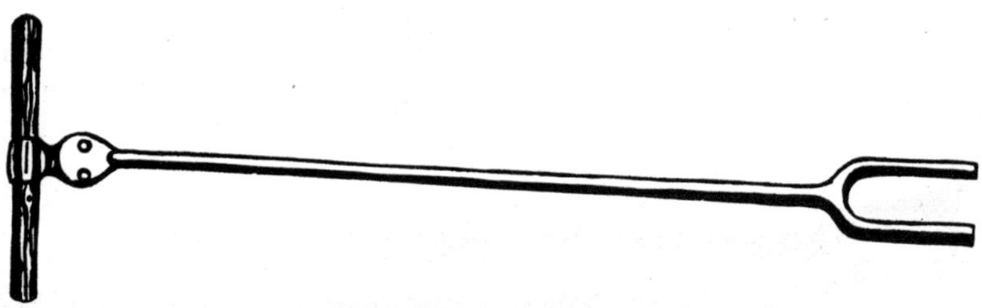

Cammerer's Torsion Fork, with Traction bar.
Cuffs for the use with the above.

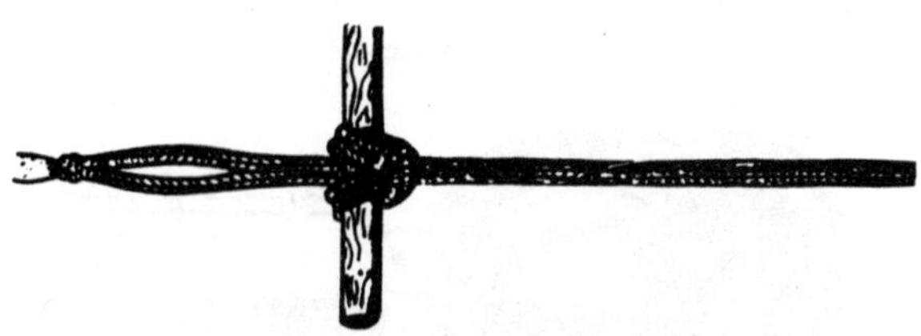

Webbing Snare, with Traction Bar.

ObstetricPulley for Cows, with 2 strong leather cuffs felt-lined, pulleys and rope.

Plate VIII

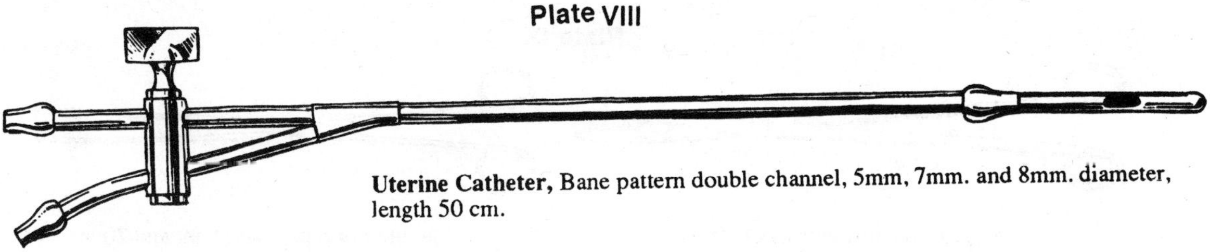

Uterine Catheter, Bane pattern double channel, 5mm, 7mm. and 8mm. diameter, length 50 cm.

Uterine Catheter, Folmer-Nielsen, 4mm. 5mm and 7mm. diameter, length 42 cm.

Uterine Catheter, Folmer-Nielsen, 4 mm and 5 mm. diameter, length 46 cm.

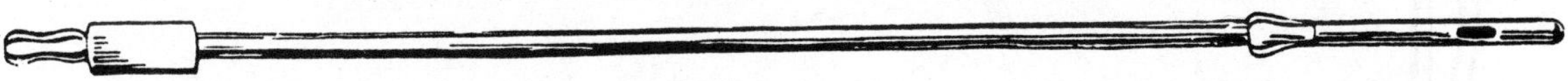

Uterine Catheter, Hagelberg pattern with cervix stop, 5mm. 7mm and 8mm. diameter, length 50 cm.

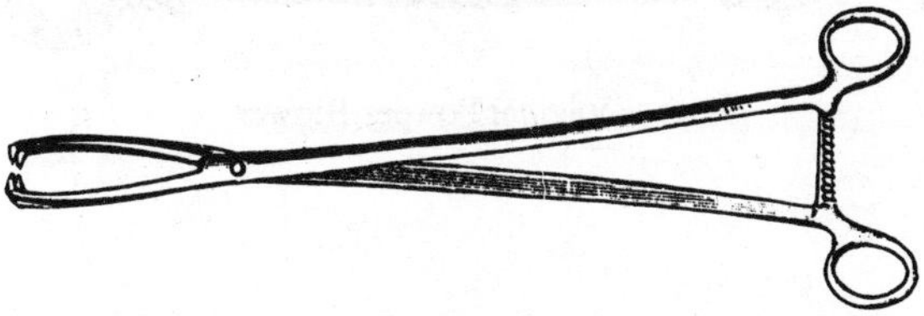

Andrews Uterine Catheter especially useful when uterus is retracted.
Smith Uterine Catheter - Return how.

Vulsellum Forceps, Albrechtsen's 2x2 prongs, 36 cm.. 42 and 46 cm. long
Vulsellum forceps, light pattern, 2 x 2 prongs, prongs
curved sideways, 24 cm. long.

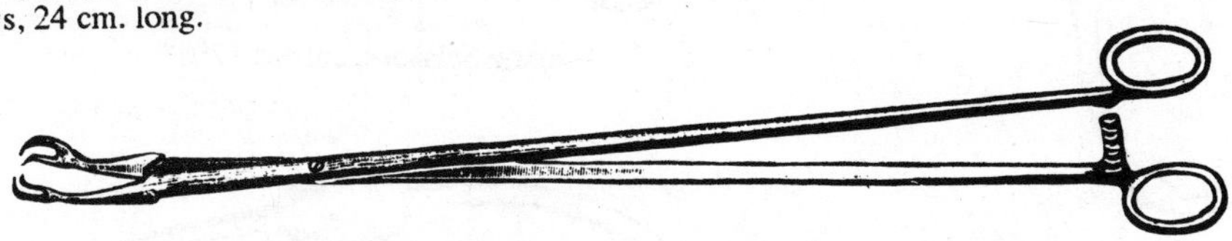

Uterine Vulsellum Forceps, Modification Of Neilsen's 2 x 2 teeth.

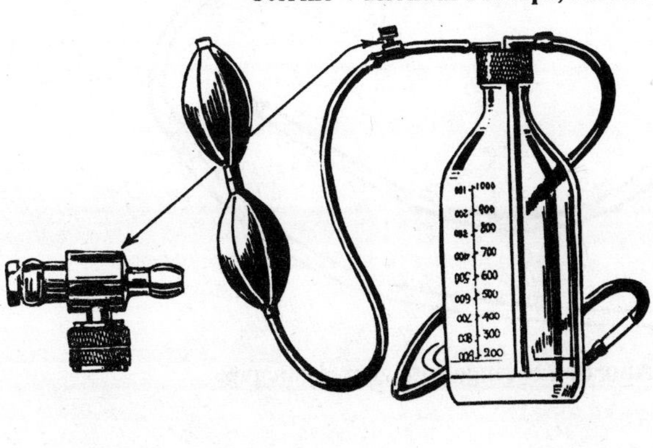

Obel Apparatus, for injection of Medicaments.

Plate IX

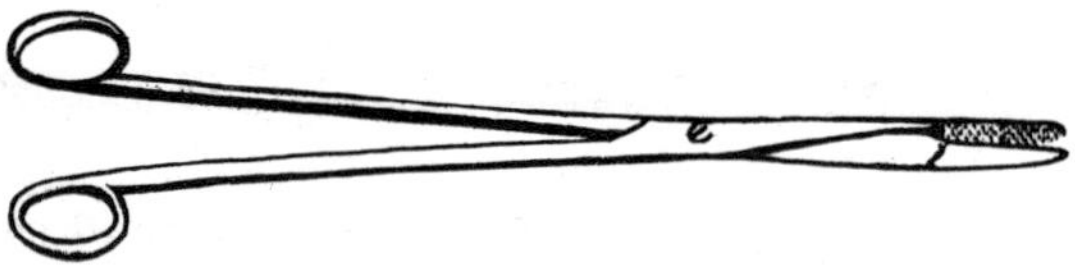

Polypus Forceps, with catch, 20 in.

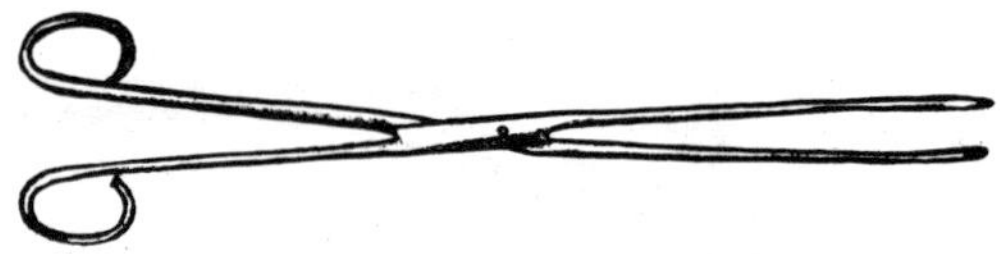

Sponge Forceps, size 15 in. and 20 in.

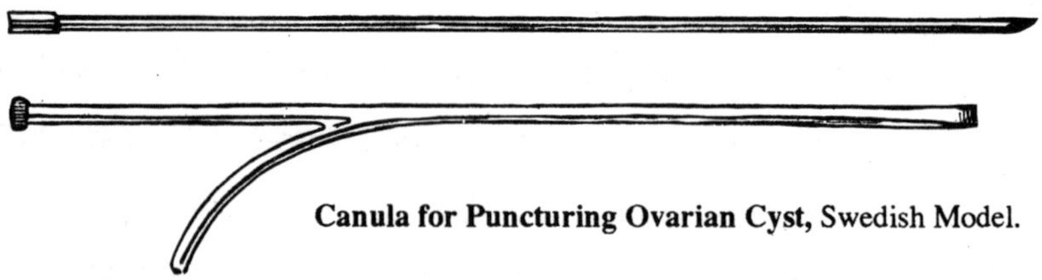

Canula for Puncturing Ovarian Cyst, Swedish Model.

Ovarian Cyst Needle, Day's

Vaginal Powder Blower.

Uterine Syringe for spraying and douching the vaginal passage and mouth of womb.

Uterine Scissors, curved $12\frac{1}{2}$"

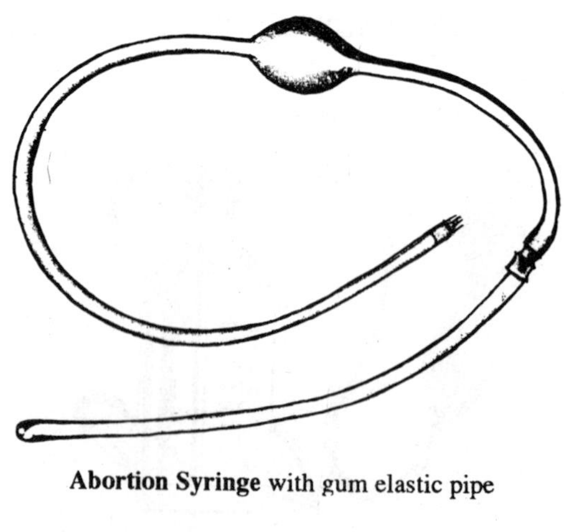

Abortion Syringe with gum elastic pipe

Plate X

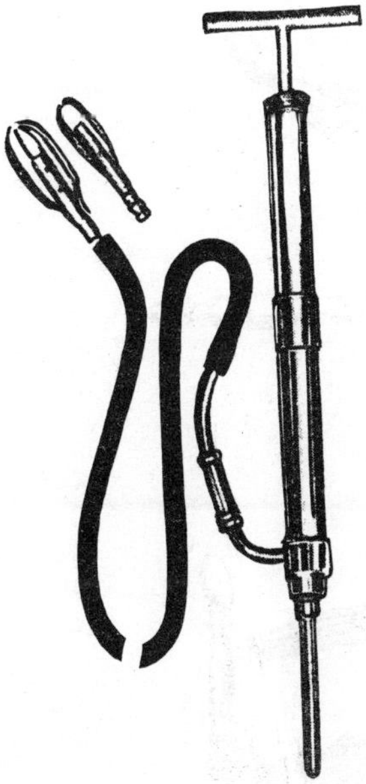

Velmelage's uterine pump,

Rudolf's Vaginal Perforator to cut the vagina when spaying mares.

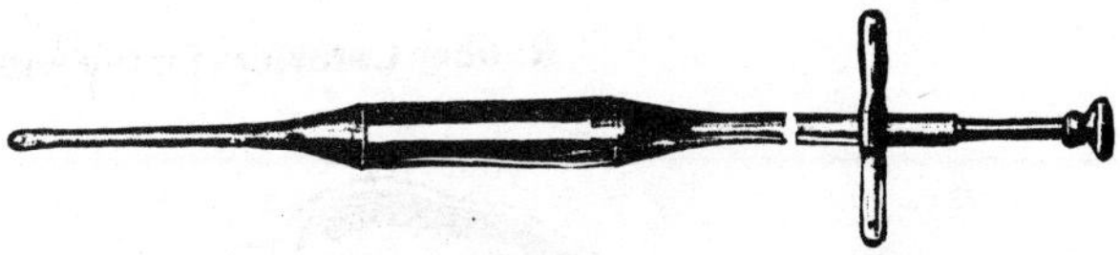

Hell's Uterine Ointment Syringe.

Spaying Hook Knife.

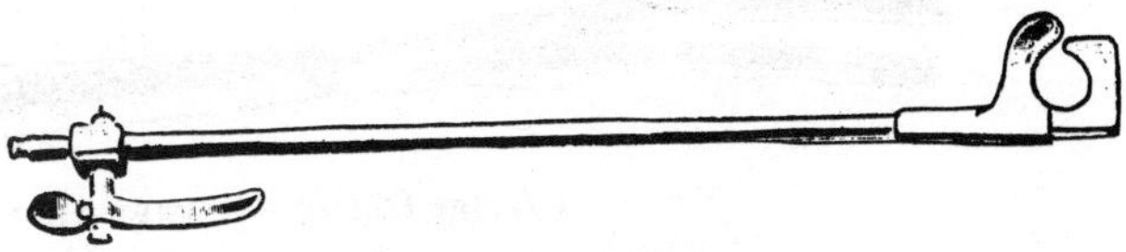

Richter's Ovariectome.

The instrument facilitates in a very short time, a safe grip on the oviduct, so that complete haemostasis is ensured.

Alton Cow Spaying Emasculator 18 in. long with sliding blade, especially useful for spaying older animals.

Speculum, All-glass, Electric attachment

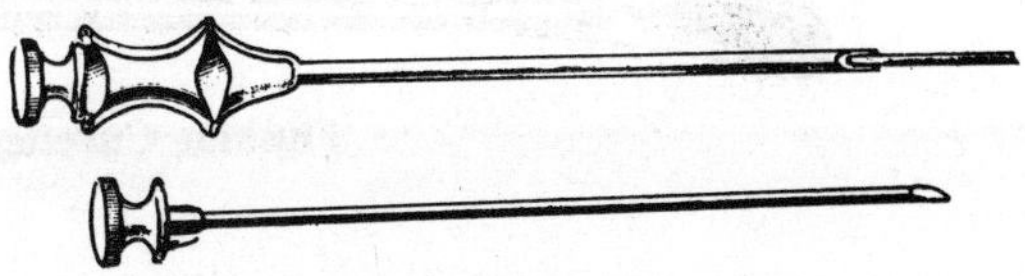

Silverman's Uterine Biopsy, adult size.

Uterine Biopsy catheter.

Plate XI

Douching Catheter, Albrechtsen's, double channel.

Mandrin for Catheters, Albrechtsen's.

Rubber Catheters for use with the above.

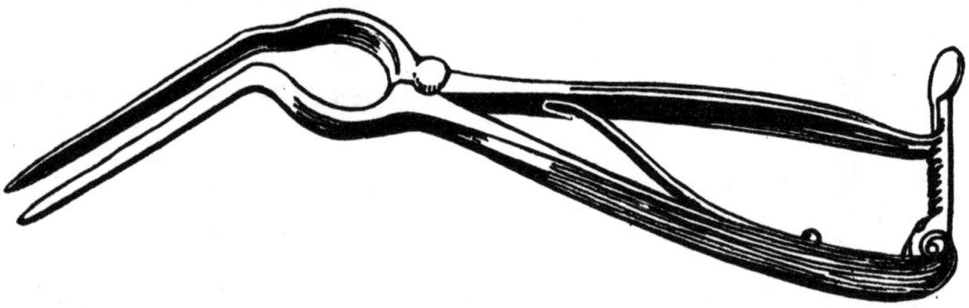

Cervix Dilator, Albrechtsen's.

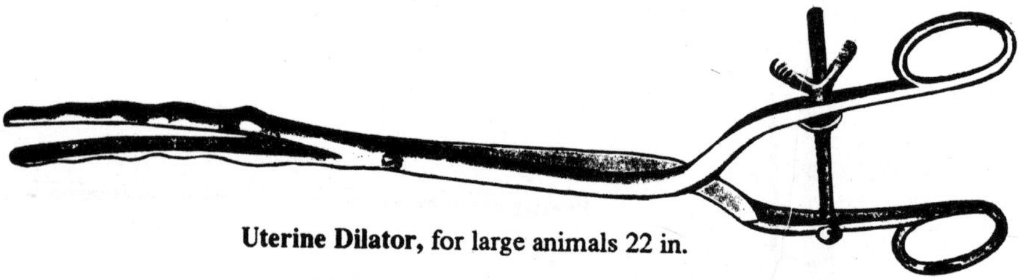

Uterine Dilator, for large animals 22 in.

Bougie, for dilating the os of mares.

Flushing Curette, 17 in. long.

Trocar & Canula, 18 in. for occlusion of the os cases.

Plate XII

Wire Handle ball-formed.

Embryotomy Knife,

Mose Embryotome

Embryotomy Knife,
sikle e shaped with ring

Embryotomy Knife, with sliding blade

Embryotomy Knife, Cowan's, with single double finger ring.

Embryotomy Knife, Stalfors pattern

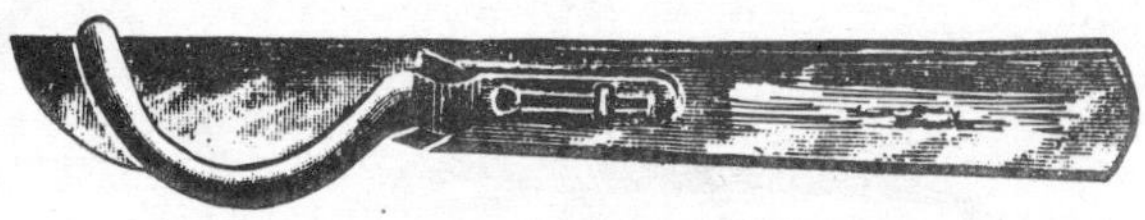

Embryotomy Knife Collins, with guarded blade.

Keller's semi-sharp spatula

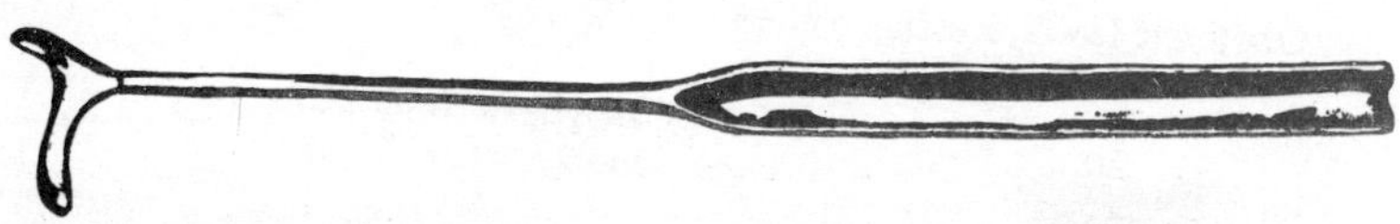

Embryotomy Knife, Cole's

Plate XIII

Obstetric Hook Harris for dead foetus.

Obermayer's Hook

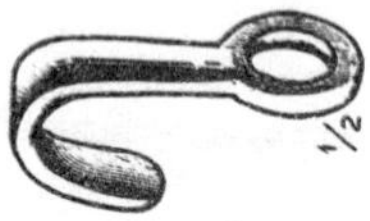

Obstetric Hook, Freyberger's for living foetus

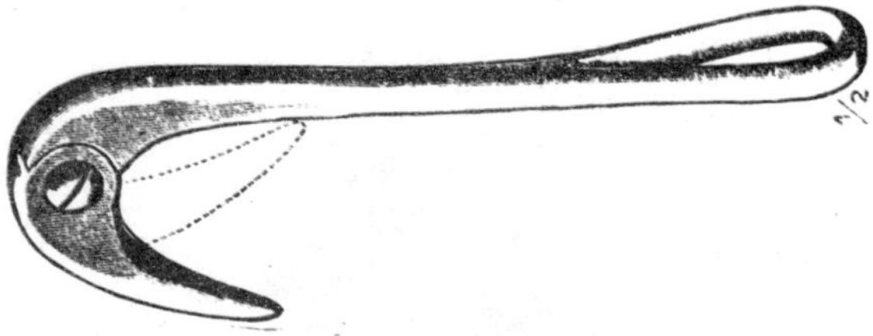

Obstetrical Hook, with joined and concealed spring, Sharp or Blunt.

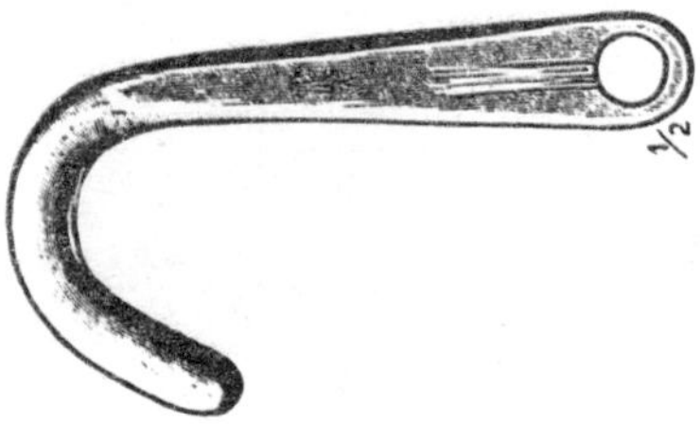

Obstetric Hook, Harms pattern,

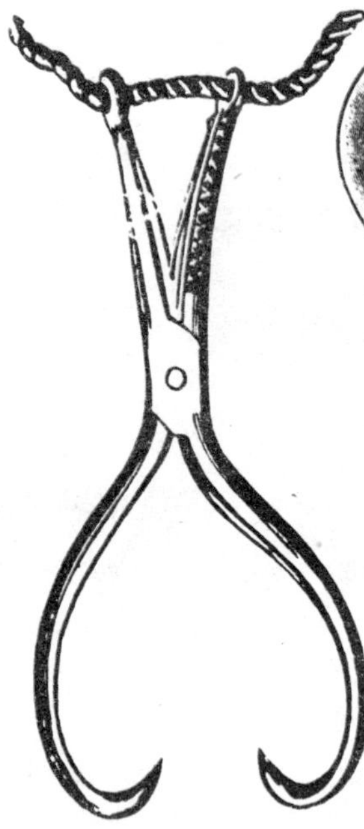

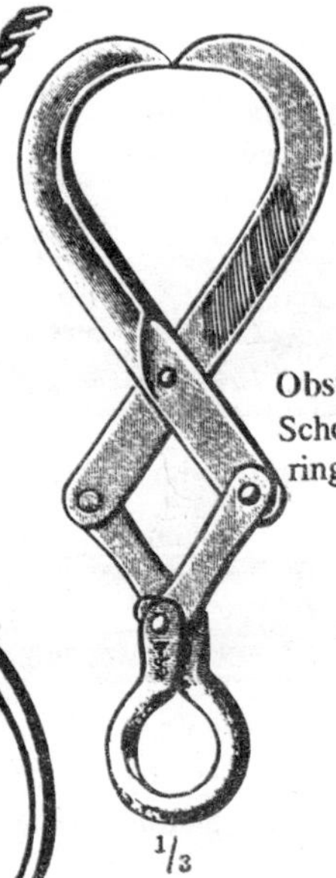

Obstetrical Hook. Krey-Schottler's, with movable ring, Sharp

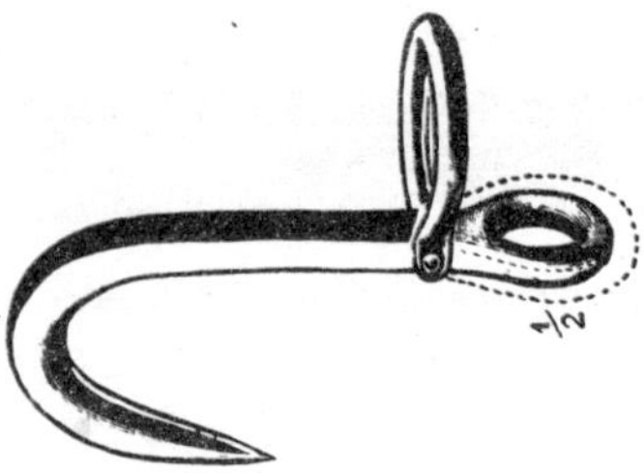

Obstetric Hook, Russian pattern

Obstetric Hook, Robert's double, sharp

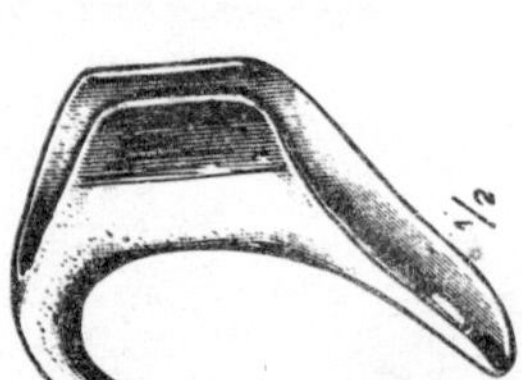

Obstetric Hook, for fixing to index

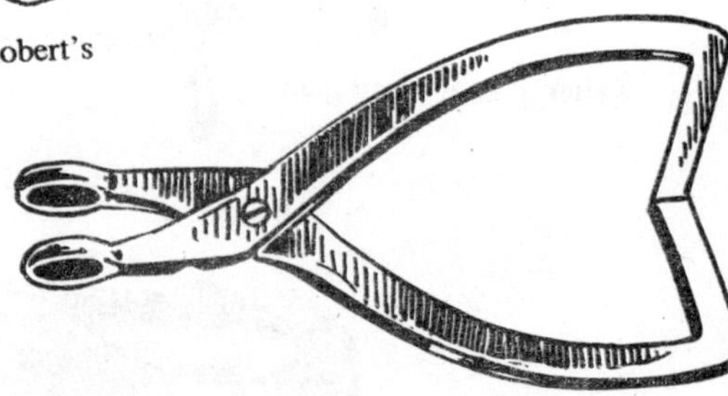

Obstetric Hook, Brante pattern

Plate XIV

Milk Siphon, self-retaining and adjustable, 2 sizes.

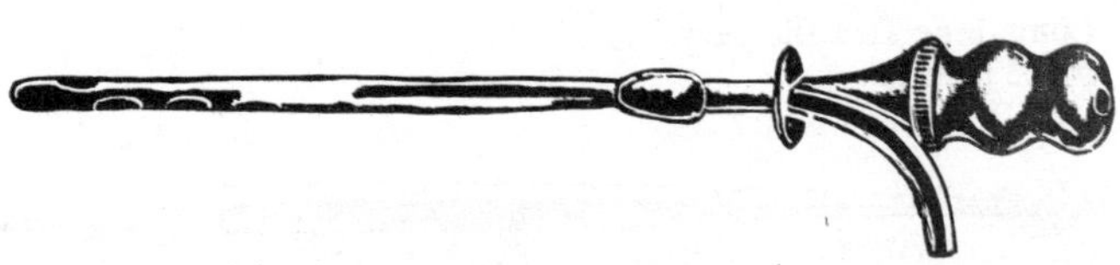

Garget Tube, double channel, for washing out the udder. Supplied with Higginson's syringe.

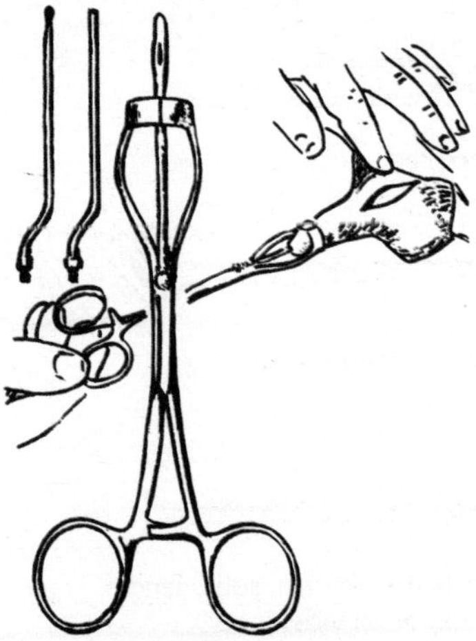

Teat Holding forceps, Fogelin pattern.

Udder Injection Tube, rounded end type

Milk Siphon, self-retaining with shield

Milk Fever Tube with valve and mount for rubber tubing for use with the Milk fever Outfit.

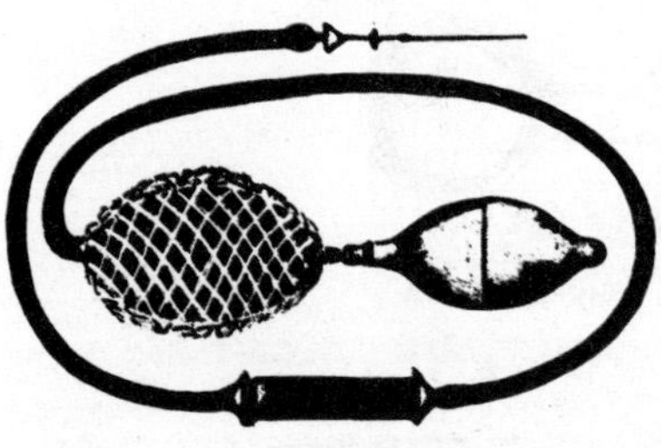

Milk Fever Outfit with double bellows, wool box and milk fever tube with valve.

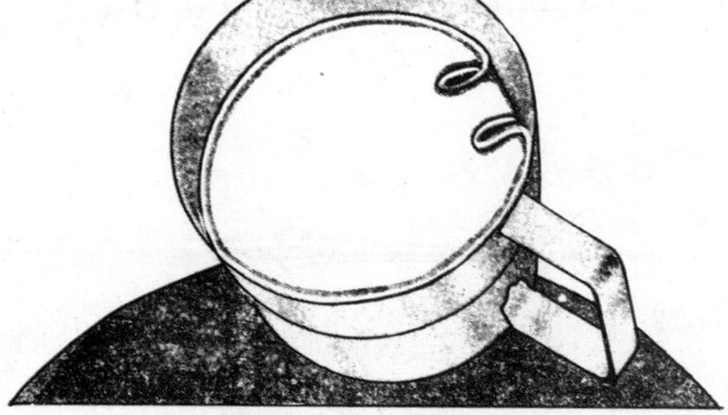

Milk Strip Cup, facilitates easy and rapid inspection of milk

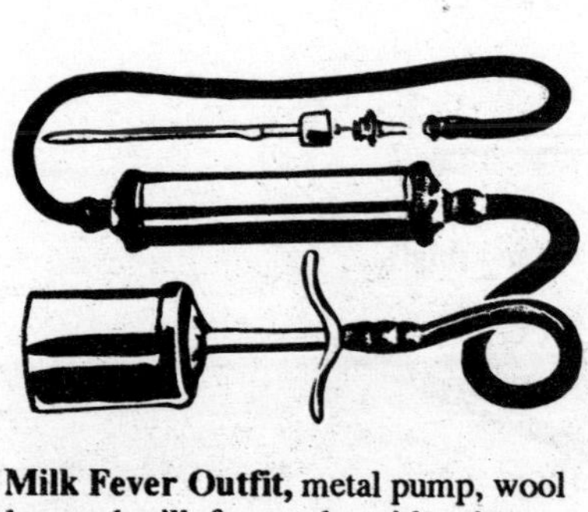

Milk Fever Outfit, metal pump, wool box and milk fever tube with valve.

Plate XV

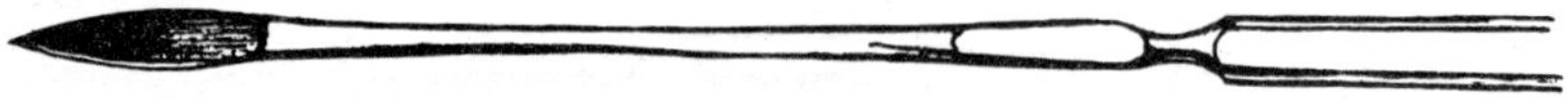

Long, Fine Teat Bistoury, 8 in. sharp pointed

Long, Fine Test Bistoury, probe pointed.

Hug's Teat lancet

Teat Knife, McLean's, for severing the sphincter muscle of the teat canal.

Teat Knife, Triffin, solid handle, with hole to wrist loop

Teat Slitter with concealed blade,

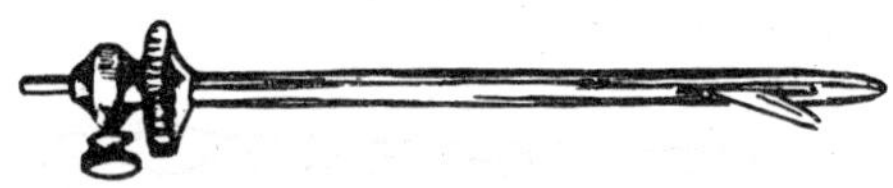

Teat Slitter, American pattern conceald adjustable blade.

Teat Slitter with twin blades, adjustable, Danish pattern

Teat Bistoury in reversible handle

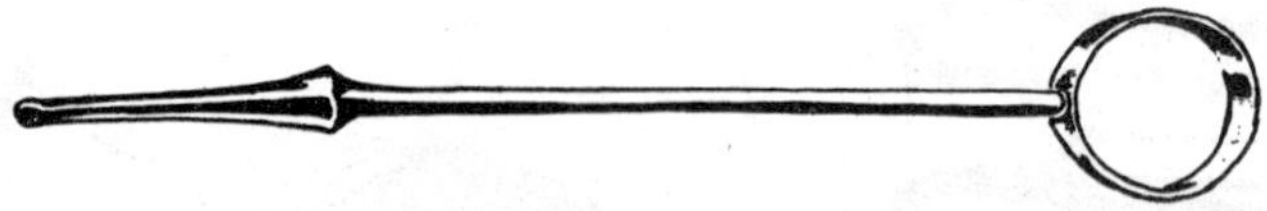

Tapering Teat Slitter, with bulbous tip and ring.

Teat Bistoury folding with catch

Plate XVI

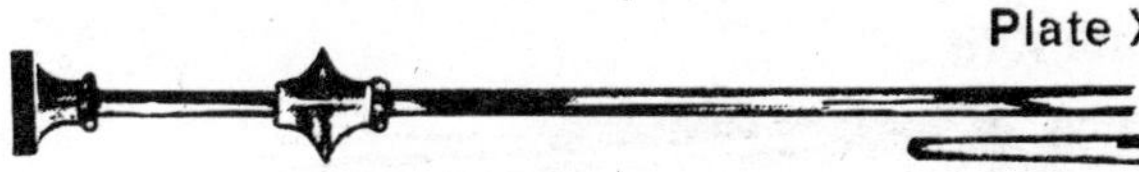

Teat Dilator, American pattern.

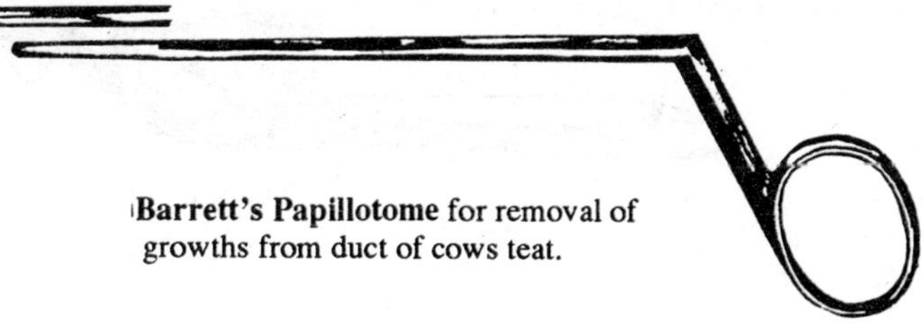

Barrett's Papillotome for removal of growths from duct of cows teat.

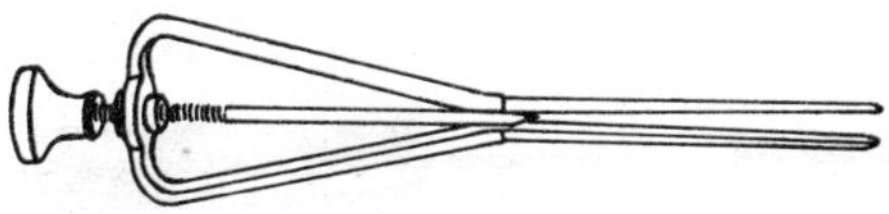

Teat Dilator with screw.

Papillotome, French model

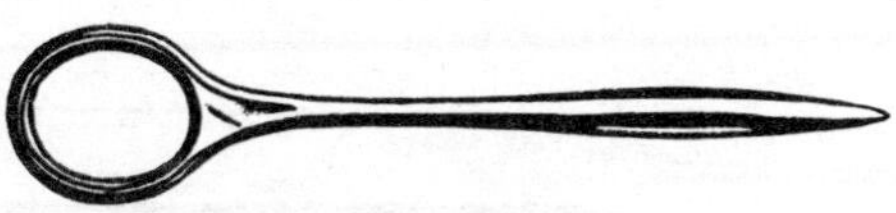

Teat Dilator especially in cases of toughness in milking.

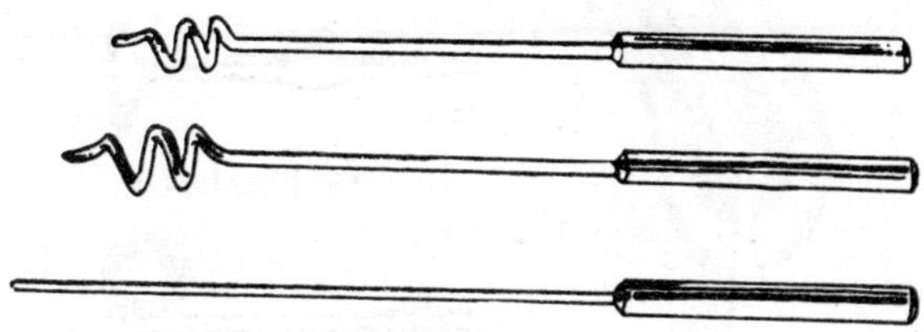

Teat Instruments Hudson's, 2 sizes dilators and 1 introducer.

Teat dilator Moore 7 in. long.

Danish Pattern

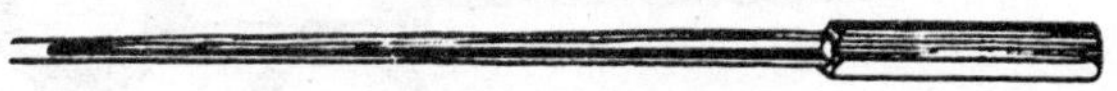

Teat Opener, grooved, American pattern.

Neilsen's Teat Canula.

Dutch type Teat Duct Opener 4 mm.

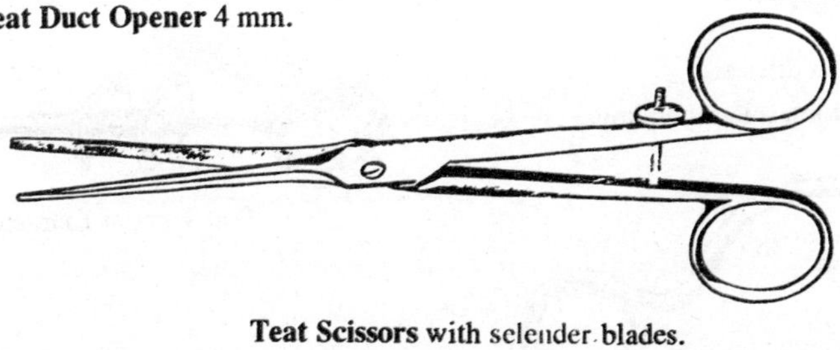

Teat Scissors with selender blades.

Fine Sharp Scoop, Double ended.

Plate XVII

Teat Knife, Swedish pattern.

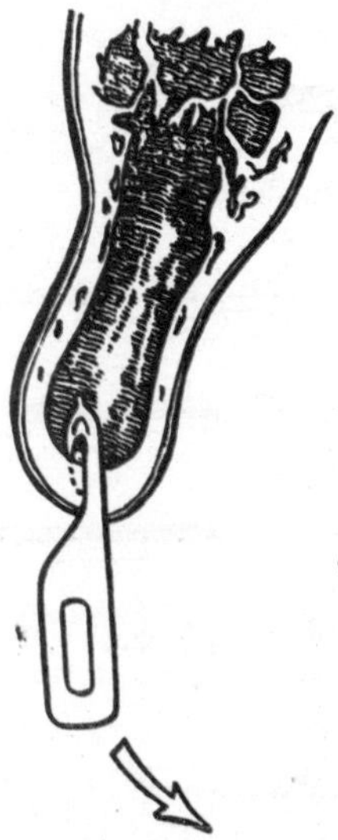

Dr. Dyekjaer's Teat Slitter is used

Teat Plug bulbous

Teat Plug with rings, self-retaining,

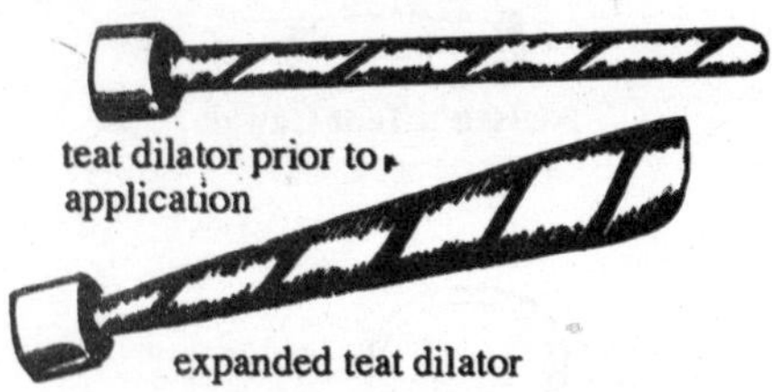

Teat Dilators, self-expanding.

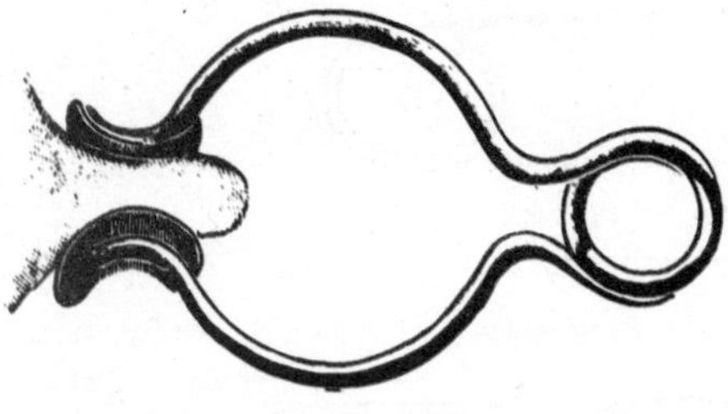

Teat Compressor

Yankee teat bistoury

Lichty teat knife

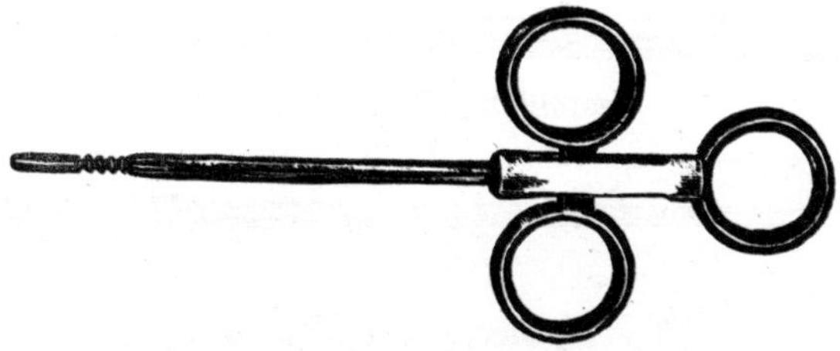

Teat Tumour Extractor with 3 rings

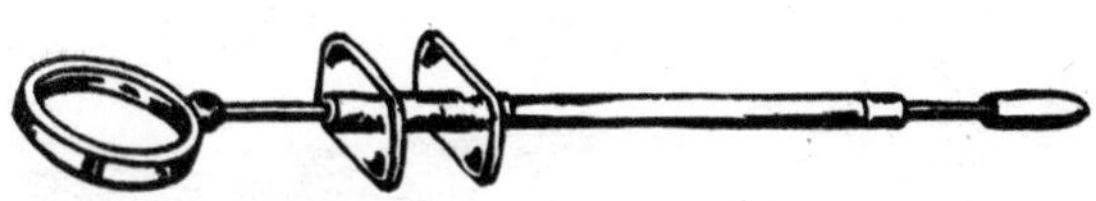

Teat Tumour Extractor American Pattern

Hugs' Tumour Extractor conical, $2^1/_2$, 3, $3^1/_2$ and 4mm.

Plate XVIII

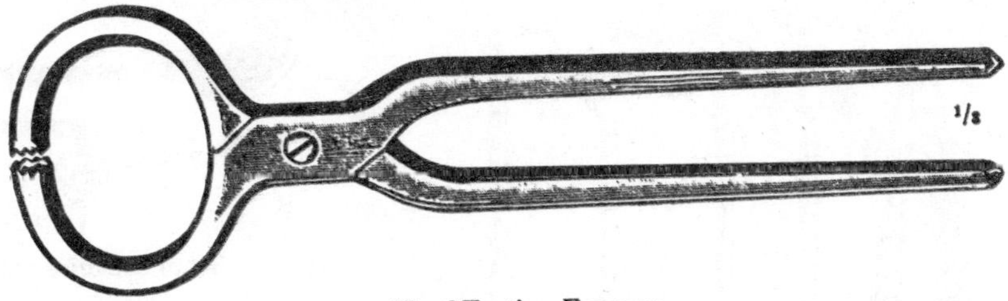

Hoof Testing Forceps

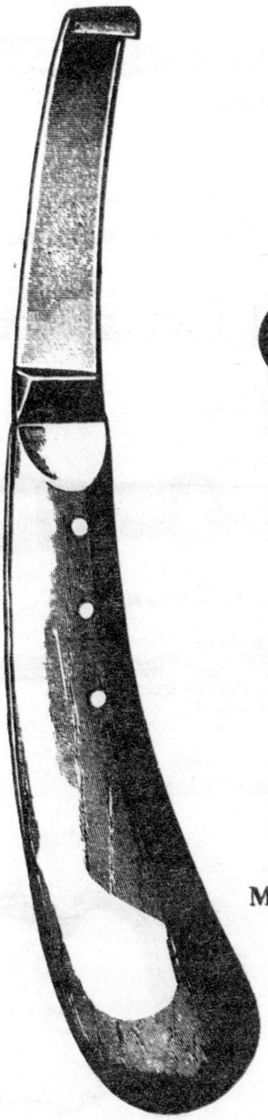

Hoof Knives wooden
right and left.

Multiple Hoof Cutter

Drawing Knife, Frehch pattern, wooden handle.
Drawing Knife, folding, spring handle, all-metal.

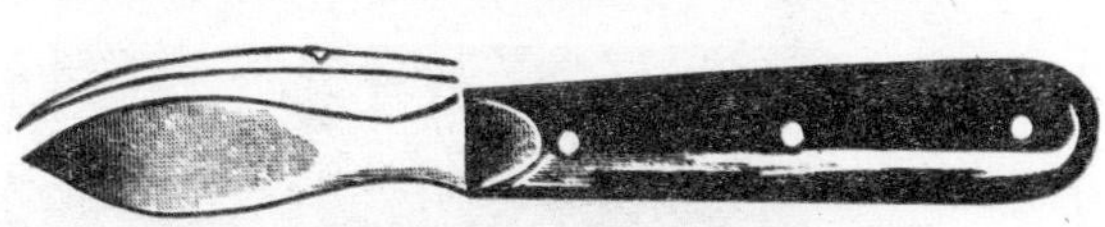

63. Hoof Sage Knife.

Farrier's Set of Tools in a Canvas bag, with strap.

Farrier's Hammer
Buffer.
R :asp.
Pincers.
Knife, right and left.
Stone for sharpening Hoof knives.

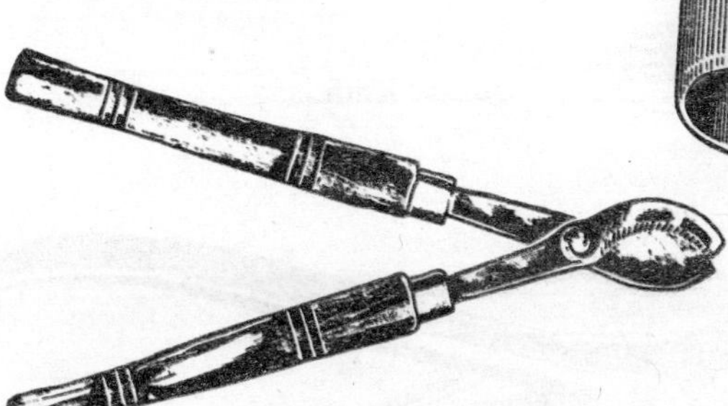

Hoof Cutter, with wooden handle.

Plate XIX

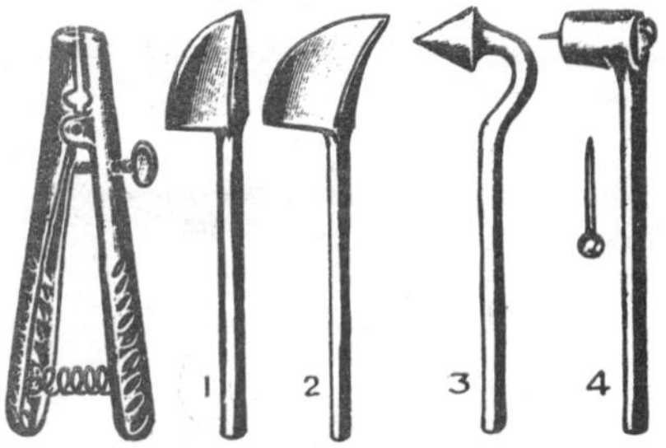

Set of Firing Irons

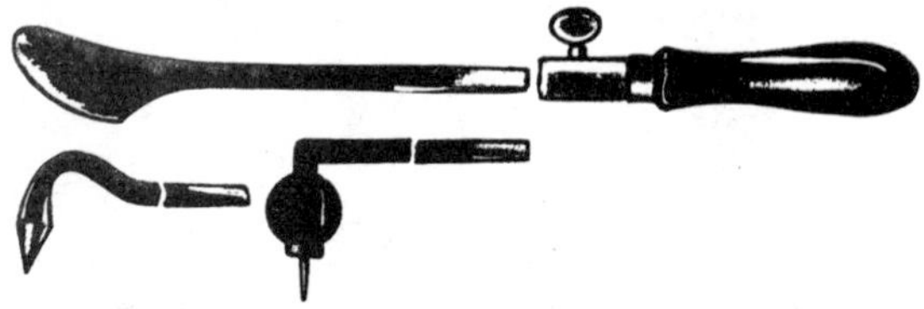

Set of cauteries with 3 firing irons, in a canvas

Hoof gouge

Hoof section saw.

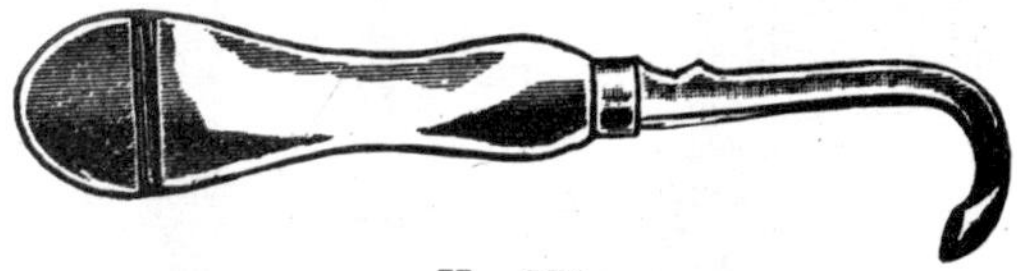

Hoof Plane.

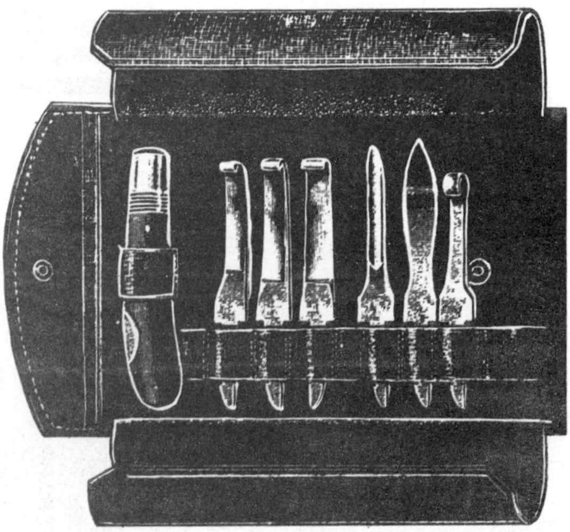

Set of 6 Hoof Knives in a leather roll with 1 handle.

Hoof Buffer.

Anticrib Biter.

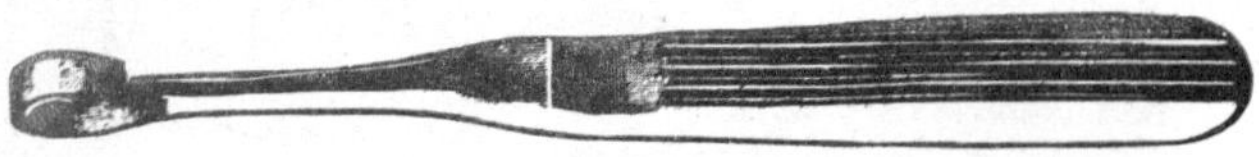

Quittor Knife.

Forceps for Tearing off Horn for Resection of the Cartilage of Hoof.

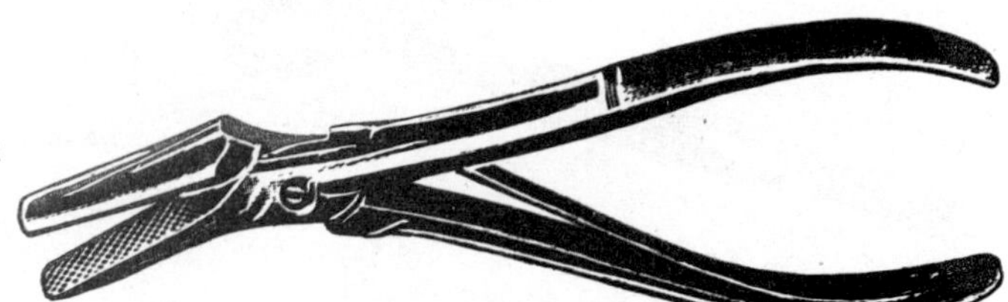

Plate XX

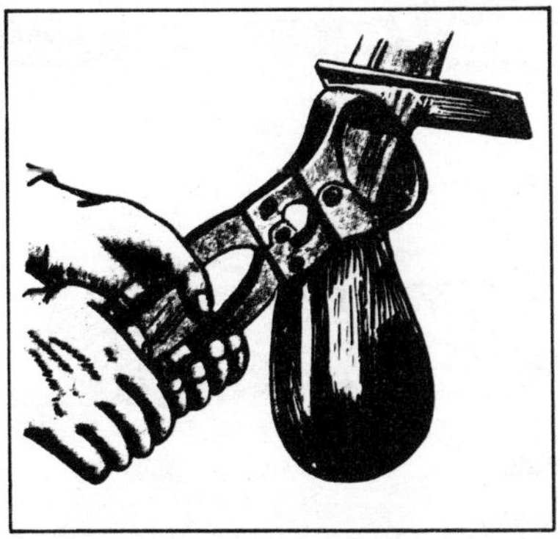

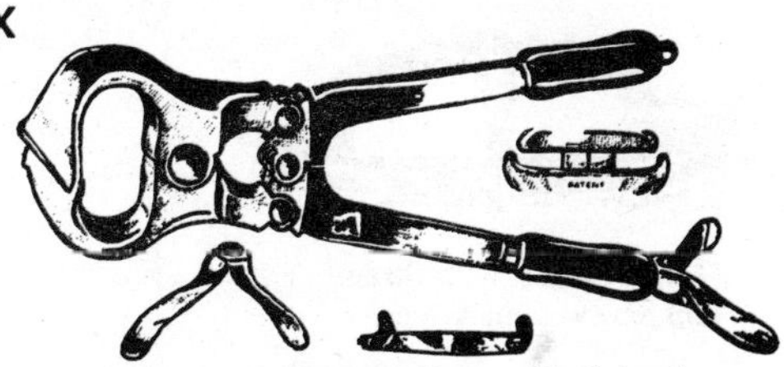

Burdizzo Castrator, Patent Cordstop Jaws, for the bloodless castration of **Sheep-Pigs - Bulls-Horses- Dogs**-etc.

Scrotum Clamps for holding the cord use in case of horses, pigs or bulls very strong and tough cords.

Castrating Knife, improved double folded

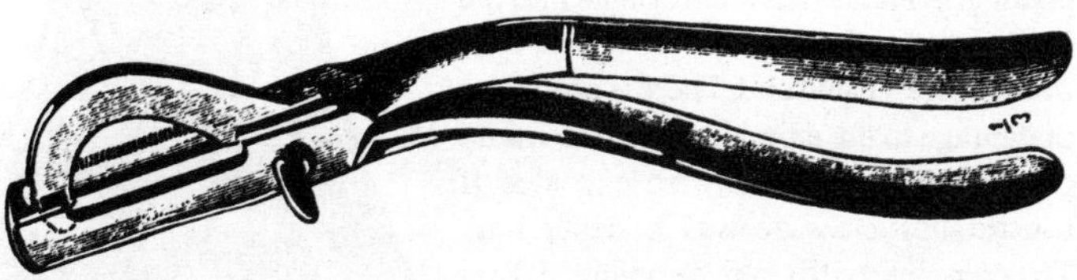

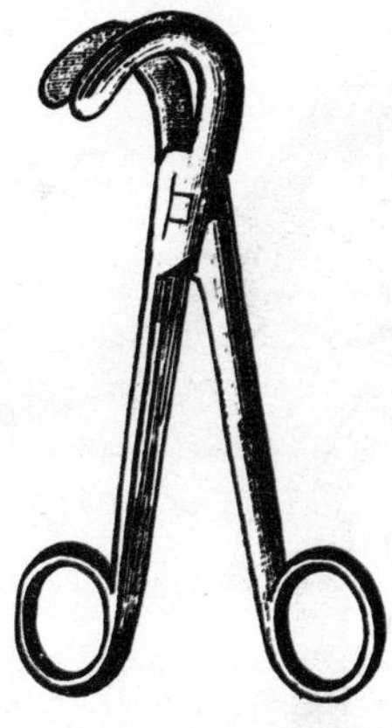

Castrating Forceps for Lamb.

Castration Tortion Forceps, Robert's

Sand's Castration Clamp.
Danish pattern.

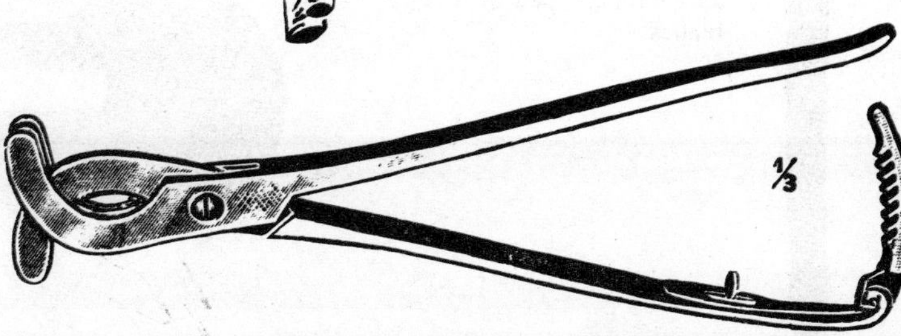

Plate XXI

Horn Trainer, with Straps and Screw adjustment.

Horn Lifter

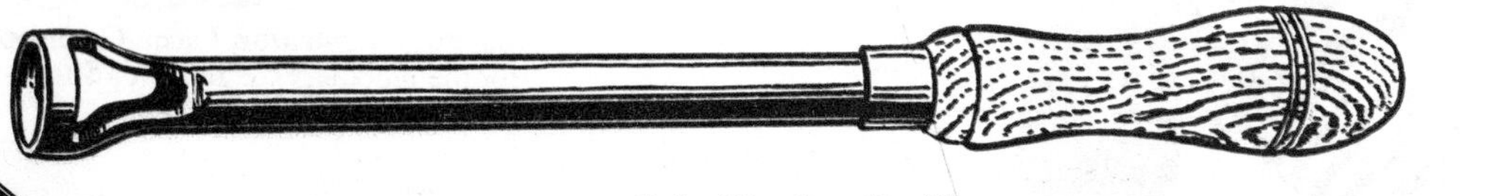

Debudding Iron Gould's

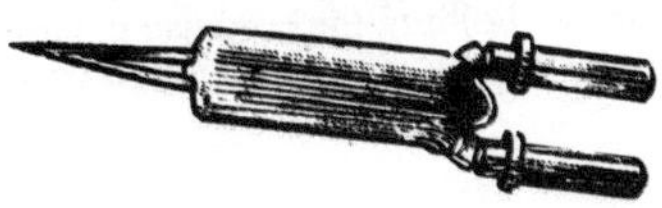

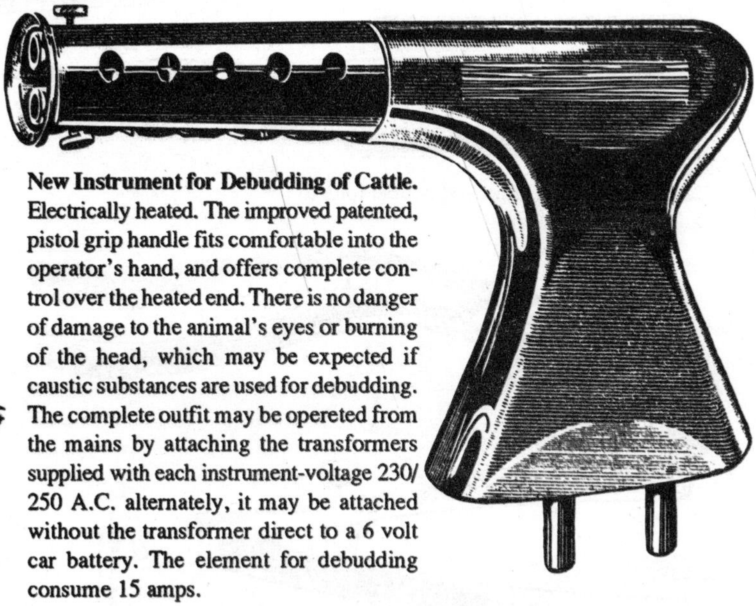

New Instrument for Debudding of Cattle. Electrically heated. The improved patented, pistol grip handle fits comfortable into the operator's hand, and offers complete control over the heated end. There is no danger of damage to the animal's eyes or burning of the head, which may be expected if caustic substances are used for debudding. The complete outfit may be opereted from the mains by attaching the transformers supplied with each instrument-voltage 230/250 A.C. alternately, it may be attached without the transformer direct to a 6 volt car battery. The element for debudding consume 15 amps.

Dishorning Shears. 76 cm long with one pair of reserve blades.

Robert Calf Dehorner

Plate XXII

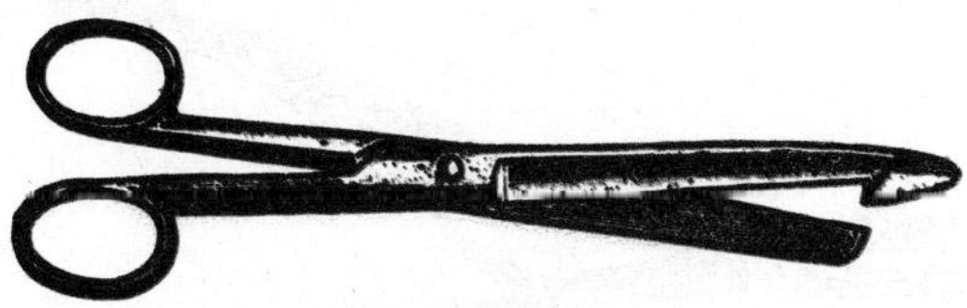

Bowel Scissors

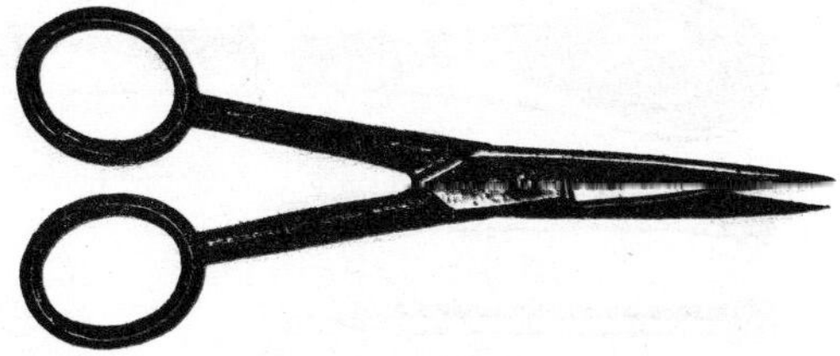

Postmortem Scissors, 6 in.

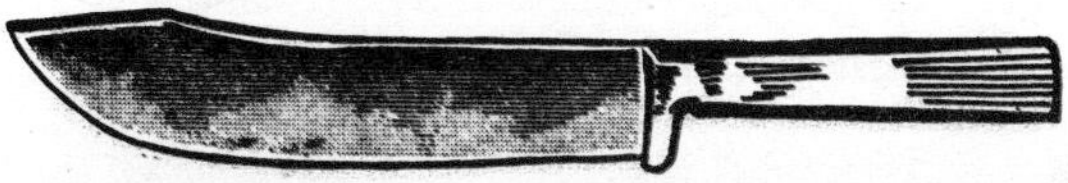

Butcher Knife, wooden handle, blades 9 in.; 10 in.

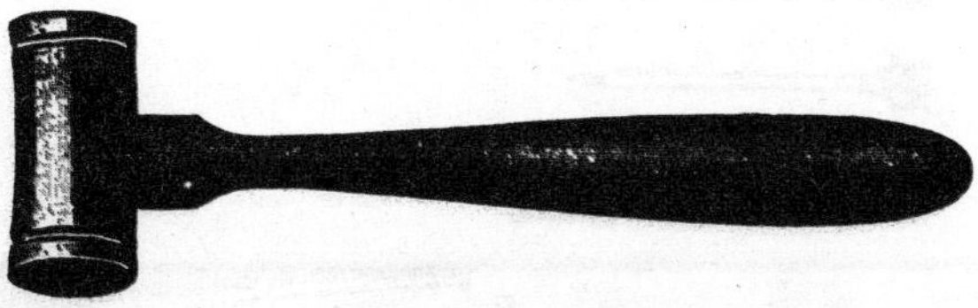

Postmortem Mallet.

Butcher Saw, with wooden handle.

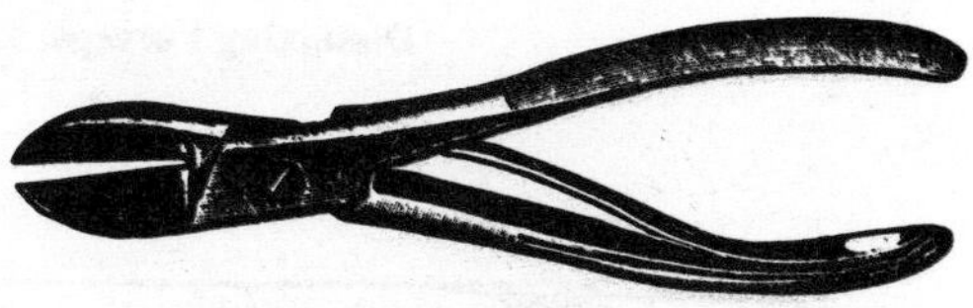

Liston's Bone Forceps, with spring, 6 in., 7 in. and 9 in.

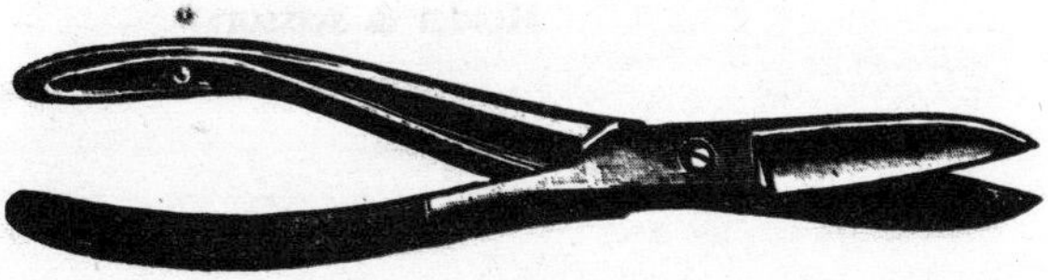

Bone Shears, straight 8 in.

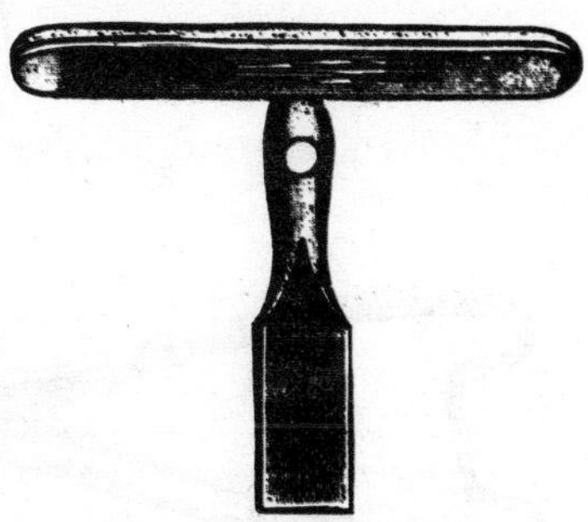

Postmortem Chisel with handle.

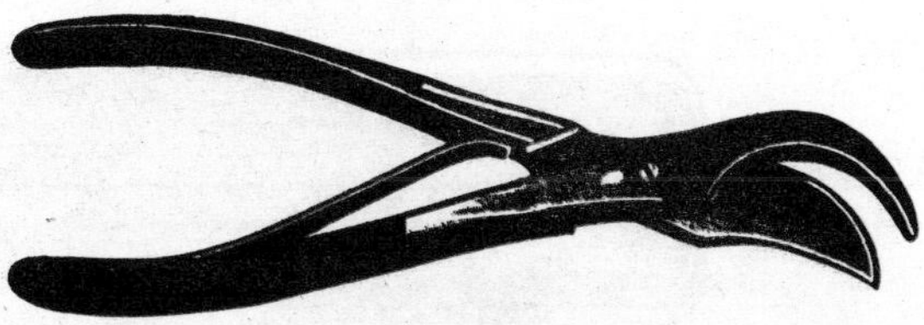

Bib Shears Pollocks 9 in.

Bone Holding Forces.

Plate XXIII

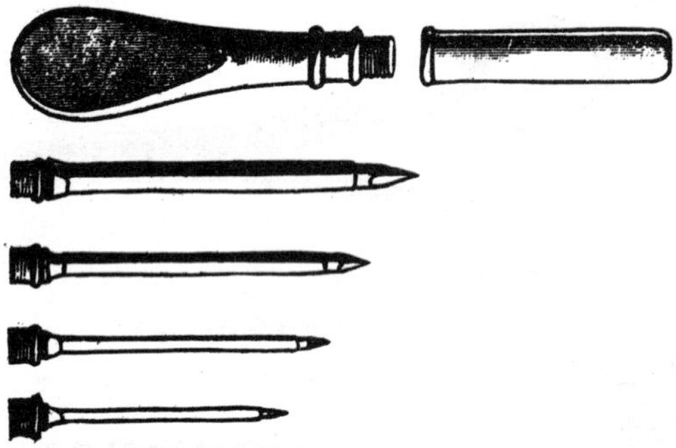

Exploring Trocars, set of 3 and 4 with stainless steel points.

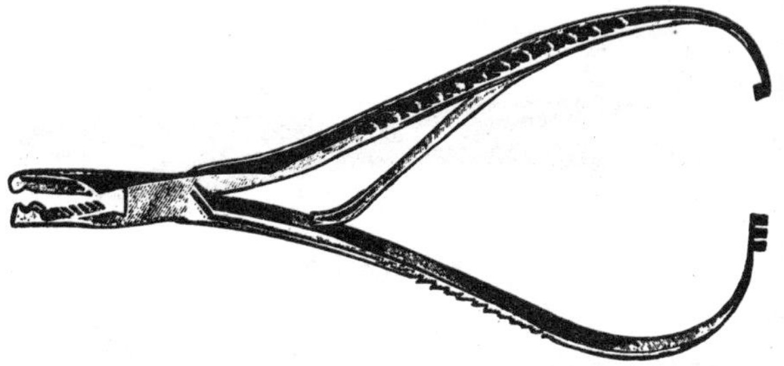

Needle Holder, Macphail's 6 in. and 8 in.

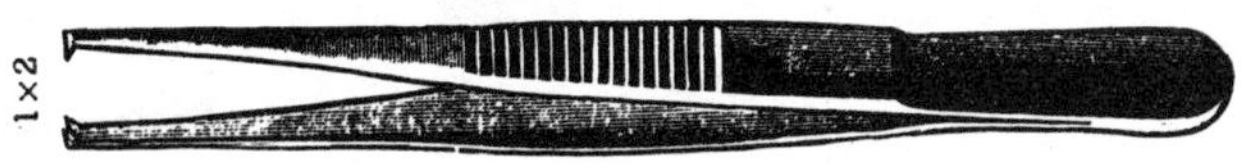

Dissecting Forceps, Rat-Tooth, sizes 5 in., $5^{1}/_{2}$ in., 6 in., 7 in.

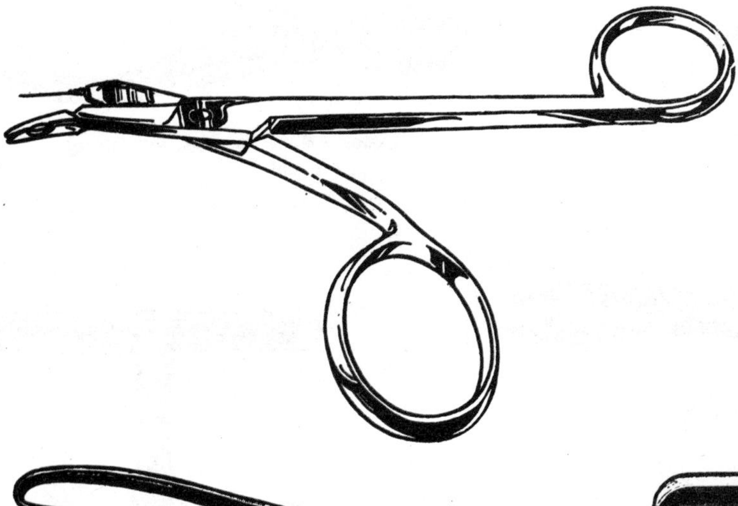

Gillies Combined Needle Holder & Scissors.

NEEDLE HOLDER MATHIEUS

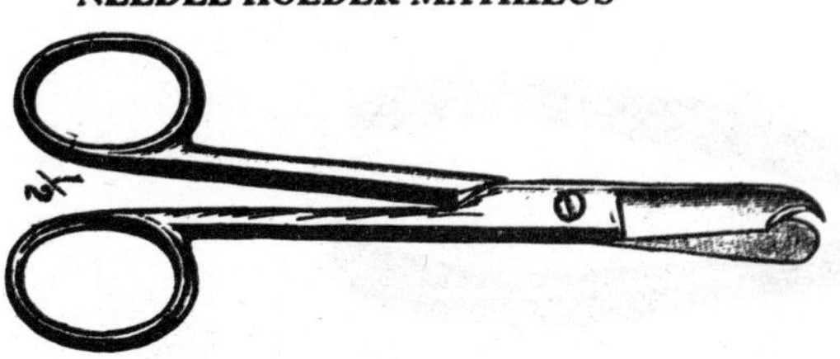

Ligature Seissors with Hook end

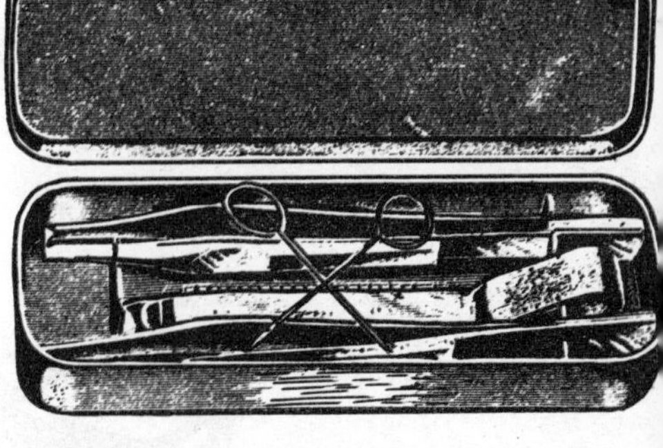

Michel's Suture set consisting of skin forceps with clip carrie r, clip fixing forceps, releasing forceps and clips in a metal case.

Plate XXIV

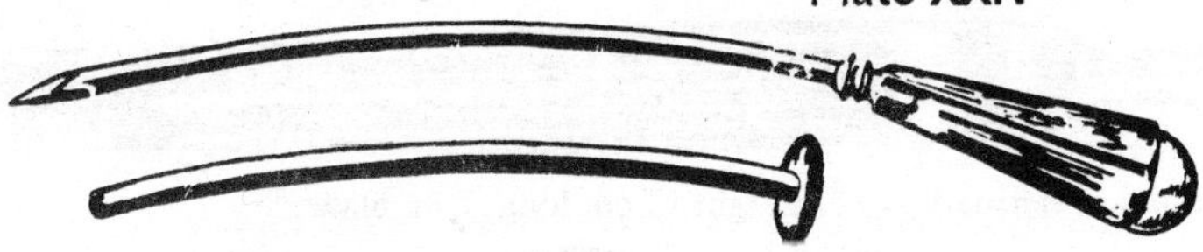

Williams Trocar and Canula for flatulent colic.

Intestinal Trocar Hanovar veterinary College model. The canula consists of two sections, each 40 cm long, which can be conncted by means of a push-on mount.. The front section alone is suitable for the puncture of the caecum from the side. In its full combined length it serves to puncture the caecum and the pelvic flexure from the rectum.

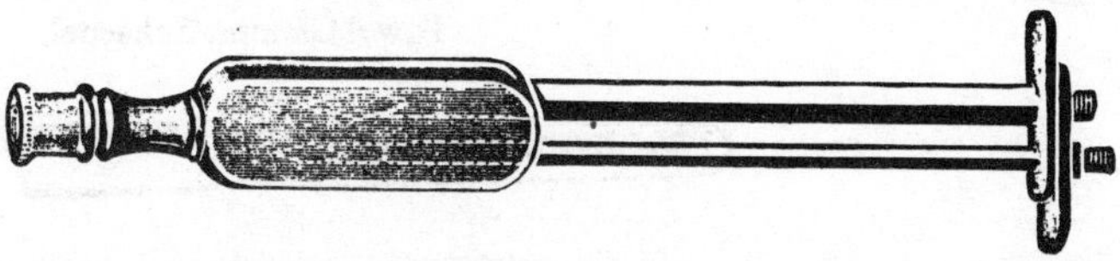

Combind Chest and **Intestinal** Trocar·. to fit instrument Case.

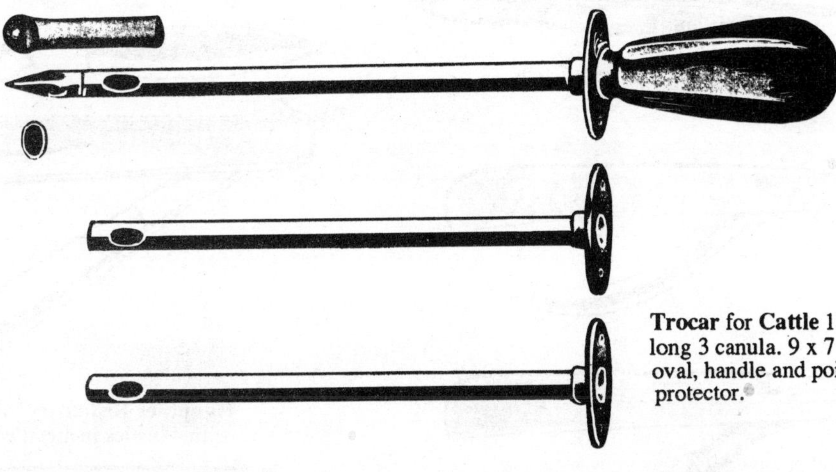

Trocar for **Cattle** 16cm. long 3 canula. 9 x 7 mm oval, handle and point protector.

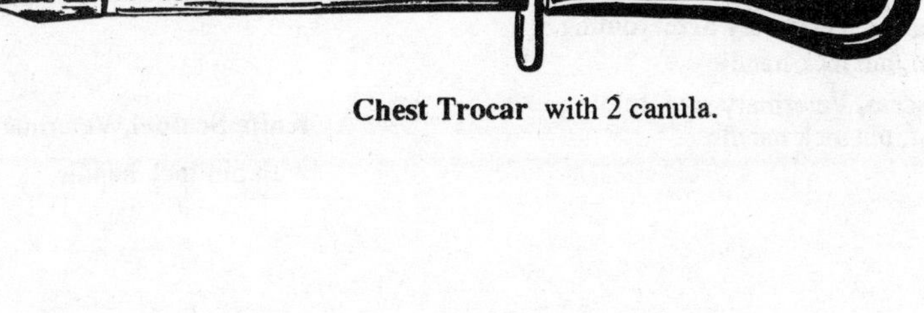

Chest Trocar with 2 canula.

Plate XXV

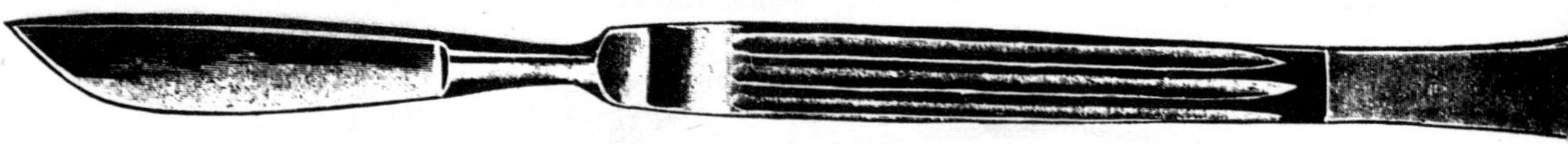

Scalpel, Veterinary size, Straight 17 cm long, 2 in. blade.

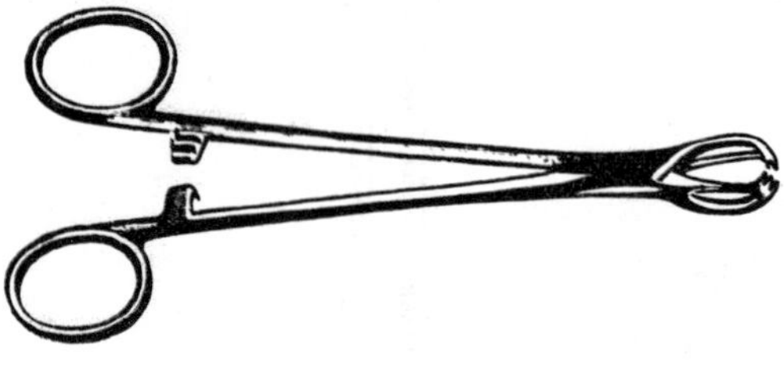

Towel Clamp, Lanes

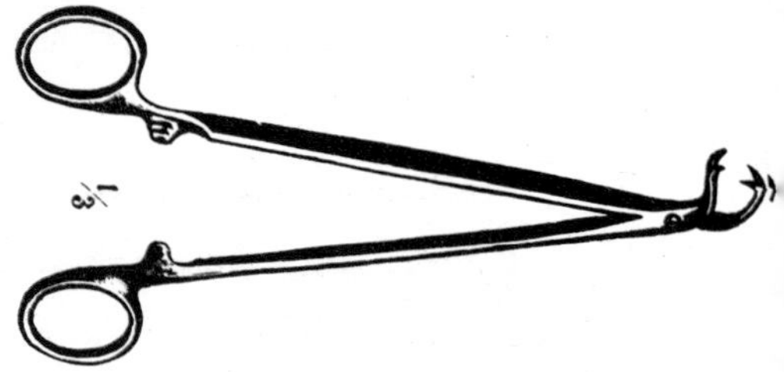

Towel Clamp's Maijnihan

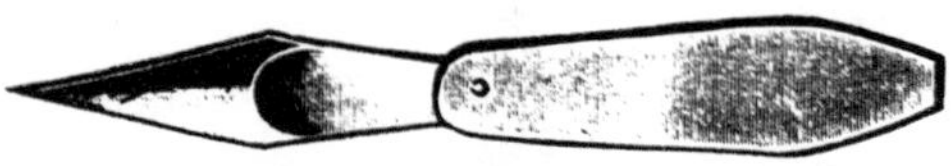

Bleeding Lancet, folding Veterinary

Towel Clamps. Schaedel.

Strong Artery Forceps with Catch.

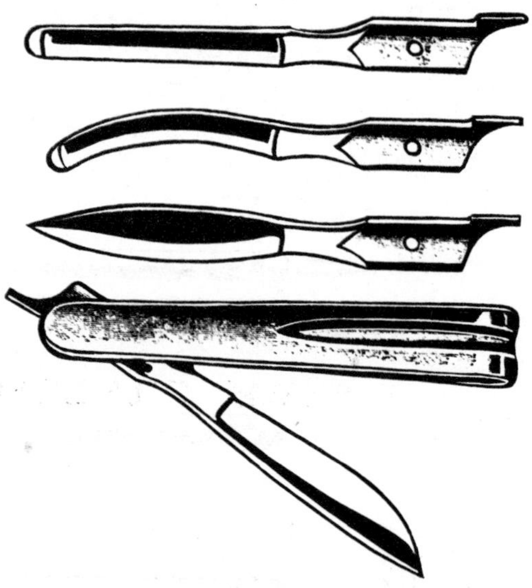

Hauptner Bistouries 'Muto'
with 4 blades in metal case

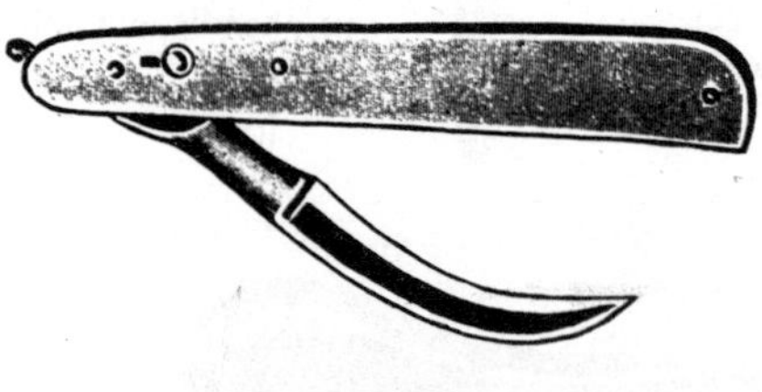

Knife Abscess, Veterinary Size. folding,
probe point, pin lock handle

Knife Abscess, Veterinary size, folding,
sharp point, pin lock handle.

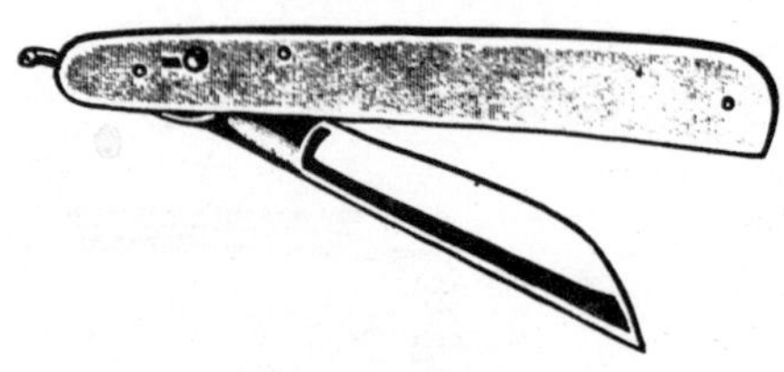

Knife Scalpel, Veterinary size, folding,
with pin lock handle.

Plate XXVI

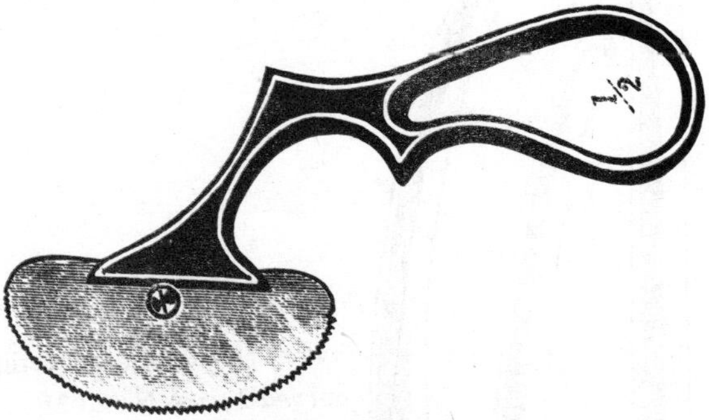

Plaster Saw Engel

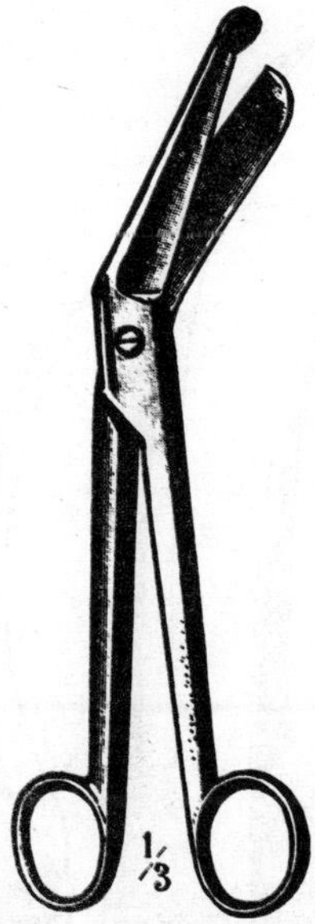

Plaster Shears.

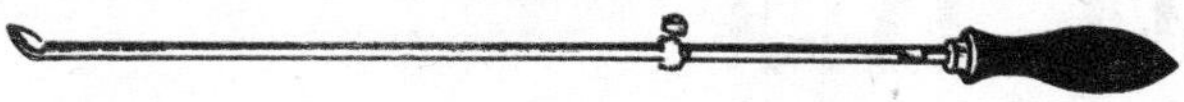

Overback's Trephining Knife, for unblocking head cavities of horses.

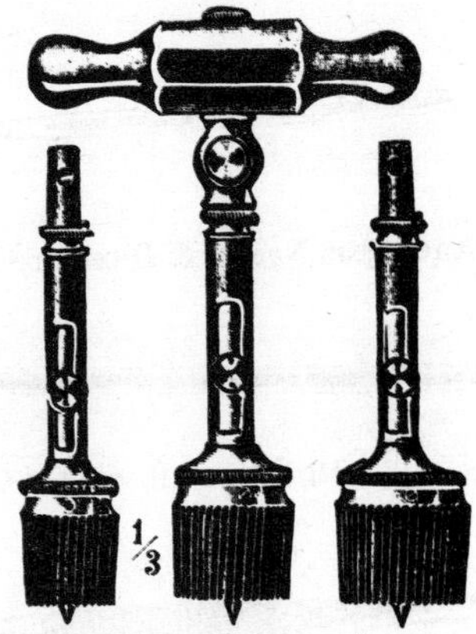

Horseley's Trephines, $^1/_2$ in., $^1/_2$ in. and 1 in., with detachable handle.

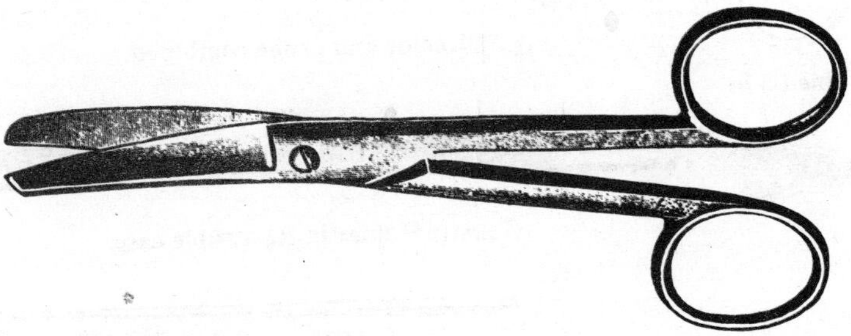

Dressing Scissors, straight, and curved on flat $5^1/_2$ in., 6 in.; 7 in; and 8 in.
Dressing Scissors Angular, 5 in.; $5^1/_2$ in. and 6 in.

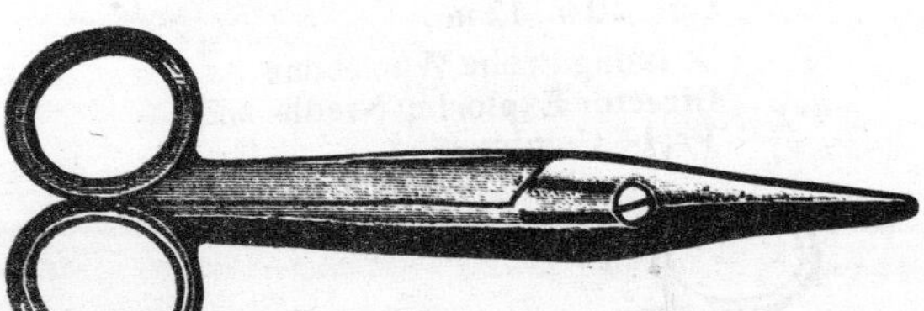

Mayo's Scissors, 14 cm and 17 cm. Straight

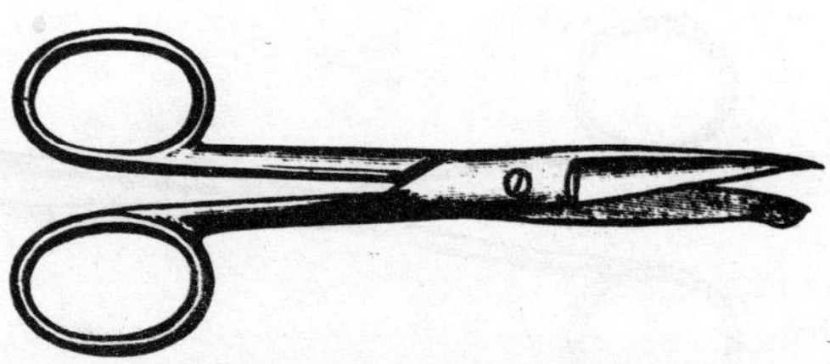

Incision Scissors one probe end.

Plate XXVII

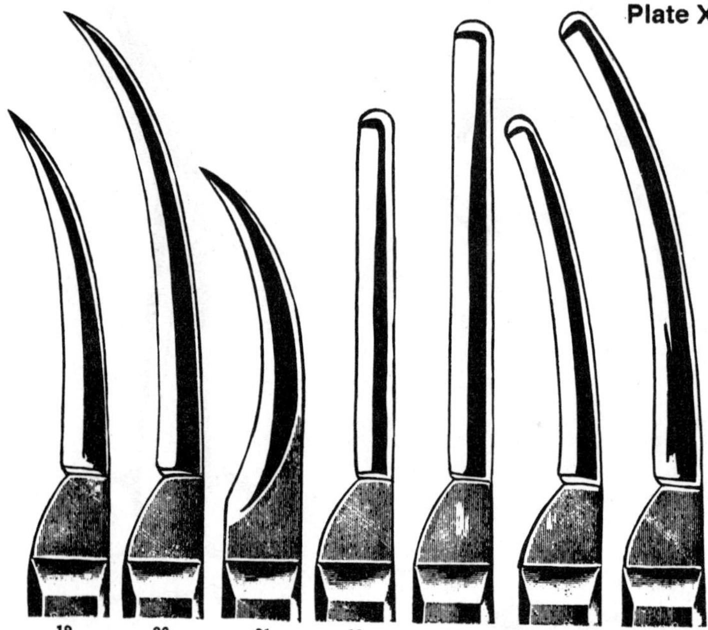

19 20 21 22 23 24 25

Symes abscess Knife Veterinary Size. No-19.
curved 2 sizes. No-20-21.
Bistoury Straight probe end 2 size No 22-23
Bistoury Curved Probe end 2 sizes No 24-25.
Straight sharp

Aneurysm Needle & Director Combined 5 in

Director and probe combined.

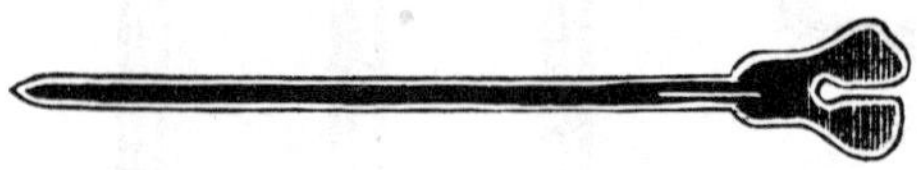

Director with **winged Grip.**

Gaustic Holder in Reversible case.

Dissecting Forceps sizes, 5 in., $5^1/_2$ in., 6 in., 7 in.,

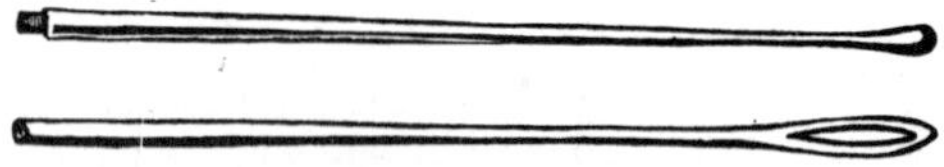

Dressing Probe with eye, sizes 5 in., 6 in., 8 in., 10 in. 12 in.,
Dressing Probe Whalebone
Director Exploring Needle and
Probe Combined

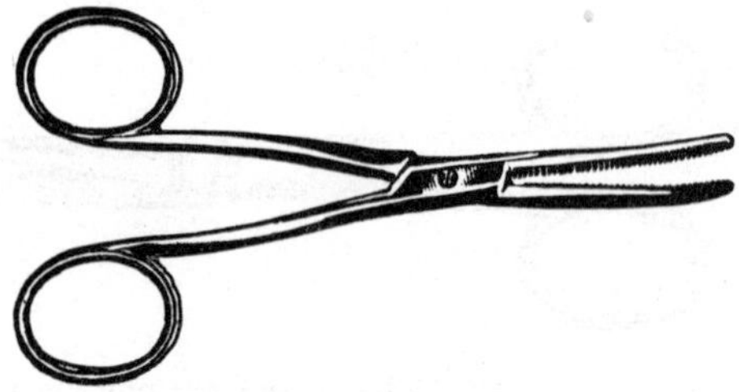

Dressing Forceps, Bryant's 5 in.

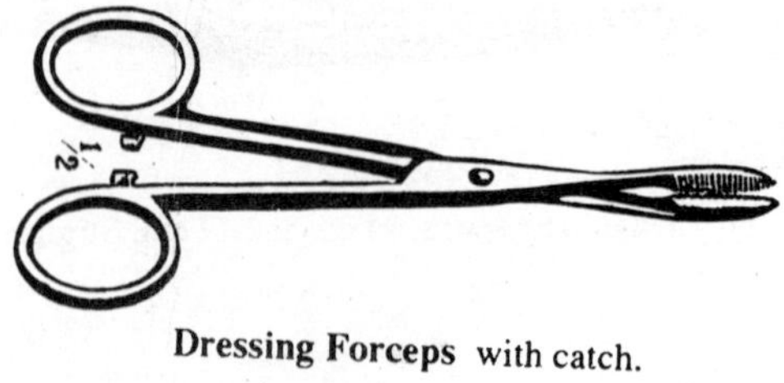

Dressing Forceps with catch.

Plate XXVIII

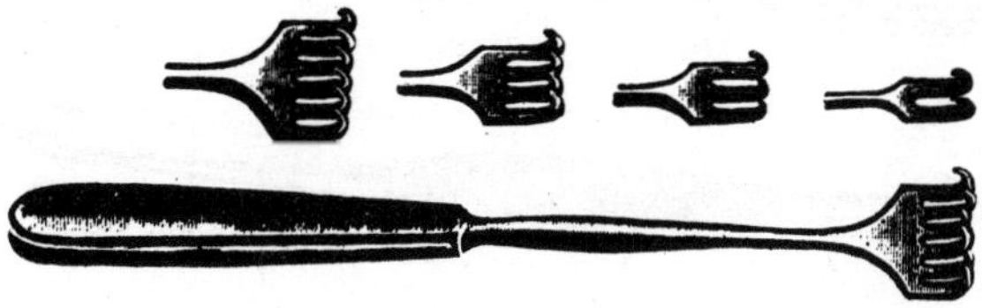

Volkmann's Retractor, Stainless steel with 2,3,4 and 5 prongs.

Guy's Retractor, $^{5}/_{8}$in. & $^{7}/_{8}$ in. wide

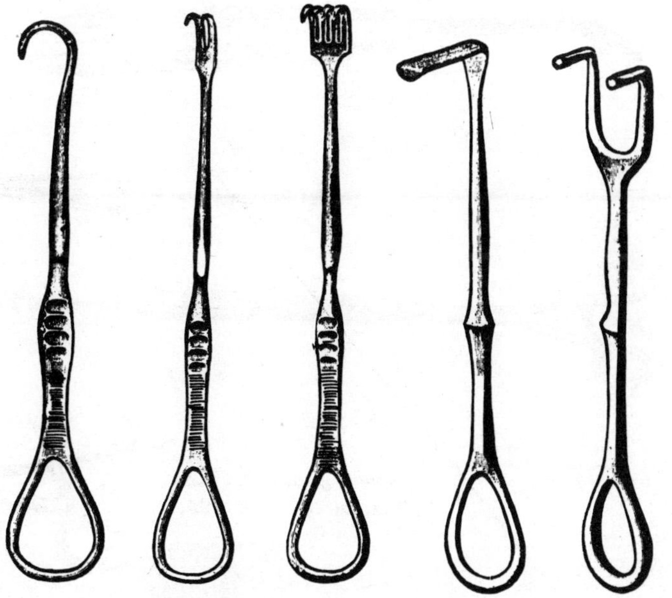

Single sharp hook retractor.

Double sharp hook retractor.

Four pronged sharp hook retractor.

Blunt hook retractor.

Double pronged blung hook retractor.

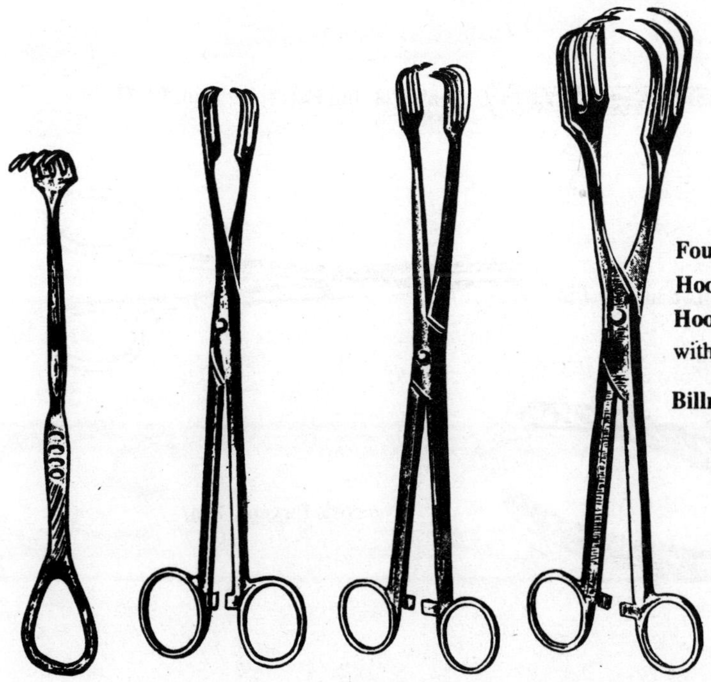

Four pronged blunt hook retractor.

Hook retractor forceps, 20 cm., with ratchet

Hook retractor forceps, 24 cm., four prongs, with ratchet.

Billroths Retractor, 26 cmlongwith ratchet.

Plate XXIX

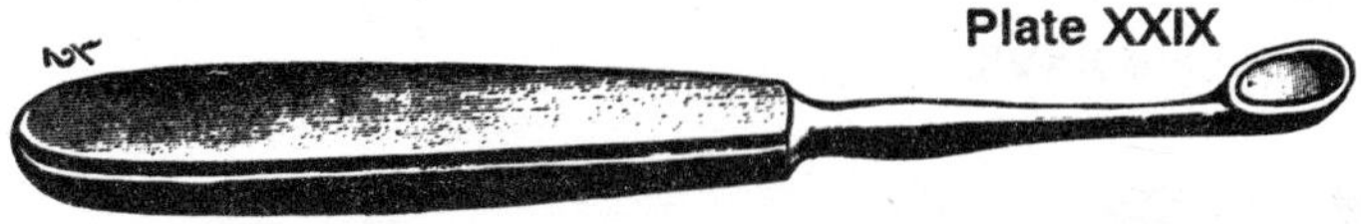

Volkmann's Scoop, single with handle

Volkmann's Scoop, double, stainless steel.

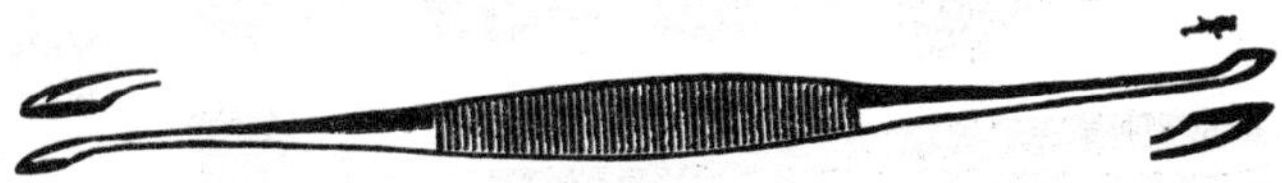

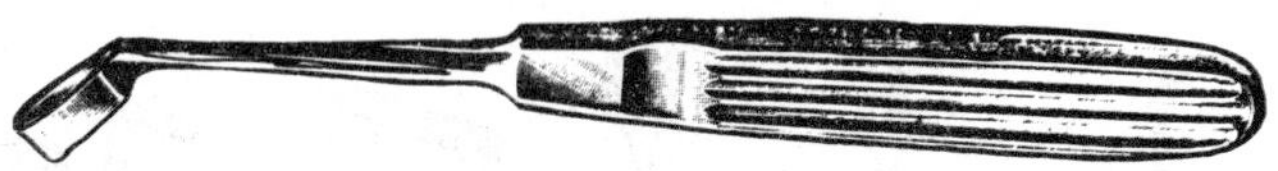

Frick's sharp Curette.

Bullet Forceps.

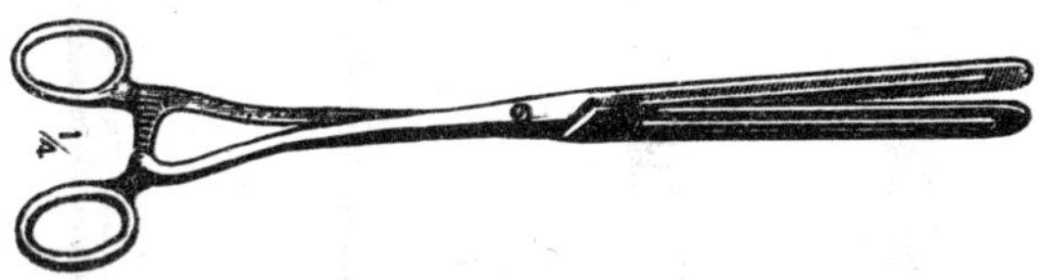

Intestinal Forceps, length 7 in.; blades $4^1/_2$ in.

Doyen's Stomach Clamp,
9 in. Curved or Straight.

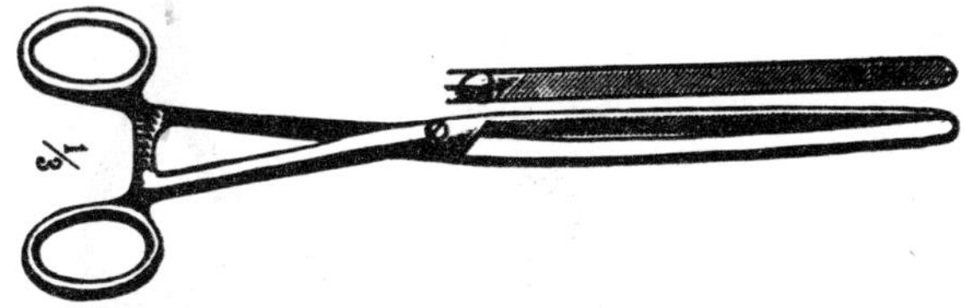

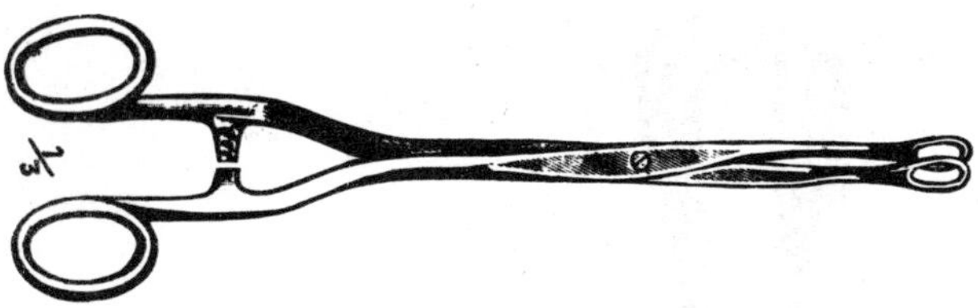

Swab Holding Forceps $9^1/_2$ in. [illegible] in.

Sinus Forceps, 5 in., 6 in. and 7 in.

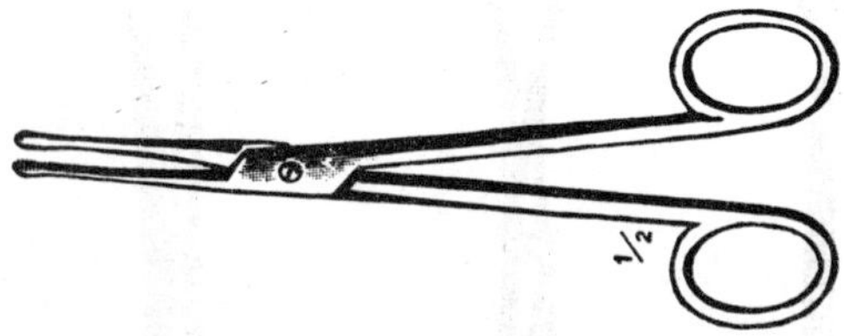

Necrosis forceps, 7 in

Plate XXX

Veterinary half curved Needles (French Model $2^3/_4$", $3^1/_4$" and $3^3/_4$" in.

Ward Finnehore's Suture Needles Curved or half Curved $2^1/_2$"$3^1/_2$"in

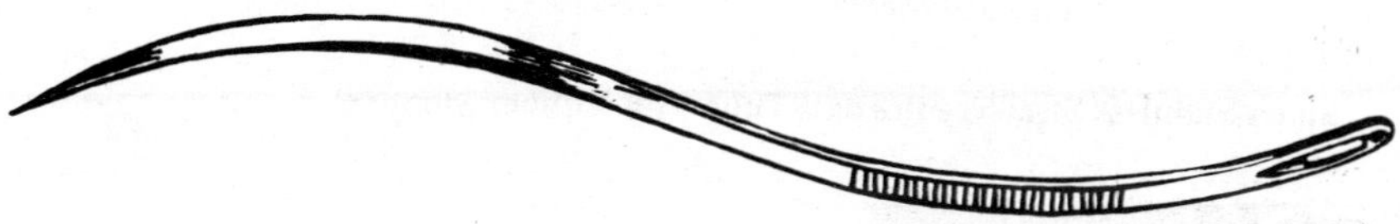

Postmortem Veterinary Needles.

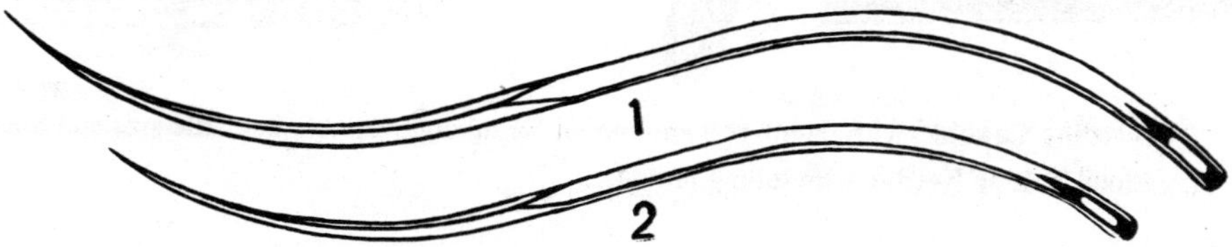

Spaying Needles, Double, Curved, large or medium.

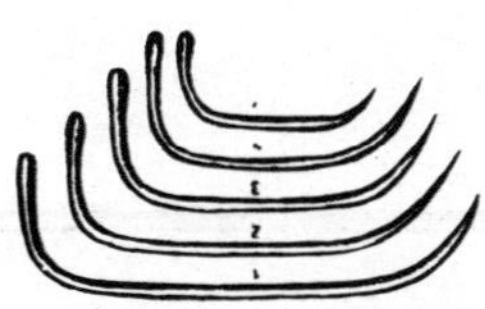

Loopuyt Needles, cutting edge to use without needle holder.

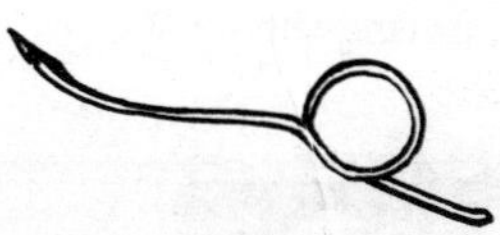

Holzhausen's suture needle with finger ring. for suturing on standing animals.

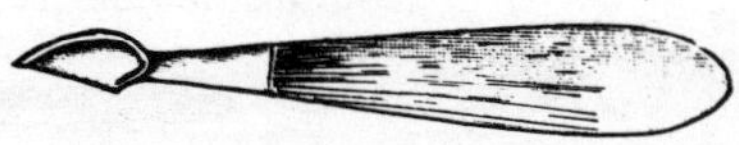

Spoon Lancet for Blood agglutination.

Plate XXXI

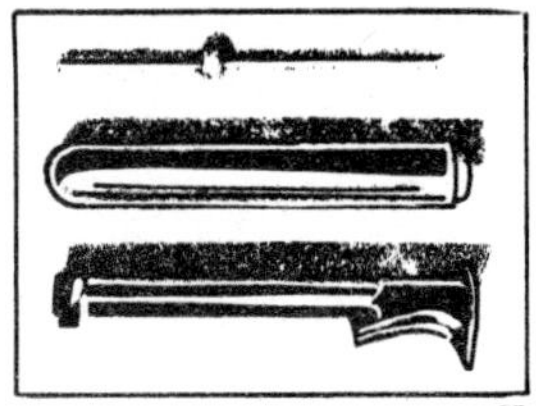

Blood Taking Needle Holder. It prevents contamination of blood sample by preceding tests and prevents transference of infectious diseases from animals while testing. Neither end of the needle can touch holder. The needle and glass tube are removed as a unit after each test. Available Holder complete with tube and needle.

Spare Stainless Steel Needles and Tube with Rubber Stoppers.

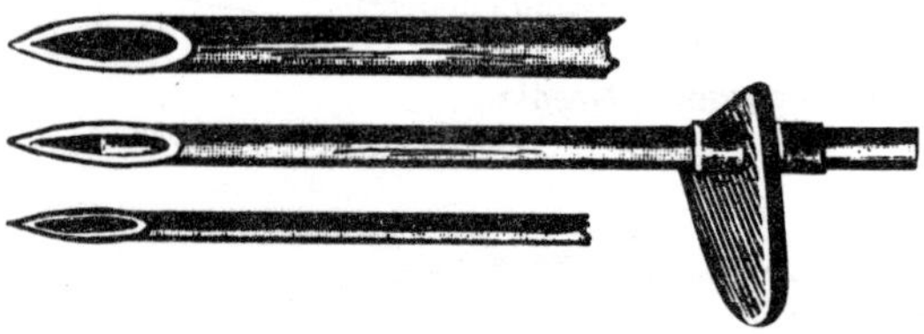

Bleeding Canulas, with thumb rest and mount for tubing available in Cattle size and Sheep size.

Blood Taking Needle with tubing mount.

Brook's Epidural Needle, for anaesthesia, for cattle, horse and dog.

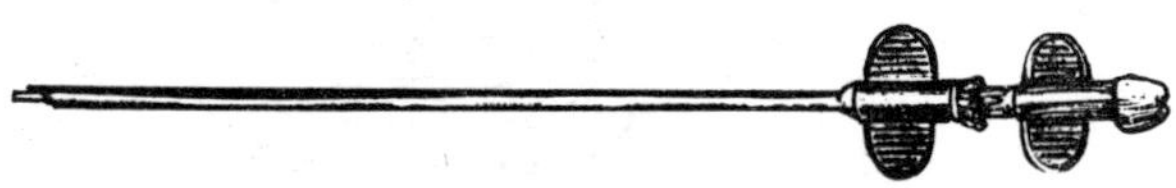

Greer's Improved Intravenous Canula, with wing mount. A combination of needle and teat siphon for bulky solutions. A half turn of the upper wing mount closes the aperture in the siphon. The principal advantages of this instrument are the elimination of risk of perforating the opposite wall of the vein and freedom from clotting the needle.

GIESEN, double safety intravenous infusion needle 7.5 cm long

Plate XXXII

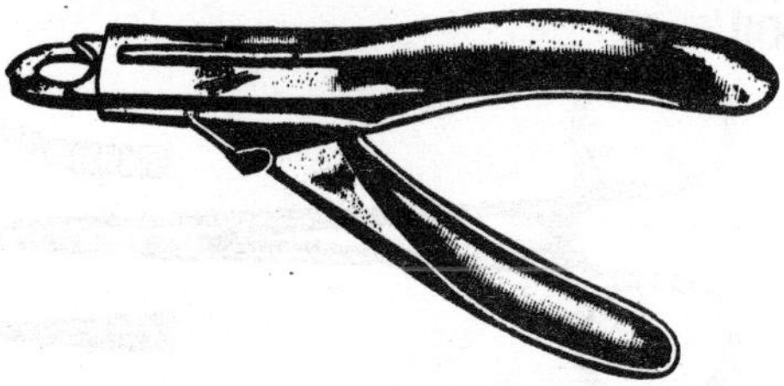

Claw or **Nail** Cutter, ensures a clean cut.

Scissors for docking puppies tails.

Nippers for Dog Claws.

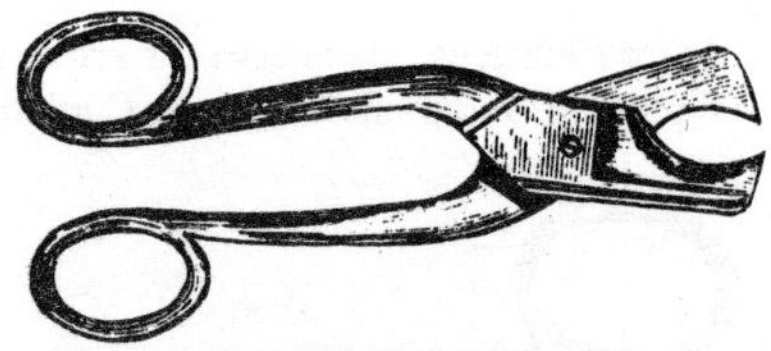

Rowelling Scissors.
Dog Tail Shears.

Wright's Ether Anaesthetic Apparatus for **Dogs** and **Cats.**

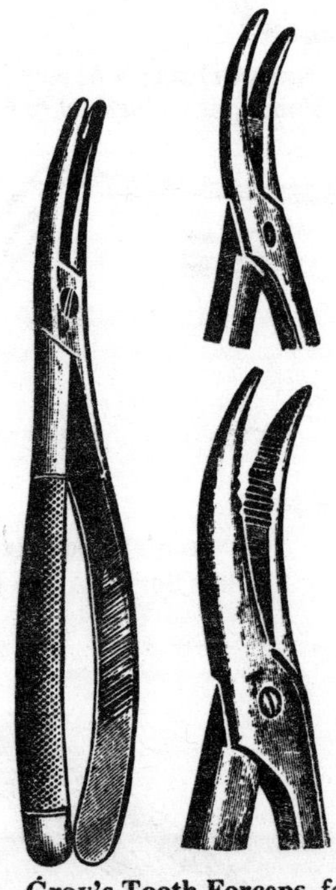

Gray's Tooth Forceps. for temporary canines; for dogs; and for tartar breaking.

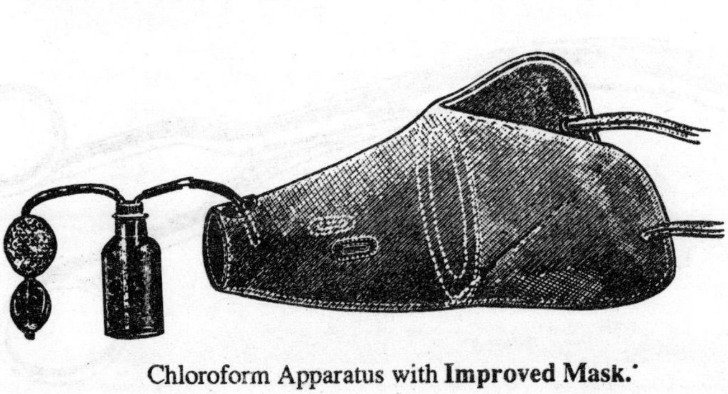

Chloroform Apparatus with **Improved Mask.**

Plate XXXIII

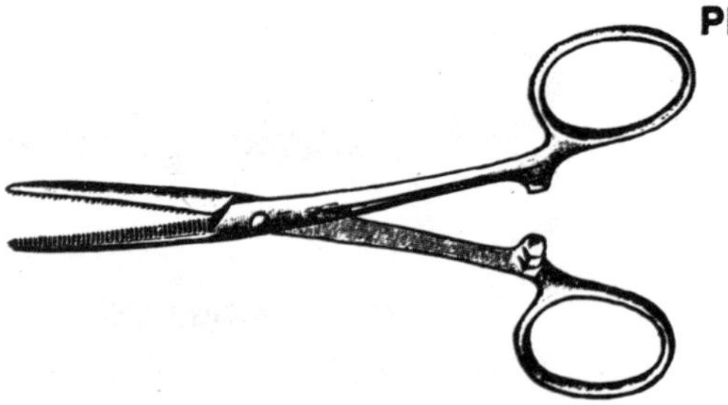

Artery Forceps, Spencerwell's screw joint, 6 in., 7 in. and 8 in. Straight or Curved.

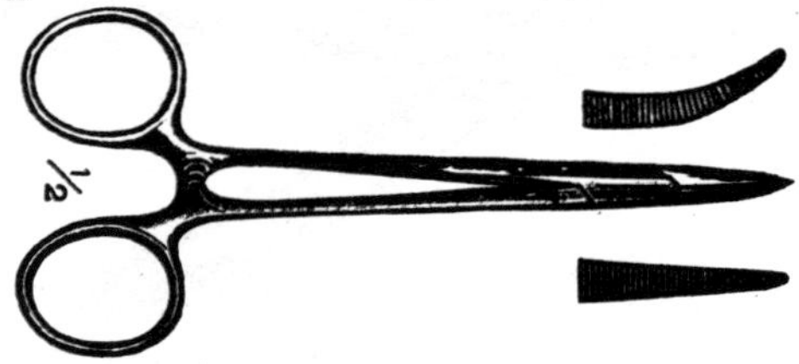

Halatead Mosquito Forceps
Straight or curved.

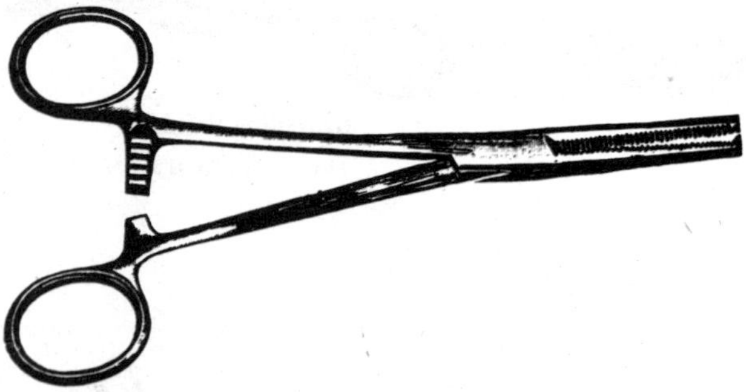

Mayo Ochsner's Artery Forceps, with **Tenaculum Points,** sizes. Straight or Curved

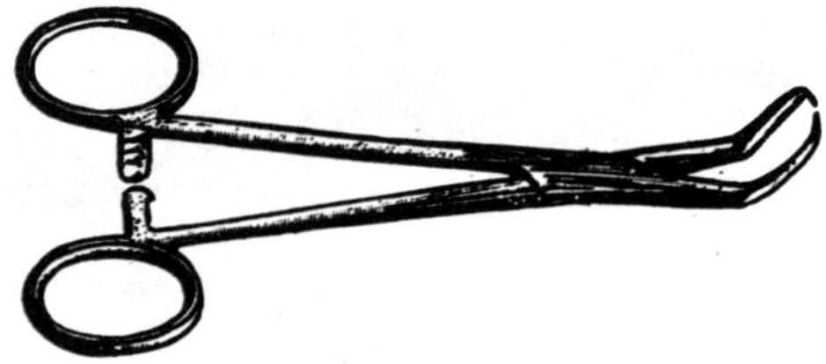

GG1. **Towel Clamp Backhaus.** 2 sizes

Artery clamps Diffenback's straight or curved.

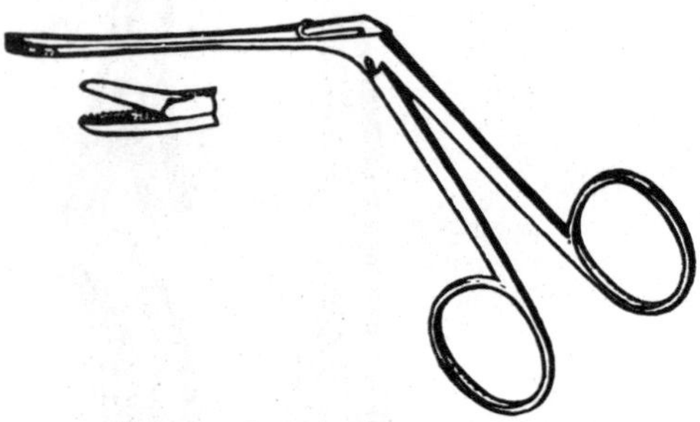

Hartman's Crocodile Ear Forceps.
Wild's Spring Aural Forceps.

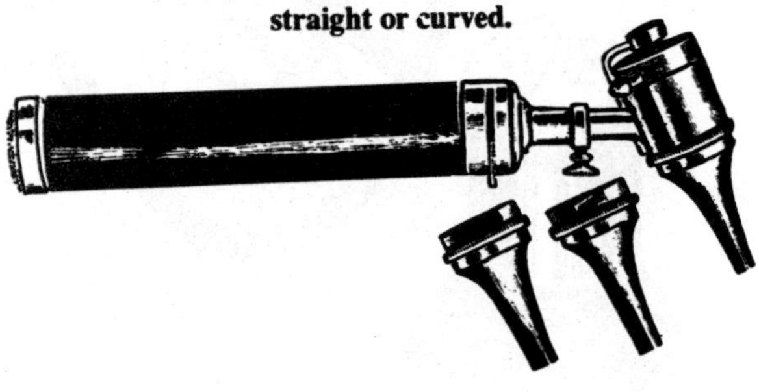

Wappler Model Auriscope with set of 3 specula.

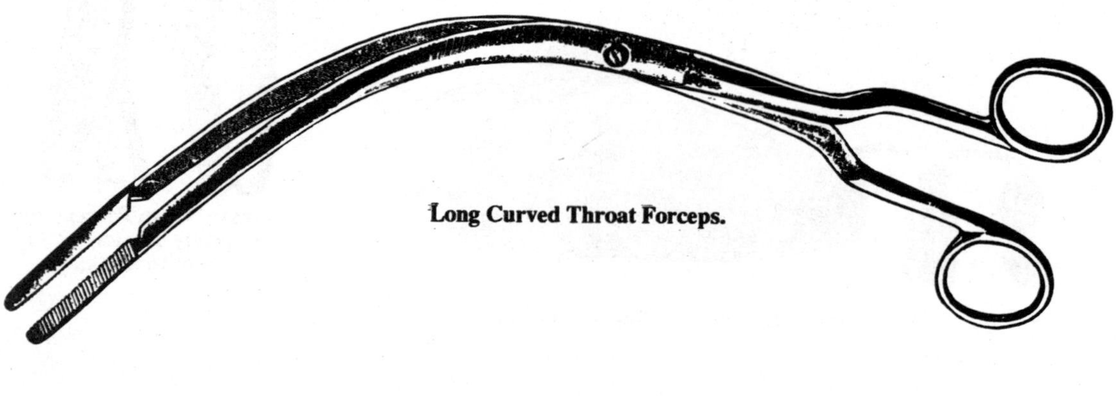

Long Curved Throat Forceps.

Plate XXXIV

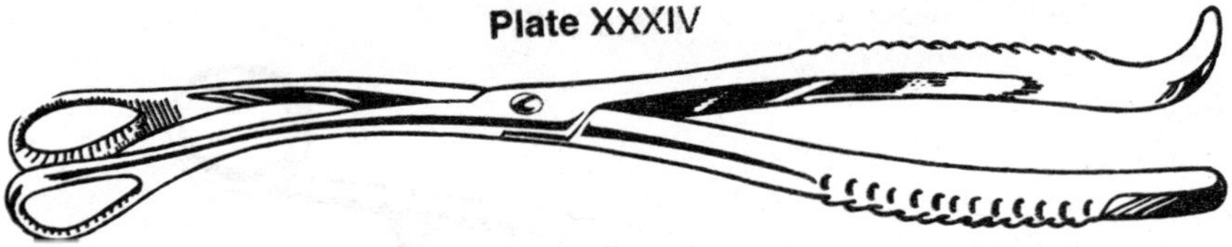

Whelping Forceps Mchean's 8", 10", 12".

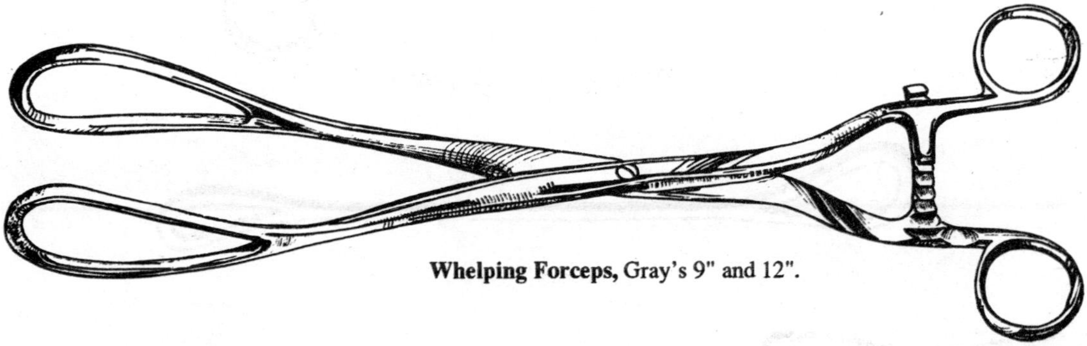

Whelping Forceps, Gray's 9" and 12".

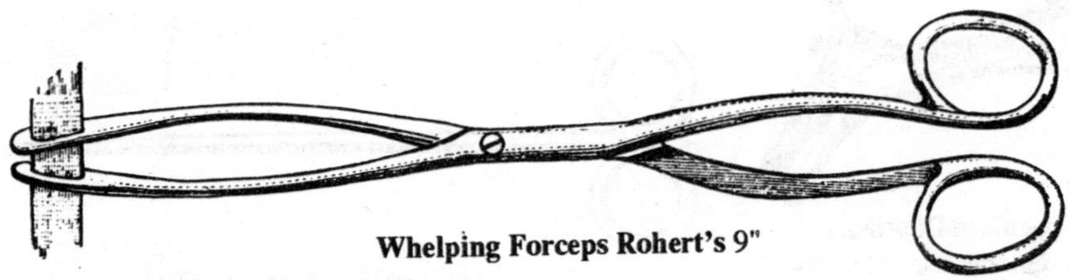

Whelping Forceps Rohert's 9"

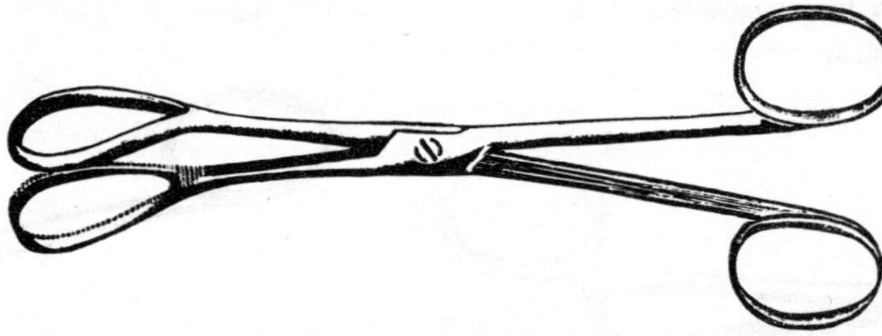

Whelping Forceps, Hobday's.

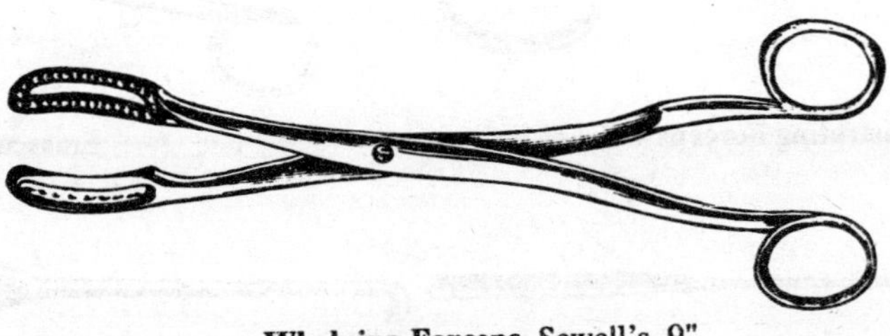

Whelping Forceps, Sewell's, 9"

Plate XXXV

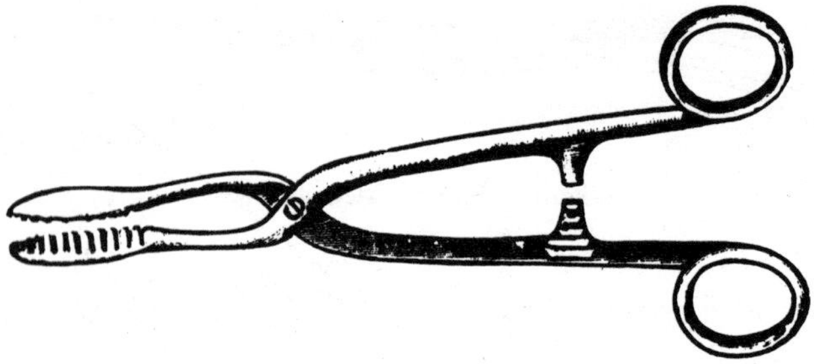

Whelping Forceps, Legette's.

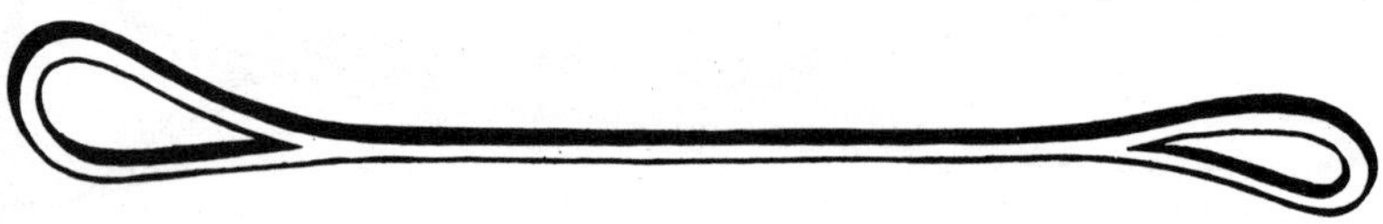

Hobday's **Vectis.**

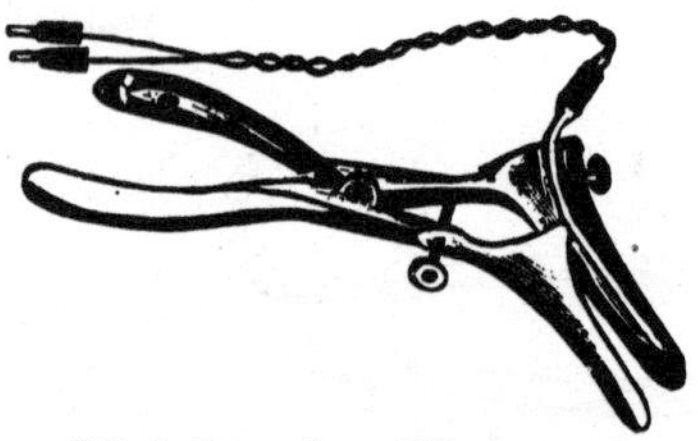

Bitch Speculum Dilating,
with solid blades and set screw.

Meyer Speculum for examination of vagina and rectum.

Obstetric Hook, 11 in.

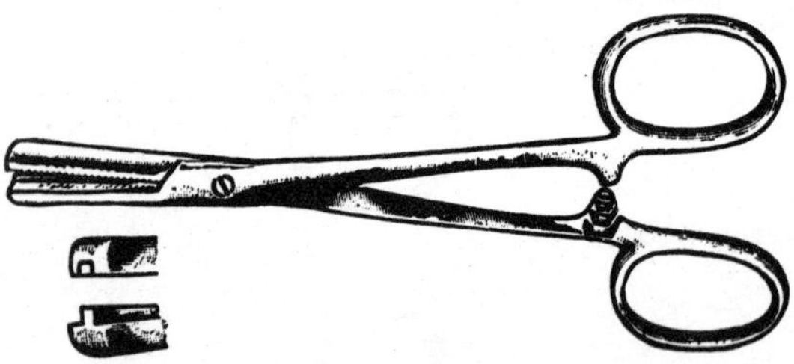

Fergusson Castrating Forceps 7-3-4 in.

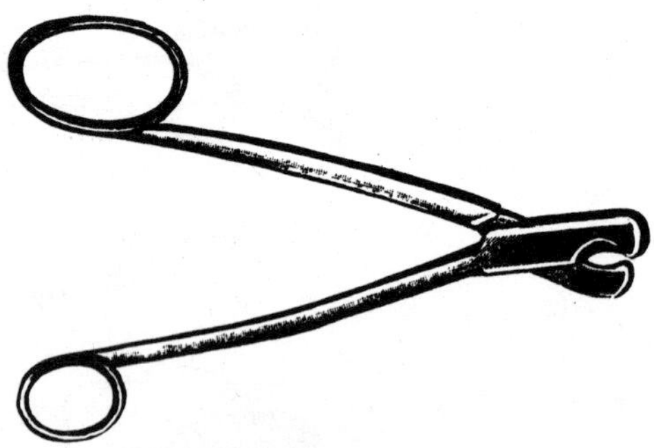

Emasculator Bitch.

Covault Ovariectomy Hook

Snook's Ovariectomy Hook

Plate XXXVI

Operation Table for Dog

Cat Catheter Grays' fine.

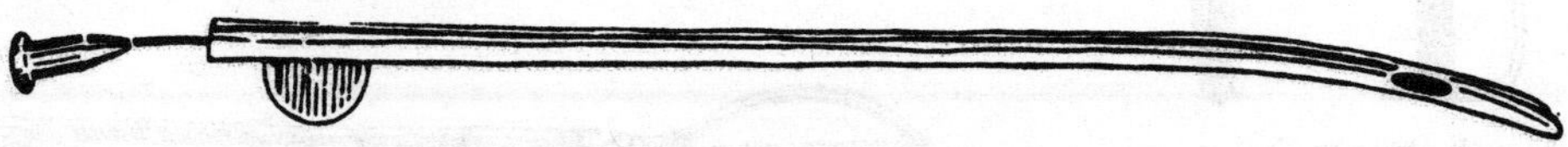

Dog Catheter, Metal.

Female Canine Catheter.

Bitch Catheter, Metal.

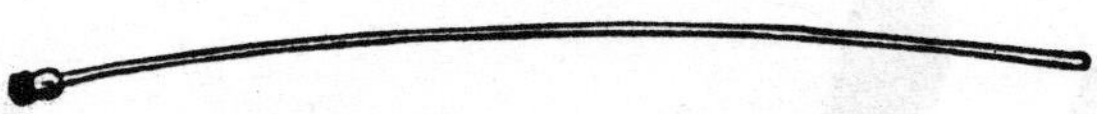

Dog Catheter, improved flexible metal, sizes

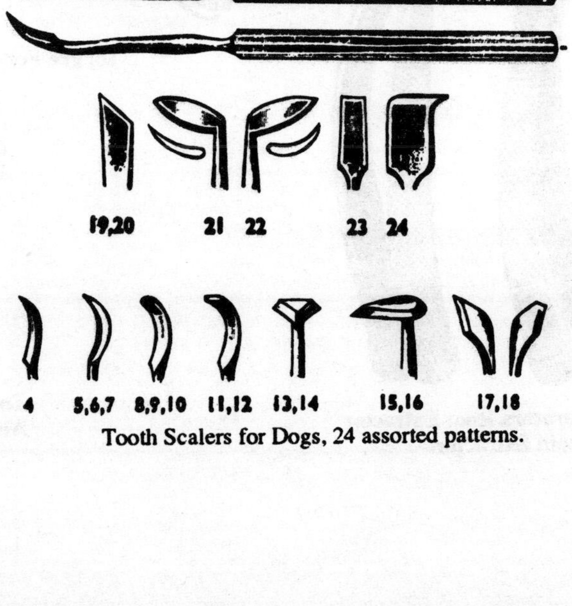

Tooth Scalers for Dogs, 24 assorted patterns.

Plate XXXVII

Dog Mouth Opener This is inserted in the angle of the mouth, pushed between the teeth and locked by

Dog ear Clamps 12 cm. operative surface.

Collar for dog.

Dog Catcher

Canine Nasal and **Ear Speculum.**

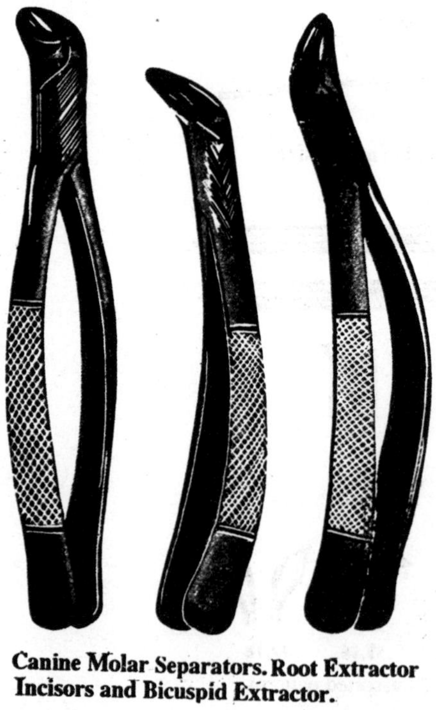

Canine Molar Separators. Root Extractor Incisors and Bicuspid Extractor.

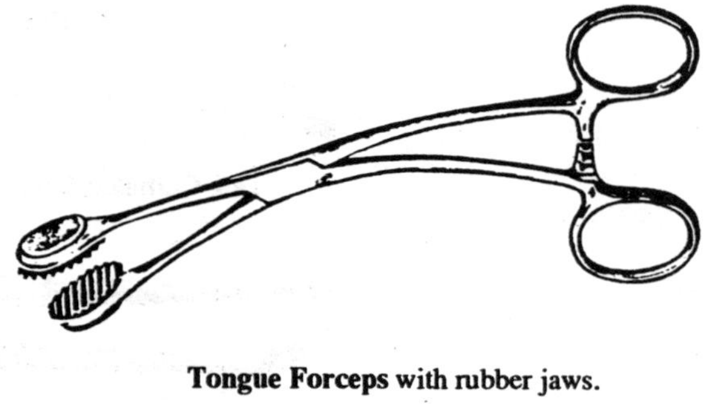

Tongue Forceps with rubber jaws.

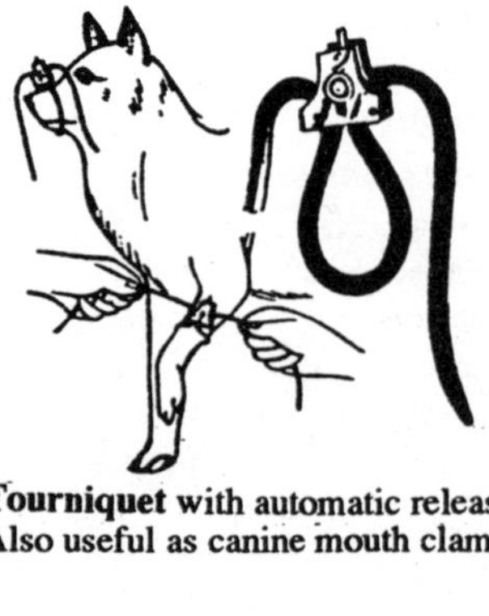

Tourniquet with automatic release. Also useful as canine mouth clamp.

APPENDIX —B

INCUBATION PERIOD OF COMMON DISEASES

Disease	Range (Days)	Average (Days)
Anaplsmosis	17-48	30
Anthrax	5-10	7
Babesiosis (equine)	7-21	-
Black quarter	1-5	-
Brucellosis	21-180	60-120
Contagious ecthyma	5-8	-
Distemper	3-7	4
Foot and Mouth disease	2-10	3
Glander	30-90	30
Haemorrhagic septicaemia	2-5	3
Influenza (equine)	3-10	4
-do-(piglet)	2-7	-
Johne's disease	30-730	90
Leptospirosis	7-9	8
Malignant oedema	2-5	3
Pox (sheep, cow)	2-7	-
Pustular dermatits	4-7	-
Rabies (all animals)	9-450	30-90
Rinderpest	3-9	3
Strangles	3-8	-
Swine erysipalus	1-5	-
Tetanus	7-21	15
Trypanosomiasis	4-13	7
Tuberculosis	30-90	30
Vibriosis	20-60	35

INDEX